The Morphology of English Dialects

Where do dialects differ from Standard English, and why are they so remarkably resilient? This new study argues that commonly used verbs that deviate from Standard English for the most part have a long pedigree. Analysing the language use of over 120 dialect speakers, Lieselotte Anderwald demonstrates that not only are speakers justified historically in using these verbs, systematically these non-standard forms actually make more sense. By constituting a simpler system, they are generally more economical than their Standard English counterparts. Drawing on data collected from the Freiburg English Dialect Corpus (FRED), this innovative and engaging study comes directly from the forefront of this field, and will be of great interest to students and researchers of English language and linguistics, morphology and syntax.

LIESELOTTE ANDERWALD is Professor of English Linguistics at the University of Kiel, Germany.

STUDIES IN ENGLISH LANGUAGE

General Editor
Merja Kytö (Uppsala University)

Editorial Board
Bas Aarts (University College London), John Algeo (University of Georgia), Susan Fitzmaurice (Northern Arizona University), Charles F. Meyer (University of Massachusetts)

The aim of this series is to provide a framework for original studies of English, both present-day and past. All books are based securely on empirical research, and represent theoretical and descriptive contributions to our knowledge of national and international varieties of English, both written and spoken. The series covers a broad range of topics and approaches, including syntax, phonology, grammar, vocabulary, discourse, pragmatics and sociolinguistics, and is aimed at an international readership.

The Morphology of English Dialects

Verb Formation in Non-Standard English

LIESELOTTE ANDERWALD

CAMBRIDGE
UNIVERSITY PRESS

CAMBRIDGE UNIVERSITY PRESS
Cambridge, New York, Melbourne, Madrid, Cape Town,
Singapore, São Paulo, Delhi, Mexico City

Cambridge University Press
The Edinburgh Building, Cambridge CB2 8RU, UK

Published in the United States of America by Cambridge University Press, New York

www.cambridge.org
Information on this title: www.cambridge.org/9781107407695

First published 2009
First paperback edition 2012

A catalogue record for this publication is available from the British Library

Library of Congress Cataloguing in Publication Data
Anderwald, Lieselotte, 1969–
  The morphology of English dialects : verb formation in non-standard
  English / Lieselotte Anderwald.
    p.   cm. – (Studies in English language)
  Includes bibliographical references and index.
  ISBN 978-0-521-88497-6 (hardback)
    1. English language–Dialects–Great Britain.   2. English language–Verb.
  I. Title.   II. Series.
  PE1736.A53   2009
  427–dc22   2009004696

ISBN 978-0-521-88497-6 Hardback
ISBN 978-1-107-40769-5 Paperback

Cambridge University Press has no responsibility for the persistence or
accuracy of URLs for external or third-party internet websites referred to in
this publication, and does not guarantee that any content on such websites is,
or will remain, accurate or appropriate.

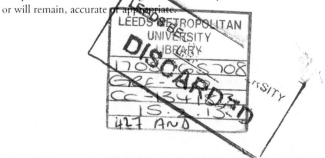

To Lucian, Eva, Julia, and Emma

Contents

List of figures   *page* xii
List of maps   xiv
List of tables   xv
Preface and thanks   xvii
Acknowledgement of sources   xviii

1   Introduction   1
    1.1 The past tense – a descriptive approach   1
    1.2 Terminology: strong–weak vs. irregular–regular   3
    1.3 Classification of strong verbs   5
         1.3.1 Ablaut series, vowel gradation   5
         1.3.2 Dental suffix   6
         1.3.3 Abstract formal identity   7
    1.4 Standard vs. non-standard English   12
    1.5 Materials employed   13

2   Past tense theories   17
    2.1 Introduction   17
    2.2 Chomsky and Halle (1968)   18
    2.3 Lexical Phonology and Morphology   21
    2.4 Optimality Theory   26
    2.5 Stochastic Optimality Theory   32
    2.6 Psycholinguistic theories   33
    2.7 Connectionist approaches   36
    2.8 Network model   38
    2.9 Natural morphology   40
         2.9.1 Universal morphological naturalness   40
         2.9.2 Language-specific morphological naturalness 42
         2.9.3 Criticism   45
         2.9.4 Compatibility with other models   45
    2.10 Conclusion   46

3   Naturalness and the English past tense system   49
  3.1 General features of the English verb system   49
  3.2 Dominant features   51
  3.3 Standard English verb classes   51
     3.3.1 Verb class 1: PRES ≠ PAST ≠ PPL   52
        3.3.1.1 VPRES ≠ VPAST ≠ VPPL   53
        3.3.1.2 <-en>-participle   53
     3.3.2 Verb class 2: PRES ≠ PAST = PPL   55
        3.3.2.1 VPRES ≠ VPAST = VPPL   55
        3.3.2.2 No vowel change   57
     3.3.3 Verb class 3: PRES = PPL ≠ PAST   58
     3.3.4 Verb class 4: PRES = PAST ≠ PPL   58
     3.3.5 Verb class 5: PRES = PAST = PPL   59
     3.3.6 Summary   59
  3.4 The central characteristics   61
  3.5 Non-standard verb paradigms as test cases   61
     3.5.1 New non-standard weak verbs   62
     3.5.2 New non-standard strong verbs   62
     3.5.3 Different non-standard strong verbs   63
        3.5.3.1 Two- instead of three-part paradigms   63
        3.5.3.2 One- instead of two-part paradigms   65
     3.5.4 Summary   65

4   *Sellt* and *knowed*: non-standard weak verbs   66
  4.1 Introduction   66
  4.2 Data from FRED: what to count?   68
  4.3 Regional comparison   69
  4.4 Individual verbs   70
     4.4.1 Northern features   73
        4.4.1.1 Past tense *gaed* and *gi'ed*   73
        4.4.1.2 Past tense *tellt* and *sellt*   73
     4.4.2 Southern features   77
        4.4.2.1 Past tense *runned*   77
        4.4.2.2 Past tense *gived*   78
        4.4.2.3 Past tense *knowed*, *growed*, *blowed* and *throwed*   79
        4.4.2.4 Historical dialect data   81
        4.4.2.5 Past tense *drawed*   82
        4.4.2.6 Relative frequencies   83
     4.4.3 Western feature   84
        4.4.3.1 Past tense *seed*   84
     4.4.4 General features   87
        4.4.4.1 Past tense *knowed*   87
        4.4.4.2 Past tense *catched*   89
  4.5 Verb classes   91

Contents

4.6 Statistical models   92
4.7 Comparison with COLT   95
4.8 Summary   96

5   *Drunk, seen, done* and *eat*: two-part paradigms instead of three-part paradigms   98
  5.1 Introduction   98
  5.2 'Bybee' verbs   98
    5.2.1 History   101
      5.2.1.1 Past tense forms of *begin*   103
      5.2.1.2 Past tense forms of *drink*   105
      5.2.1.3 Past tense forms of *sink*   106
      5.2.1.4 Past tense forms of *sing*   107
      5.2.1.5 Past tense forms of *ring*   108
    5.2.2 Historical dialects   109
    5.2.3 Data from FRED   110
      5.2.3.1 Verbs   110
      5.2.3.2 Singular vs. plural?   110
      5.2.3.3 Regions   111
    5.2.4 Comparison with COLT   113
    5.2.5 Cognitive explanation   114
  5.3 Past tense *seen*   120
    5.3.1 Introduction   120
    5.3.2 History   120
    5.3.3 Historical dialects   121
    5.3.4 Data from FRED   121
    5.3.5 Conclusion   125
  5.4 Past tense *done*   125
    5.4.1 Introduction   125
    5.4.2 History   126
    5.4.3 Previous studies   127
    5.4.4 Historical dialects   127
    5.4.5 Data from FRED   129
    5.4.6 Data from COLT   132
    5.4.7 *Done* in American English   133
    5.4.8 Cognitive explanation   134
  5.5 Counterexamples: past tense *eat, give* and *see*   136
    5.5.1 Introduction   136
    5.5.2 Past tense *eat*   136
      5.5.2.1 History   137
      5.5.2.2 Historical dialects   137
      5.5.2.3 Data from FRED   138
      5.5.2.4 Conclusion past tense *eat*   140

5.5.3   Past tense *give*   141
      5.5.3.1 History   141
      5.5.3.2 Historical dialects   141
      5.5.3.3 Data from FRED   142
5.5.4   Past tense *see*   144
      5.5.4.1 Historical dialects   144
      5.5.4.2 Data from FRED   144
      5.5.4.3 Data from COLT   145
5.5.5   Conclusions   146
5.6   Chapter conclusion   147

6   *Come* and *run*: non-standard strong verbs with a
    one-part paradigm   149
    6.1   Past tense *come*   149
        6.1.1   Introduction   149
        6.1.2   History   150
              6.1.2.1 Regular development   150
              6.1.2.2 Standard English past tense *came*   153
        6.1.3   Historical dialects   158
        6.1.4   Data from FRED   163
        6.1.5   Data from COLT   165
        6.1.6   Summary and explanation   166
    6.2   Past tense *run*   168
        6.2.1   Introduction   168
        6.2.2   History   168
              6.2.2.1 Present tense   168
              6.2.2.2 Past tense   174
        6.2.3   Historical dialects   176
        6.2.4   Data from FRED   176
              6.2.4.1 Procedure   176
              6.2.4.2 Quantification   178
        6.2.5   Data from COLT   179
        6.2.6   Cognitive explanation   179
    6.3   Chapter conclusion   180

7   Conclusion: supralocalization and morphological theories   183
    7.1   Summary of findings   183
    7.2   Supralocalization?   185
    7.3   Morphological theories revisited   188
        7.3.1   Rules vs. representations   188
        7.3.2   The role of frequency   191
        7.3.3   Accounting for diachronic developments   191
        7.3.4   Non-standard data   194
    7.4   Summary   197

Contents

Appendix 1: Verb classification   198

Appendix 2: SED localities and list of counties   205

Bibliography   207

Index   216

List of figures

Figure 1.1	Formal identity of forms	8
Figure 1.2	Verb patterns, ordered by functionality	11
Figure 2.1	Dual-route models	34
Figure 2.2	Product-oriented schema for past tense forms	39
Figure 2.3	Inflection class classification (after Wurzel 1990)	46
Figure 3.1	Internal structure of verb class 1	54
Figure 3.2	Internal structure of verb class 2	59
Figure 3.3	Summary of verb class structures	60
Figure 3.4	Features and class membership	62
Figure 3.5	Pervasive patterns in non-standard tense paradigms	64
Figure 4.1	Non-standard weak verbs per dialect area (normalized)	70
Figure 4.2	A-curve for non-standard weak verbs	72
Figure 4.3	A-curve for non-standard weak verbs excluding *knowed*	72
Figure 4.4	Verb class 1 affected by non-standard weak forms	92
Figure 4.5	Relative vs. absolute frequencies for non-standard weak verbs in FRED	93
Figure 4.6	Scatterplot of relative vs. absolute frequencies of non-standard weak verbs	94
Figure 4.7	Curve estimation on relative vs. absolute frequencies of non-standard weak verbs	95
Figure 5.1	Past tense, Bybee verbs	100
Figure 5.2	Diachronic development of past tense *begun* (Helsinki, ARCHER)	104
Figure 5.3	The demise of past tense *sunk* (ARCHER)	107
Figure 5.4	Diachronic development of past tense *rung* vs. *rang* (Helsinki, ARCHER)	109
Figure 5.5	The five most frequent Bybee verbs per dialect area in FRED	112
Figure 5.6	Schema for past tense *begun*	116
Figure 5.7	Schema for past tense *rung*	116
Figure 5.8	Schema for past tense *sung*	116
Figure 5.9	Schema for past tense *sunk*	117
Figure 5.10	Schema for past tense *drunk*	117

List of figures

Figure 5.11	Stable word class as attractor	117
Figure 5.12	Prototypical structure of verb class (Bybee verbs)	119
Figure 5.13	Past tense *seen*, *seed* and *see* per dialect area in FRED	124
Figure 5.14	Past tense *done* (main verb) per dialect area in FRED	132
Figure 5.15	Schema for past tense *done*	135
Figure 5.16	Prototypicality grid of Bybee verbs including *done*	135
Figure 5.17	Past tense *eat* per dialect area in FRED	140
Figure 5.18	Past tense *give* per dialect area in FRED	143
Figure 5.19	Standard English three-part paradigm	148
Figure 5.20	Non-standard English two-part paradigms	148
Figure 6.1	Postulated regular development of present and past tense *come*	151
Figure 6.2	Marked regular development of past tense *coom*	153
Figure 6.3	Phonological development of *come*	153
Figure 6.4	The rise of past tense *came* (Helsinki corpus, normalized figures)	158
Figure 6.5	Past tense *come* per dialect area in FRED	164
Figure 6.6	Paradigm of non-standard *come*	166
Figure 6.7	Schema for past tense *come*	167
Figure 6.8	*Come* as a Bybee verb	167
Figure 6.9	Present tense *run* (Helsinki corpus)	173
Figure 6.10	Past tense *run* per dialect area in FRED	178
Figure 6.11	Schema for past tense *run*	180
Figure 6.12	*Run* as a Bybee verb	180
Figure 6.13	Prototypicality grid of Bybee verbs including *come* and *run*	181
Figure 7.1	New Bybee verbs	190
Figure 7.2	Extension of network model to variable data	196

List of maps

Map 1.1   English counties sampled in FRED   15
Map 4.1   Past tense *sellt* and *tellt* in the EDD   75
Map 4.2   Past tense *growed* in the SED (Basic Material)   82
Map 4.3   Past tense *seed, seen* and *see* in the SED (Basic Material)   86
Map 4.4   Past tense *catched* in the SED (Basic Material)   90
Map 5.1   Past tense *seen* in the EDD   122
Map 5.2   Past tense *seed, seen* and *see* in the SED (Basic Material)   123
Map 5.3   Past tense *done* in the EDD   128
Map 5.4   Past tense *done* in the SED (by counties)   130
Map 5.5   Past tense *done* in the SED (Basic Material)   131
Map 5.6   Past tense *eat* in the SED (Basic Material)   139
Map 5.7   Past tense *give* in the EDD   142
Map 5.8   Past tense *see* in the SED (Basic Material)   145
Map 6.1   Past tense *came* in LALME   155
Map 6.2   Past tense *come* in LALME   156
Map 6.3   Past tense *comed* in the EDD   159
Map 6.4   Past tense *coom* in the EDD   160
Map 6.5   Past tense *come* in the EDD   161
Map 6.6   Past tense *coom* in the SED (Basic Material)   163
Map 6.7   Present tense *run* metathesis in LALME   170
Map 6.8   Present tense *rin* in LALME   171
Map 6.9   Past tense *run* in LALME   175
Map 6.10   Past tense *run* in the EDD   177

List of tables

Table 1.1	FRED words per dialect area	16
Table 2.1	Example 1 OT tableau	29
Table 2.2	Example 2 OT tableau	29
Table 2.3	Example 3 OT tableau	29
Table 2.4	Schematic comparison of morphological theories	47
Table 4.1	Non-standard weak verbs per dialect area (normalized)	70
Table 4.2	Individual weak verbs per dialect area	71
Table 4.3	Relative frequencies of *tellt* in FRED	76
Table 4.4	Relative frequencies of *sellt* in FRED	77
Table 4.5	Relative frequencies of *drawed* in FRED	84
Table 4.6	Relative frequencies of *blowed* in FRED	84
Table 4.7	Relative frequencies of *throwed* in FRED	84
Table 4.8	Relative frequencies of *growed* in FRED	84
Table 4.9	Relative frequencies of *seed* in FRED	86
Table 4.10	Relative frequencies of *knowed* in FRED	88
Table 4.11	Relative and absolute frequencies of *know* etc. in FRED	88
Table 4.12	Relative frequencies of *catched* in FRED	91
Table 4.13	Relative and absolute frequencies of all non-standard weak verbs in FRED	93
Table 5.1	Diachronic development of past tense *began* vs. *begun* (Helsinki, ARCHER)	104
Table 5.2	Diachronic development of past tense *sank* vs. *sunk* (ARCHER)	106
Table 5.3	Diachronic development of past tense *rang* vs. *rung* (Helsinki, ARCHER)	108
Table 5.4	New 'Bybee' verbs in FRED	110
Table 5.5	Singular referents of Bybee verbs	111
Table 5.6	The five most frequent Bybee verbs per dialect area in FRED	112
Table 5.7	New Bybee verbs in COLT	114
Table 5.8	Relative frequencies of *seen* in FRED	124
Table 5.9	Past tense *seen* in COLT	125
Table 5.10	Past tense *done* (main verb) in FRED	132

Table 5.11   Past tense *done* (main verb) in COLT   133
Table 5.12   Past tense *eat* in FRED   140
Table 5.13   Past tense *give* in FRED   143
Table 5.14   Past tense *see* in FRED   146
Table 5.15   Past tense *see* in COLT   146
Table 6.1   Past tense (*he/she/it*) *come* in FRED   164
Table 6.2   Past tense (*he/she/it*) *come* in COLT   165
Table 6.3   Diachronic development of present tense *run* (Helsinki corpus) 173
Table 6.4   Past tense *run* in FRED   178
Table 7.1   Supralocalization features   187

Preface and thanks

While tense and aspect in general have always interested me since my days as a student at the Free University Berlin and a class on the topic by Ekkehartd König, my interest in the non-standard past tense arose purely coincidentally. I was asked to write an overview of the morphology and syntax of the South East of England (Anderwald 2004), when – in the pursuit of some little-documented feature – I fell to reading whole texts from our corpus FRED from this area, especially those from London, noting down rather informally all non-standard features I came across. Many questions that this article raised could not be answered immediately, but I thought they deserved a more thorough investigation. In particular, the many and varied non-standard past tense forms had never been investigated in their regional extension, and I had the feeling that this would make a satisfying research topic.

I have to thank countless colleagues, whom I pestered with sometimes incomprehensible questions about verbal paradigms, in particular Øystein Vangsnes in Norway for answering questions on Old Norse, Nynorsk and Icelandic; Karel Gildemacher from the Fryske Akademie in the Netherlands for information on past and present-day Frisian; Ton Goeman for information on Dutch (standard and dialects); my colleague Richard Matthews for discussing the history of *come* with me; Christian Mair and Bernd Kortmann for discussion and suggestions during the infamous Oberseminar, and elsewhere, and support and coaching in the most general ways; Peter Trudgill for (very entertaining) anecdotal evidence on East Anglian verb forms; Benedikt Szmrecsanyi and Douglas Biber for helpful suggestions on some statistical procedures and some number crunching; my good friends Marianne and Andrea; Georgie, my favourite native speaker of no dialect at all ☺ (thanks also for proofreading); Lucian not just for help with soft-, hard- and other -ware problems; and, most of all, Eva and Julia and Emma for making life fun – my family to whom this book is dedicated.

Acknowledgement of sources

Thanks to Joan Bybee for letting me name a whole verbal class after her.

Maps are based on the *Survey of English Dialects* overview map indicating the location of their informants in Orton and Halliday (1962–64: 30). Counties in these maps are numbered. For easier reference, a complete list of county names and numbers can be found in Appendix 2. I gratefully acknowledge that Hodder Education have no objections to my using the basic map in this book.

It has to be noted here that every effort has been made to secure necessary permissions to reproduce copyright material in this work, though in some cases it has proved impossible to trace copyright holders. If any omissions are brought to our notice, we will be happy to include appropriate acknowledgements on reprinting or in any subsequent edition.

I   Introduction

But it was in the verbal conjugation that the Ablaut found its peculiar home, and there it took formal and methodical possession. (Earle 1892: §124)

1.1   The past tense – a descriptive approach

PAST is the most frequently marked verbal category by far (e.g. according to Sampson 2002, based on figures from the British National Corpus), accounting for around 25 per cent of all verb forms in contemporary spoken British English. In comparison, the two next categories, negation or modals, both only account for roughly 12 per cent of verb forms, the perfect for around 8 per cent, and the progressive for under 6 per cent. The passive finally is at best marginal with a text probability of under 1 per cent.

Past tense formation in English appears to be a very simple matter. Nevertheless – or perhaps because of this simplicity – great theoretical significance has been attached to an analysis of the past tense because it is used as the prime example in a long-standing debate in morphological theory (more on which in Chapter 2).

Putting it in simple descriptive terms (although no description is of course theory-free, or truly pre-theoretical), the majority of English verbs today have past tense forms that consist of the present tense stem plus <-ed>.[1] <-ed>, the weak past tense marker, is exactly parallel to the weak past tense in all other Germanic languages and is indeed one of the characterizing features of Germanic. English here is no exception. There are several theories, each deficient in its own terms, of how this common dental suffix evolved with the specific past tense meaning – among them the '*tun* theory' and the '*-tó-* theory'[2] – but a consensus cannot as yet be presented. Although it is probably generally true that, from an Indo-European perspective, the

---

[1] In contrast to most reference grammars, I disregard variation in spelling here, although I will refer to the graphemes for simplicity's sake.
[2] For a short overview, see West (2001: 53).

weak verbs are the more recent innovation,[3] inside the weak verb class there appear to be different layers: some weak verbs are very old and can be traced to Indo-European roots (and thus constitute rather untypical weak verbs), whereas the majority are probably younger.[4]

Today, for the weak past tense forms, in English we have three regular allomorphs: /əd/ or /ɪd/ after the two alveolar stops /t/ and /d/, /t/ after all other voiceless sounds, and /d/ after all other voiced sounds. This case of phonologically determined allomorphy is perfectly regular and equally productive. The rarer verbs in particular, as well as neologisms and loan words, are weak today. The number of paradigms of weak verbs is very large (because of possible new coinages probably infinite), so that a high type frequency is here coupled with a low token frequency.

A small number of verbs in contemporary (standard) English – Quirk et al. list '250 or so' (Quirk et al. 1985: 104), Huddleston and Pullum have exactly 176 (Huddleston and Pullum 2002: 1608–9), although other linguists name considerably fewer – are irregular and have retained strong past tense forms. This group has been gradually decreasing in number, as strong verbs have changed verb classes and become weak verbs since Old English times (see in particular Krygier 1994 for a detailed analysis through the centuries until Early Modern English). Nevertheless, strong verb forms are still highly visible in present-day English because the frequent verbs in particular have retained their strong forms. Indeed, some text counts put the figure for strong verbs in running text as high as 70 to 75 per cent.[5] For strong verbs, then, low type frequency is coupled with a very high token frequency.[6]

Incidentally, Quirk et al.'s classification seems to be the most inclusive. For them, all verbs that are not regular are irregular. While regular verbs can be defined positively, irregular verbs simply constitute 'the rest' (a rather heterogeneous category that will be discussed further below). Perhaps for this reason, the terms *strong verb* and *weak verb* do not appear in Quirk et al. (1985). Other authors, especially those arguing from a historical point of view, are more discriminatory. Stockwell and Minkova, for example, quoting

---

[3] As opposed to the strong verbs, which can be shown to re-use the old aorist; for a recent treatment in terms of exaptation, see Lass (1990).

[4] The Newcastle Weak Verb Project aims to shed light on this layering (see West 2001). First studies for Old High German suggest that about 70 per cent of weak verbs are neologisms, 18 per cent are West Germanic, 10 per cent are Germanic and around 2 per cent could be pre-Germanic (West 2001: 54). Figures for Old English were not available at the time of writing.

[5] E.g. in transcripts of parental speech, see Pinker (1999: 227). Based on Sampson's CHRISTINE corpus, a subcorpus of the British National Corpus (BNC), Dahl (2004: 300–1) quotes even more striking figures. Of all verb forms, regular verbs only make up around 9 per cent of all tokens. If one disregards *be*, *have* as well as modals, regular verbs still make up only around 24 per cent of all lexical verb tokens, figures very similar to Pinker's.

[6] This is an oversimplification. In fact, some of the very frequent verbs are weak (*look*, *ask*, *seem*, *want*, *turn* …), while many strong verbs have a very low token frequency. As a statistical trend, however, this statement holds.

Baugh and Cable (1978), only mention sixty-eight strong verbs (Stockwell and Minkova 2001: 130), i.e. those that form the past tense by vowel gradation, going back to similar processes in Indo-European, plus thirteen that are both strong and weak today; Carstairs-McCarthy occupies some middle ground in claiming that 'in all, 150 or so verbs are irregular in that they do not use the -*ed* suffix' (Carstairs-McCarthy 2002: 40), without, however, supplying a list.

As Quirk et al. do provide a comprehensive list of all strong verbs and their various forms, this will constitute the point of departure for my study, the foil against which any non-standard forms will be compared. However, from their list of 250 verbs I excluded 83 which were either morphologically complex (e.g. *deepfreeze*; the simplex *freeze* is included) or behaved as if they were (e.g. *become*, cf. *come*).[7] These were mostly verbs with the prefixes *a-*, *be-*, *for(e)-*, *mis-*, *out-*, *over-*, *re-*, *un-*, *under-*, *up-* and *with-*. Clearly in most cases the prefixes are not semantically transparent today, and many verbs are thus arguably monomorphemic. For our purposes it is important to note, however, that they behave morphologically *as if* they were derivational forms. To avoid skewing due to frequent prefixation of some bases in the later quantitative comparisons, these seemingly derivational forms were excluded. Incidentally, these exclusions bring Quirk et al.'s list very close to the figure '150 or so' mentioned by Carstairs-McCarthy above, namely to a total of 167.[8] Quirk et al.'s complete list of strong verbs with all exclusions can be found in Appendix 1.

1.2   Terminology: strong–weak vs. irregular–regular

A brief note on terminology: in this book, I will use the terms *strong* and *weak verbs* for the verbs that in more modern terminology (see Quirk et al. 1985; Huddleston and Pullum 2002) are usually called *irregular* and *regular*. In particular, *strong verb* will be used as a cover term not only for verbs that display the characteristic Indo-European vowel gradation, but for any other irregular verb as well. The reason for this choice is twofold. Firstly, we will have to have recourse to the concept of *regularization*, an abstract cognitive

---

[7] Huddleston and Pullum also stress that 'verbs with complex bases' have 'irregular forms matching those of the simple verb in final position' (2002: 1609), pointing out that 'the inflectional-morphological relationship is thus maintained long after the semantic connection has been lost' (2002: 1610). Aronoff goes further and in fact takes 'the inheritance of irregular morphology from a root or morphological head, even in the absence of compositionality' as proof for a level of analysis 'between morphosyntax and morphophonology', i.e. as morphology in the narrow sense, claiming that 'in each case, the set of irregular forms is obviously not a single lexeme ... so their unity must be expressed at a purely morphological level' (Aronoff 1994: 28).

[8] Huddleston and Pullum's list is slightly longer with a total of 176 verbs (2002: 1608–9); in contrast to Quirk et al., they include *bid* twice, and add *bust*, *earn*, *fit*, *gird*, *sneak* and *thrive*, as well as the four modals *can*, *may*, *shall* and *will*. On the other hand, their list does not include *knit*, *shit* or *sweat*.

process that can apply at a number of different linguistic levels. As regularization is not necessarily confined to the process of turning irregular verbs into regular verbs, to avoid utter confusion the terms *irregular* and *regular verbs* will not be used in this book after this introduction. If the following sections and chapters mention *strong verbs*, then, it should be borne in mind that this does not only include strong verbs in the narrower sense, i.e. those verb paradigms displaying Indo-European vowel gradation, but also verbs that Stockwell and Minkova call strong and weak, i.e. any verbs that are not weak verbs.[9]

Secondly, the term *regular* (at least in some frameworks) might presuppose, based on perhaps overzealous etymologizing, that a *rule* (Latin *regula*) is involved in the production of this form. This is a presupposition that I will be trying to avoid. In particular, in Chapter 5 and throughout the book I will be arguing that there can be both *weak* ('regular') verbs that are not created through a rule, and, more importantly, *strong* verbs ('irregular' verbs) that nevertheless follow a rule, or pattern, in their formation.

Finally, the data employed here are mainly historical as well as dialectal. While in historical studies it is of course still the case that the terms *strong* and *weak* verbs are used, the situation in dialectology is a little different. Again, works with a strong historical focus tend to avoid the terms *regular* and *irregular* and use *strong* and *weak* instead (despite the title, for example, Cheshire uses 'strong' and 'weak' in her analysis of the English irregular verbs: see Cheshire 1994; see also Miller 2003: 74). When I chart the progress of individual verb forms through history to their dialectal status today, it will be particularly useful to be able to use the same terms, rather than switch from *strong – weak* to *regular – irregular* at some arbitrary point in time (e.g. the change from Middle English to Modern English; the change from historical linguistics to synchronic linguistics; the change from dialectology to sociolinguistics; and what would be the respective dates for these important changes?).

Nevertheless, I am aware of several complications in this choice of terminology. Words that were weak in Old English (like *teach*) would have to be treated as having 'jumped' to the strong verb class, whereas what 'really' happened was of course a series of sound changes that resulted in opacity and, indeed, irregularity for this form.[10] Clearly *taught* is not perceived

---

[9] Cf. McMahon's terminology, which is similar: 'The Modern English strong verbs ... will be defined for present purposes as all those verbs which do not simply add a dental suffix {D} ... to mark the past tense, but also, or instead, change the quality of the stem vowel ... The term "strong" therefore designates not only historically strong verbs, but also historically weak verbs which now exhibit a vowel mutation in the past tense' (McMahon 2000: 129). In her analysis, it is not clear whether she really wants to exclude paradigms like *hit – hit*.

[10] The Germanic spirant law (or Primärberührung) resulted in the spirantization of /k/ > /x/ before the alveolar in the past tense, but not the present, whereas the vowel change is due to 'reverse vowel gradation' (usually known by its German name of Rückumlaut).

today any longer as containing the regular weak ending <-ed>, and so it would be misleading (for a synchronic analysis) to classify *teach* as a 'weak' verb today." On the other hand, a modern interpretation of 'strong verb' as identical to 'irregular' verb stresses for example the vowel change that takes place between *teach* and *taught*. Although of course it does not go back to an Indo-European ablaut schema, and indeed should not be called ablaut, vowel change between present and past tense stems is still one of the most frequent characteristics in the group of strong verbs (although not all of them, as we shall see in section 3.3).

1.3 Classification of strong verbs

1.3.1 Ablaut series, vowel gradation

Among the strong verbs, several classifications have been proposed. Classically, divisions are historical in nature, but among Germanic scholars it seems widely accepted that 'the English strong verbs are probably the most difficult of any modern West Germanic language to classify in any systematic way' (Durrell 2001: 13), no doubt because English has moved furthest away from its typological relatives German or Dutch in many respects. Typically, for example, verbs are grouped together by the same vowel changes they contain, according to present-day English, Old English, West Germanic, or indeed Indo-European ablaut series (e.g. /ɪ/~/æ/~/ʌ/ *sing – sang – sung; begin – began – begun* vs. /e/~/ɔ/ *bear – bore – borne; tear – tore – torn*, etc.). For present-day English, but clearly based on Old English schemas, this classification typically yields seven verb classes (e.g. Katamba 1993: 102):

Class I:	/aɪ/ /əʊ/ /ɪ/	rise	rose	risen
Class II:	/iː/ /əʊ/ /əʊ/	freeze	froze	frozen
Class III:	/ɪ/ /æ/ /ʌ/	shrink	shrank	shrunk
Class IV:	/eə/ /ɔə/ /ɔː/	bear	bore	borne
Class V:	/ɪ/ /eɪ/ /ɪ/	give	gave	given
Class VI:	/əʊ/ /uː/ /əʊ/	know	knew	known
Class VII:	/æ/ /ʊ/ /ʊ/	stand	stood	stood

The problem with this classification according to ablaut series is that it accounts for only a minority of strong verbs today, even though it is specifically written for present-day English, not historical stages of the language. Katamba's classification, for example, can only include 49 strong verbs – that is less than 30 per cent of the 167 strong verbs today. It neglects many vowel series of verbs that were strong in Old English and have remained so until

---

" Some synchronic descriptions resort to classifying these verbs as 'partial suppletion'; see Aronoff and Fudeman (2005: 168–9), as almost the complete stem /tiːtʃ/ is 'replaced' in /tɔːt/ (with the exception of the initial consonant).

today (e.g. *choose – chose – chosen* or *take – took – taken* or *break – broke – broken*). A classification according to vowel series in general also cannot account for paradigms that have three identical forms, because here the vowel can be quite different from verb to verb (e.g. *cast – cast – cast* vs. *hit – hit – hit* vs. *put – put – put* vs. *cost – cost – cost* vs. *shed – shed – shed*) – nevertheless it would be desirable to capture their intuitive similarity by classifying them together in one class.

Other verbs used to be weak in Old English times, but today have become irregular through devoicing (e.g. *spill – spillt – spillt* or *bend – bent – bent*). A second class of weak Old English verbs (particularly the weak class III verbs) today are still differentiated by their consonants, while the vowel has remained the same (e.g. *make – made – made* or *have – had – had*). A third group of weak Old English verbs have become strong through the regular process of Middle English open syllable lengthening (MEOSL), so that the Great Vowel Shift operated on different forms of the same paradigm differently. These regular phonological processes have resulted in markedly irregular paradigms with vowel changes as well as sometimes an added suffix (e.g. *mean – meant – meant* or *bite – bit – bitten*) that should be included in a present-day classification like Katamba's above. Finally, some verbs that were weak in Old English have undergone both vowel and consonant changes such as the Germanic spirant law, turning /g/ or /k/ into /x/ before the past tense alveolar stop (but not in the present tense), and deleting any preceding nasal; vowel changes even in Old English were due to *Rückumlaut* (or 'reverse vowel gradation'); with the subsequent deletion of /x/ in the majority of verbs this again results in present-day verb paradigms with a clear vowel change, but with very different present tense forms (e.g. *buy – bought – bought* with present tense /aɪ/; *teach – taught – taught* with present tense /iː/; or *catch – caught – caught* with present tense /æ/). As we have seen above, synchronically these verbs are today classified by many as 'partial suppletion' (see Aronoff and Fudeman 2005: 168–9) because their past tense forms are so radically different from their bases. Clearly, the intuitive similarity between these past tense forms is poorly accounted for in the form of vowel series.

Finally, it is no great help to start from the seven Old English strong verb classes either, as some verbs switched verb classes, many became weak, a large number simply fell into disuse, and of course some verbs entered the system after Old English times (for Old English verb classes, see Cassidy and Ringler 1971; and of course Krygier 1994. For sound change, see Campbell 1959).

1.3.2   Dental suffix

A second classificatory criterion generally applied is the presence or absence of a (dental) suffix in the past tense and (or) the past participle – the advantage is that this criterion can also be applied to all weak verbs, in addition to those strong verbs (former weak verbs) like *dream – dreamt – dreamt* which do have a suffix; some authors also include a nasal suffix here and would therefore classify *shake – shook – shaken* as belonging to this special group. As the examples already show, this criterion cuts across the first one of ablaut series, as dental or nasal suffixation may go hand in hand with vowel alternation (but need not do so). Clearly, however, this criterion on its own does little to structure the group of strong verbs, as almost half of them – around 47 per cent – have either a dental or a nasal suffix; if employed, this criterion probably always has to be combined with other criteria to result in a workable classification.

1.3.3   Abstract formal identity

A third, more interesting criterion characterizing verb paradigms today is the formal identity or non-identity of forms, and this is the one that will be chiefly applied in this book. Quirk et al. for example – if only in passing – distinguish five patterns of paradigms[12] (Quirk et al. 1985: 103), as do Nielsen (1985) and Hansen and Nielsen (1986: 181) in some more detail: (a) all forms are the same (e.g. *cut – cut – cut*); (b) only past tense and past participle are identical (e.g. *meet – met – met*); (c) infinitive and past tense are identical (e.g. *beat – beat – beaten*); (d) infinitive and past participle are identical (e.g. *come – came – come*); and (e) all three forms are different (e.g. *speak – spoke – spoken*) (Quirk et al. 1985: 103).[13] These are the five patterns that are logically possible, and as the examples already show, all five (one one-form pattern, three two-form patterns, and one three-form pattern) are actually attested in English.

Diagrammatically, the five logically possible patterns are displayed in Figure 1.1.

Quirk et al. list these possibilities without further qualification (Quirk et al. 1985: 103). It has to be stressed, however, that these five possibilities are by no means equivalent functionally (and they are also not equally distributed

---

[12] I use the term paradigm to refer to what has traditionally been known as the principal parts of the verb, i.e. present tense stem – past tense stem – past participle.

[13] Quirk et al. go on to use a mixture of all three criteria (presence/absence of suffix, identity/non-identity only of past tense and past participle, and vowel identity across all three forms). This mixture results in a very detailed classification, nevertheless again with seven main classes and many subclasses. They do not, however, justify their use of only employing identity of past and past participle as a criterion. Huddleston and Pullum in contrast use four criteria: (1) secondary *–ed* formation, (2) vowel alternation, (3) participle <-en>, (4) 'other formations', where these four are not mutually exclusive (Huddleston and Pullum 2002: 1600–8). In their Student Grammar, by contrast, they have reduced irregular verb classes to just two: those where simple past and past participle are identical (with eight subtypes, including a 'miscellaneous' class), and those where simple past and past participle are not identical (with six subtypes, again including a 'miscellaneous' one) (Huddleston and Pullum 2005: 274–7).

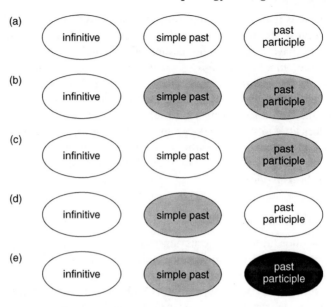

Same shading implies identity of forms

Figure 1.1 Formal identity of forms

across the English vocabulary, as Nielsen 1985 points out, and as will become apparent shortly).

The first type of verbs they mention – equality of all forms – is clearly not optimal in functional terms. Verbs without any morphological tense distinctions certainly have moved furthest on their way towards the 'isolate word'. For them, temporal distinctions can be recovered by the context only. Nevertheless, twenty-four verbs of Quirk et al.'s list fall into this class (i.e. around 14 per cent of all strong verb paradigms listed there – certainly a sizeable subgroup). However – not surprisingly, considering the less than optimally functional nature of this class in the system – for many verbs weak alternatives are recorded (e.g. *rid – rid – rid* but also *ridded*; *bet – bet – bet* but also *betted*), and thus this subclass seems at present to be diminishing. (That historically this pattern has been quite attractive is stressed by Bauer 1997.)

The second group of verbs (e.g. *say – said – said; find – found – found*) – despite having identical past tense and past participle forms – is not dysfunctional at all. Any tense contrasts that might involve the past tense forms and the past participle must also involve further auxiliaries, so that the tenses can always be unambiguously decoded, even if the form of the lexical verb is identical. In particular, the past participle is used for the perfect (obligatorily with forms of HAVE) as well as for the passive (obligatorily with forms of BE); cf. *I found* vs. *I have found/I was found* or *he said* vs.

he had said/it was said. Although this pattern is not the prototypical pattern of strong verbs, half of all strong verbs do pattern like this (81 in Quirk et al.'s reduced list of 167, or over 48 per cent); this is indeed the largest group of strong verbs. More importantly, despite of course forming the past tense by a different process, all weak verbs also follow this abstract pattern. One can therefore say that this type constitutes the prototypical weak verb pattern. As we shall see, in non-standard dialect systems this pattern acts as a powerful attractor for a range of strong verbs, and the weak verb pattern receives additional support in the system from the large subgroup of strong verbs that already pattern alike. This pattern also seems attractive from a cross-linguistic perspective. Durrell, for example, notes for Dutch that here more strong verbs have been retained and indeed more verbs have entered the strong verb classes than in other West Germanic languages, and that these stable strong verbs 'all ... have the same vowel in the preterite and the past participle. This levelling seems to have simplified the paradigms and stabilized them, facilitating analogical levelling towards these classes' (Durrell 2001: 13).

Group (c), although at first glance perhaps a little similar, is really quite different. Here, the identity lies between infinitive and the simple past. In contrast to the prototypical weak verb pattern above, the simple present – employing the base form – and the simple past are never further distinguished by auxiliaries; present tense and past tense are after all the only purely morphological (i.e. inflectional) tenses of English (indeed, of the Germanic languages). Similar to those patterns that have identical forms everywhere, therefore, the context is the only source for clues about the temporal reference. Only one formal difference exists between present tense and past tense, namely in the third person singular. Here the present tense regularly has the suffix *–s*, whereas the past tense does not; cf. *I beat* (present? past?) vs. *she beats me* (present)/*she beat me* (past). For spoken language, in particular, the importance of this criterion should not be underestimated, as much discourse is in fact in the third person singular.[14] Again not surprisingly, this type does not contain too many verbs (in Quirk et al.'s list, *beat* is

---

[14] The figures from FRED are as follows:

Pronoun	Occurrence	% of total	Pronoun	Occurrence	% of total
I	61,458	23.4%	we	27,240	10.4%
he	29,733	11.3%	you	54,163	20.6%
she	9,418	3.6%	they	38,608	14.7%
it	41,776	15.9%			
			Total	262,396	

In other words, even in FRED – heavily biased towards first person narratives – the third person singular accounts for around a third of all pronouns. In addition, of course, all singular noun phrases are in the third person singular.

in fact the only verb, and thus accounts for only around 0.6 per cent of all strong verb types).

Quirk et al.'s fourth pattern – with identity of base form and past participle (e.g. *come – came – come; run – ran – run*) – along the same lines of argument is not particularly non-functional, at least not for the expression of tenses, as there is no possible area of confusion between the simple present (*I come/she comes, you run/we run*), and any perfect form (*I have come, she has come; you have run, we have run*); the important morphological distinction between simple present and simple past is maintained for this verb type. Nevertheless, this pattern is also very much a minority pattern, accounting basically for only the two verbs *come* and *run* (and a number of derivational forms which, as detailed above, have been excluded from these calculations) together making up just over 1 per cent of all strong verbs. Low type frequency is here obscured by extremely high token frequency, with *come* and *run* being some of the most frequent words in general.[15] This is no doubt the reason that this pattern appears intuitively quite common. Although it cannot really be called non-functional, there is a very strong trend in non-standard systems to 'level' the morphologically distinct past tense forms of both *come* and *run*, resulting in three identical forms. A detailed analysis of past tense *come* and *run* (in Chapter 6) aims to shed more light on this phenomenon.

The final pattern – three distinct forms for base form, past tense and past participle, e.g. *sing – sang – sung; eat – ate – eaten; fall – fell – fallen* – results in a maximally distinct three-way paradigm and constitutes the prototypical strong verb pattern. In Quirk et al.'s list, 59 out of 167 or around 35 per cent – a little more than a third – of all verbs conform to this pattern. Not surprisingly, the Old English ablaut series have survived in this pattern especially. Although it is certainly not dysfunctional in any way, the three-way contrast is redundant. In particular, a formal distinction between past tense and past participle is not necessary to assign tenses unambiguously (from the viewpoint of the listener), and perhaps for this reason many non-standard systems tend to 'level' the simple past–past participle contrast for these verbs – at least and especially for one particular subgroup, like *sing – sang – sung*, or *drink – drank – drunk*, namely to *sing – **sung** – sung* or *drink – **drunk** – drunk*. In other words, these verbs become more like prototypical weak verbs, the most frequent group, in particular like a subgroup of these, provisionally designated *Bybee verbs*. These are verbs like *cling – clung – clung, win – won – won* or *stick – stuck – stuck* and they have in common a certain phonological shape (to be detailed in Chapter 5), in particular a past tense form in /ʌ/. These

[15] In Francis and Kučera's adjusted frequency list for the Brown corpus (American English), *come* has rank 60, *become* rank 99 and *run* rank 204 (Francis and Kučera 1982: 465–7). This means that *come* is the 60th most frequent word in the corpus, *become* the 99th most frequent, and *run* the 204th most frequent. In fact, *come* is the 11th most frequent verb after *be*, *have, do, will, say, make, can, could, go* and *take*.

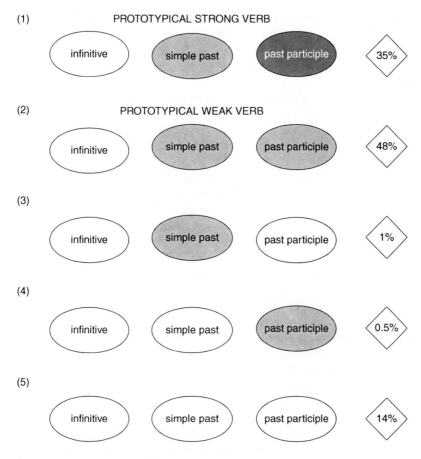

(1) PROTOTYPICAL STRONG VERB

infinitive | simple past | past participle | 35%

(2) PROTOTYPICAL WEAK VERB

infinitive | simple past | past participle | 48%

(3)

infinitive | simple past | past participle | 1%

(4)

infinitive | simple past | past participle | 0.5%

(5)

infinitive | simple past | past participle | 14%

Same shading implies identity of forms

Figure 1.2 Verb patterns, ordered by functionality

verbs seem to act as a very strong attractor for the very similar subgroup – cf. *sing – cling* or *drink – slink* – such that many, if not most non-standard systems also have a tendency to form the past tense of these verbs with /Λ/, resulting in the formal identity of past tense and past participle.

Re-grouped according to 'functionality', rather than in logical order, Quirk et al.'s classification then looks as in Figure 1.2 (percentages have been added[16]). Again, same shading implies identity of form.

What is important in the assignation of functionality is only the present and past tense forms. In particular, the prototypical strong verbs and the

---

[16] To recall, percentages are of type frequency, not token frequency, based on the list in Quirk et al. (1985: 103ff.).

prototypical weak verb patterns as well as the marginal pattern (3) are characterized by the fact that infinitive (thus the simple present) and the simple past tense are morphologically distinct. The non-functional verb patterns on the other hand are characterized by an identity of present and past tense forms.

While, in general, percentages accord quite well with the respective functionality of the class – such that the most functional classes do in fact also have the most members, most surprising is the high number of class 5 verbs. As Pinker, for example, points out, all verbs in this class (*hit, slit, split, quit, knit, fit, spit, shit; rid, bid, forbid; shed, spread, wed; let, bet, set, beset, upset, wet; cut, shut, put; burst, cast, cost, thrust; hurt*)[17] have stems ending in /t/ or /d/, i.e. in the (probably) prototypical weak past tense phonemes, and there are several plausible psycholinguistic explanations why 'we don't like to put or keep a suffix on a word that looks like it already has the suffix' (Pinker 1999: 60). Although Pinker claims that 'the no-extra-suffix habit is alive and well in modern speakers' (Pinker 1999: 60), and historically this class has actually gained, rather than lost, members, as the figures show (see Bauer 1997 for an analysis of this class as a productive pattern), there seems to be a definite regularization tendency. Indeed, those verbs that can be traced back to Old English were historically weak with apocope (practically all these forms are attested with a geminate <t> in the past tense which, after all, was still phonemic in Old English, cf. *let* < *lætan – lette – (ge)læten* or *sweat* < *swætan – swætte – swæt*). Today at least some of these verbs tend to form 'new' weak forms. Nevertheless, the high number of members in this class might be an indication that this less than optimally functional pattern might not be so bad in terms of functionality after all.

Another interesting feature is the fact that the 'most' functional class is only the second largest class of verbs. Whether non-standard systems remedy this situation, or whether there may be explanations for these two oddities will also be a topic to be discussed in this book.

1.4   Standard vs. non-standard English

While this study is mainly concerned with various patterns in non-standard English, the standard will be referred to as a point of comparison in many places. Terminology here basically follows dialectological practice, which implicitly assumes a shared concept of 'standard English' between readers and researchers. Many, especially corpus-linguistic, studies of recent

---

[17] This list is Pinker's, and there are some inconsistencies, some of which may be due to differences between American and British standard English. *Forbid* has the past tense forms *forbade, forbad* according to Quirk et al.(1985), the OED and all other dictionaries I have consulted. *Fit* is not included by Quirk et al. (cf. *fitted*), but by Huddleston and Pullum (2002), neither is *spit* (cf. past tense *spat*). This does not change Pinker's main point, of course.

years have demonstrated that 'the standard' is not a monolithic entity (see especially register differences in Biber et al. 1999), and these insights are not contested here. Since in Great Britain (or, indeed, the United States) no language academy was ever established that would settle disputed questions over what constitutes 'good' English or that could officially sanction language behaviour, the question of what exactly 'standard English' is can only be answered much more indirectly than, say, for French, where such an academy exists. Nevertheless, 'standard English' is much more than a mythical entity or chimera which would dissolve if you look at it too hard, although its exact borders may be fluid. Native speakers' awareness of what constitutes 'acceptable' language forms (even if they might not always use them themselves) is mirrored by the vast range of publications that deal with the subject, not to mention the huge number of dictionaries – always a bestseller when a new edition is marketed. As this study is mainly concerned with individual verb forms, I would claim that – especially for the very frequent verbs discussed in this book – native speakers of English have very clear intuitions which of these forms are officially sanctioned (through their use in school, self-help guides, in formal registers and laid down in dictionaries), and which forms constitute deviations from this norm. Wherever 'standard English' is referred to in this study, then, these shared intuitions by native speakers are meant. Individual paradigms will be based on dictionary evidence.

1.5 Materials employed

The present study relies heavily on the *Oxford English Dictionary* (OED 1994) for historical information on verb forms, paradigms and meanings, as well as the Helsinki and ARCHER corpora for quantitative analyses of diachronic developments.[18] Dialectal data come from several sources, in particular the *Linguistic Atlas of Late Mediaeval English* (LALME), Wright's *English Dialect Dictionary* from 1898 (EDD, Wright 1898–1905), Wright's *English Dialect Grammar*, based on the same material as the EDD (EDG, Wright 1905), the *Survey of English Dialects*, in particular the published Basic Material (SED, Orton and Barry 1969–71; Orton and Halliday 1962–64; Orton and Tilling 1969–71; Orton and Wakelin 1967–68), and FRED (in rough chronological order). For some current trends, material from FRED is also compared to the (regionally restricted) COLT corpus (the Corpus of London Teenage Speech).[19] While most of these sources are well known, FRED deserves a few words by way of introduction.

---

[18] For details on the diachronic part of the Helsinki corpus, see Kytö (1996) and contributions in Rissanen et al. (1993). The Helsinki corpus is available on the ICAME CD (http://icame.uib.no/). For ARCHER 1, see Biber et al. (1994).

[19] For details see Stenström et al. (2002). COLT was compiled by the University of Bergen in 1993 and is available on the ICAME CD.

The Freiburg English Dialect corpus FRED is the first corpus that makes quantitative analyses across British English dialects possible. It was compiled between 1999 and 2003 under the supervision of Bernd Kortmann[20] and contains free conversational material, mainly from oral history projects recorded during the 1970s and 1980s across Great Britain, carefully chosen for its authenticity (only dialect speakers that had several well-known dialect features in their speech were included), for regional representativeness (speech from the nine large dialect areas as detailed in Trudgill 1999 was collected) and from a roughly homogeneous age group (around 90 per cent of informants were born before 1920).[21] FRED is thus explicitly not a socially representative sociolinguistic corpus, but a corpus of traditional dialect speakers. The English counties sampled are detailed in Map 1.1.[22]

In particular, FRED contains material from the northern counties of Northumberland [1], Durham [3], Westmoreland [4], Lancashire [5], Yorkshire [6] and the Isle of Man; from the Midlands counties of Shropshire [11], Nottinghamshire [9], Leicestershire [13] and Warwickshire [17]; the southwestern counties of Cornwall [36], Devon [37], Somerset [31] and Wiltshire [32]; and the southeastern counties of Middlesex and London [30] and Kent [35]. FRED also contains material from Oxfordshire [25], which in this book has been included in the South West dialect area, and from Suffolk [22], which has been included in the South East dialect area. (All figures shown in square brackets relate to the county numbering in the *Survey of English Dialects* and a full list, both alphabetical and numerical, can be found in Appendix 2.)

All material was transcribed where no previous transcriptions existed, or where they were of poor quality. In some cases, it was re-transcribed, where we possessed some transcriptions for other purposes. These usually left out many interesting dialect phenomena (oral history project members were typically more interested in *what* was being said, rather than *how* it was being said) which could relatively easily be re-inserted into the text. (For details on the corpus compilation and transcription, see Anderwald and Wagner 2007.) All texts were digitized and are available in simple .txt-format and are thus compatible with a number of text retrieval programs. In particular, I conducted all searches with the help of WordSmith.

All searches were conducted on a pre-final version of FRED from August 2003. This was the first version which contained all the final texts, even though not all of these were necessarily edited in the final format. While there may thus be some inconsistencies inside and especially across texts, a

---

[20] With the help of grants from the German Science Foundation DFG grants Ko 1181-1/1-3.

[21] Details can be found at the project website www.anglistik.uni-freiburg.de/institut/lskortmann/ FRED/.

[22] All county designations in this book refer to the pre-1974 counties before the great reforms. Not only does much of the material come from the time before 1974, the traditional names (and borders) still seem to carry great weight in people's perceptual geography even today. A full list of county names and numbers can be found in Appendix 2.

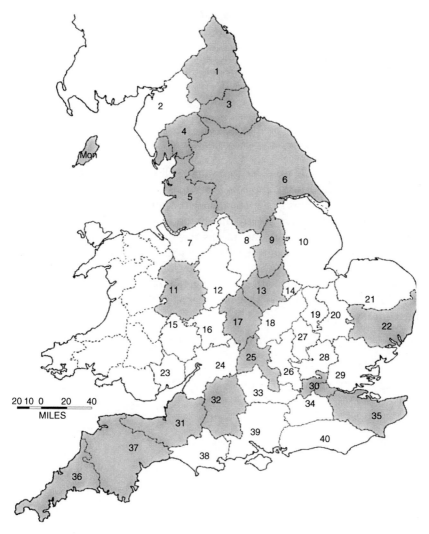

Map 1.1 English counties sampled in FRED

fixed date had to be chosen to guarantee comparability across analyses, and of course to get started in the first place, and thus I chose the latest possible version of FRED for these analyses.

FRED contains almost 2.5 million words (excluding interviewers' utterances), which are distributed across the six major dialect areas as detailed in Table 1.1. (Scotland has been further subdivided into the Hebrides, the Highlands and the Lowlands. Where appropriate, these will be referred to separately.)

Table 1.1   *FRED words per dialect area*

	Words
South East	652,871
South West	569,969
North	432,214
Midlands	358,318
Scotland	339,917
Wales	89,018
Total	**2,442,307**

The focus in FRED on older informants telling their life stories – and, in general, on oral history projects – means of course that there are certain inherent limitations in the material. For example, it can be shown that present tense contexts are greatly underrepresented in FRED (Anderwald 2002b). On the other hand, this means that past tense contexts are more frequent than in spontaneous discourse – a highly welcome skewing for the present study.

But before we continue with an investigation of past tense forms in these materials, the following two chapters will explore the past tense from a more theoretical perspective.

2   Past tense theories

> Like fruit flies, regular and irregular verbs are small and easy to
> breed, and they contain, in an easily visible form, the machinery
> that powers larger phenomena in all their glorious complexity.
> (Pinker 1999: ix)

> No-one has ever dreamed of a universal morphology, for it is
> clear that actually found formatives, as well as their functions
> and importance, vary from language to language to such an
> extent that everything about them must be reserved for special
> grammars. (Jespersen 1924: 52)

2.1   Introduction

After the short descriptive overview in the previous chapter, this chapter
will concentrate on the role of weak vs. strong past tense formation in various theoretical frameworks. Indeed, past tense formation has served and is
serving as the test case for or against individual theoretical constructions,
and this fact already merits a closer look at the various theories. In turn,
different theories may make different predictions about what to expect in
non-standard tense paradigms, and new observations from non-standard
past tense paradigms in the remainder of the book may support or revise
specific theories.

   Although the systematic study of morphology goes back at least to Indian
linguists like Panini (ca. fifth or sixth century BC), this tradition has not had
a great impact on Western theorizing (although, as we shall see, some ideas
have – without acknowledgement – found their way into generative theories). Neogrammarian linguistics, to which we owe the distinction of weak
and strong verbs, as well as the detailed Indo-European ablaut classes, was
not much concerned with theoretical questions of morphology, so that the
following overview will concentrate on current morphological theories since
the second half of the twentieth century. This is the current debate and will
therefore take prominence in this chapter. For reasons of space, I will only
try to do justice to this debate as it concerns the English past tense. Whole

books could be and indeed have been written on the subject (I point again to Pinker 1999).[1]

2.2   Chomsky and Halle

Chomsky and Halle (1968) on the surface do not belong in this overview, as they do not propose a morphological theory, nor do they take the English past tense as a prime example. Even the title is misleading, as *The Sound Pattern of English* is intended as an introduction to topics of relevance to Universal Grammar. Nevertheless, on the way they also sketch a possible (and radical) solution to the past tense problem, which is why I have chosen to include them here briefly. In addition, they are an important precursor to Lexical Phonology and Morphology presented below, perhaps the most important generative theory to date that deals with morphology.

Arguably, Chomsky and Halle (1968) is the first attempt at deriving the different past tense forms in a generative framework. Quite characteristically, however, they do not propose a morphology module (which is why on the surface this is not a morphological theory). On the other hand, this in itself is an interesting theory about morphology. Morphological processes are divided between the syntax module, delivering the input for the phonology module, and phonology itself. Rules are employed to derive the actual surface form (the 'phonological representation') for strong and weak verbs alike, as the following quotation makes clear:

the verb *sing* will appear in the lexicon as a certain feature matrix [of phonological features, LA], as will the verb *mend*. Using letters of the alphabet as informal abbreviations for certain complexes of features, i.e., certain columns of a feature matrix, we can represent the syntactically generated surface structure underlying the forms *sang* and *mended* as $_V[_V[sing]_V past]_V$ and $_V[_V[mend]_V past]_V$, respectively, where *past* is a formative with an abstract feature structure introduced by syntactic rules. The readjustment rules would replace *past* by *d*, as a general rule; but, in the case of *sang*, would delete the item *past* with the associated labeled brackets, and would add to the *i* of *sing* a feature specification indicating that it is subject to a later phonological rule which, among other things, happens to convert *i* to *æ*. Designating this new column as *, the readjustment rules would therefore give the forms $_V[s*ng]_V$ and $_V[_V[mend]_V d]_V$, respectively.

(Chomsky and Halle 1968: 11–12)

Note in particular that the past tense forms are 'syntactically generated' and the past tense morpheme ('formative') is introduced by 'syntactic rules'. This

---

[1]   The following list should by no means be taken as inclusive, but rather as exemplary. For a good overview, especially of the development inside the generative paradigm, see Carstairs-McCarthy (1992). As his overview only goes up to 1990, however, many interesting developments are not surveyed and his book is therefore slightly dated.

has also been stated more generally in the claim that 'the syntactic component of a grammar assigns to each sentence a "surface structure" that *fully
determines* the phonetic form of the sentence' (Chomsky and Halle 1968: 6,
my italics). As there is no morphology to perform the role of an interface
between syntax and phonology, the syntactic input [*past tense*] has to act
directly on the phonology of the verbs. For weak verbs, this is not problematic (at least not for English): a stipulated, general rule 'would replace
past by *d*'; purely phonological rules would then take account of the three
allomorphs (for a discussion of the underlying form, see Zwicky 1975). For
strong verbs, however, Chomsky and Halle have to assume a direct influence of syntax on the phonology of the verb stem, and indeed, they propose a range of phonological vowel-change rules that take account of strong
verbs. The vowel change *sing – sang*, for example, is described in more detail
as follows. Incidentally, Chomsky and Halle's Vowel Shift Rule should not
be taken as equivalent to the historical Great Vowel Shift, even though the
Great Vowel Shift is clearly their starting point;[2] cf. the postulated changes
for tense vowels (Chomsky and Halle 1968: 50–5, 187):[3]

ī	ū	ē	ō	ǣ	ɔ̄
↓	↓	↓	↓	↓	↓
ǣ	ɔ̄	ī	ū	ē	ō
ride	loud	see	boot	name	boat

As these rules do not suffice, however, to derive the actual present-day
forms, 'the reflexes [æ] and [ɔ̄] of original [ī] and [ū] are subject to further
rules … which adjust backness and rounding (and possible tenseness) and
result in the *required* [āy] and [āw] or [æw]' (Chomsky and Halle 1968: 187,
note 121, my emphasis).

As this still does not take account of our *sing–sang* variation, Chomsky
and Halle extend their Vowel Shift Rule from tense to lax vowels:

Consider first the nonback high vowel [i]. If this were to undergo Vowel
Shift, it would become [æ], just as [ī] becomes [ǣ]. (We continue to restrict
Diphthongization and Backness Adjustment to tense vowels, so that the
alternation [i] – [æ] for lax vowels is parallel to the alternation [ī] – [āy] for
tense vowels.) The alternation [i] – [æ] is, in fact, found in a certain class
of irregular verbs in English, e.g. *sit – sat, sing – sang*. These verbs will

---

[2] Chomsky and Halle explicitly say that what they 'call the Vowel Shift rule … is, in fact,
a synchronic residue of the Great Vowel Shift of Early Modern English' (Chomsky and
Halle 1968: 184). In general, it is clear that they try to build as much diachrony into the
synchronic description of English as possible. Whether this is desirable from a theory-
internal, not to mention a theory-external position is debatable. For an eloquent criticism,
see Blevins (2004). This discussion is taken up again in Chapter 7.

[3] The illustrating lexemes are mine.

be marked in the lexicon as belonging to a special lexical category, and by Convention 2 ... this lexical category will be distributed as a feature of each segment of these verbs, in the appropriate context. Thus, in particular, the vowel of *sit* will have a certain feature [+F] when it is in the syntactic context — *past* ... We can then account for the alternation that gives the past tense form by permitting the Vowel Shift Rule to apply also to vowels in the following specially marked context:

$$
\left[\begin{array}{c} \overline{} \\ +F \end{array} \right]
$$

(Chomsky and Halle 1968: 201)

In other words, memorized forms play no role in past tense formation whatsoever, as only the morpheme ('formative') *sing* is stored in the lexicon. After past tense affixation, *sing* undergoes a stipulated readjustment rule, and this form can then undergo the special case of the Vowel Shift Rule, leading to the correct output *sang* (or *sat* for *sit*). As Chomsky and Halle say, 'we can find a small "subregularity" in the class of irregular verbs by generalization of the Vowel Shift Rule to *certain* lax nonback vowels' (Chomsky and Halle 1968: 201, my emphasis).

This rule applies to *sing – sang*; another verb, *tell – told*, is not accounted for, however, as here we have a change not only in vowel quality, but also in quantity, as well as a suffix. The similar-looking *bring* would have to undergo yet another specific rule to rule out a wrong form like *brang*, and we could probably go on like this for the majority of English strong verbs. Chomsky and Halle have of course been criticized theory-internally for a number of other problems with their theory (underlying forms that are widely divergent from actual surface manifestations, a 'battery of rules' (Spencer 1998: 125), including free rides and cyclical applications, extrinsic ordering, unconstrainedness, and others), but for our purposes it is clear that Chomsky and Halle cannot account for the majority of standard English past tense forms employing rules without adding a range of ad hoc rules. Even if we grant this, however, the claim that both weak and strong verbs are formed by the same kind of process (in this case: a phonetic rule) obscures an important difference between the two verb classes. It is very clear that the history of English is to blame for processes like ablaut, strong–weak verbs, irregularities arising through MEOSL and so on. As Bybee puts it, 'much of what we analyze as morphophonology is fossilized sound change from bygone areas' (Bybee 1996: 247). This diachronic residue can only with the greatest difficulty be captured by synchronic rules, as through phonological attrition most, if not all, of the original conditioning factors have disappeared. Hence the many difficulties encountered in a rules-based account, and the intuitive implausibility.

Even for a purely synchronic description, however, (any) rule that derives a past tense form from the present tense form cannot account for similarities between past tense forms that have different present tense forms. Taking account of this similarity is, however, not only intuitively desirable, but also necessary if we want to accurately explain the (limited) productivity some strong verb classes apparently still have today.

2.3 Lexical Phonology and Morphology

Still in the generative school, the most widespread theory today is probably Lexical Phonology and Morphology. Katamba (1993) is a good introduction to some of the general issues; see also Carstairs-McCarthy (1992). Lexical Phonology and Morphology assumes that the lexicon is arranged in several layers or levels, called strata.[4] More precisely, lexicon entries (e.g. the lexical roots in many theories) are stored at the base, and are then moved through the different strata to form words. Morphological (and their concomitant phonological) rules are stored at different strata, which serves to explain some very distinctive differences that obtain between otherwise quite similar processes, e.g. of derivation. Linguists are generally not agreed on the number of strata – Katamba presents a consensus model of just two strata, Kiparsky (1982) has proposed three, others have even argued for four distinct strata including loops (Halle and Mohanan 1985; Mohanan 1986 – I will not go into details of the loop discussion here).

For the sake of exposition, I will describe Katamba's two-stratum model here. It is important to note that the different strata do not directly correspond to the difference between inflection and derivation, or between derivation and compounding. Rather, some inflectional processes are stored at stratum 1, some at stratum 2. Some derivational processes operate at stratum 1, some at stratum 2. Only compounding is confined to stratum 2, whereas conversion again operates on both levels. Where theorists have proposed more strata, these are of course filled differently. Kiparsky (1982), for example, proposed that on stratum 1 there would be irregular inflection and derivation; on stratum 2 only regular derivation and compounding; and on stratum 3 only regular inflection, and that past tense t/d is affixed twice, once to strong verbs like *kneel – knelt* on level 1, and once to weak verbs on level 2. Halle and Mohanan (1985) divide the tasks between their four strata: stratum 1 contains irregular inflection and derivation as in Kiparsky's and Katamba's models; stratum 2 contains only regular derivation, but also some non-cyclic inflectional rules; stratum 3 contains only compounding; and stratum 4 only regular inflection. It seems that the mid-1980s saw the high

---

[4] Singh (2001) consistently calls this type of constraint-rich morphology *Paninian*, rightly pointing out that level ordering is not an invention of the twentieth century, but can be traced back to the Indian linguist Panini (sixth or fifth century BC). However, this source is generally not openly acknowledged by generativists.

point of this proliferation of strata; since then theorists have been reducing their strata because of insurmountable problems, and most theorists seem to be content to assume only two strata these days. See also the more recent discussion in Giegerich (1999). To return to Katamba's two-stratum model, for derivation, stratum 1 contains (rules about) non-neutral affixes, i.e. those affixes that change the stress pattern or affect the base phonologically in other ways, whereas stratum 2 contains neutral ('regular') affixes. This is basically equivalent to the difference between strong and weak boundaries in Chomsky and Halle (1968), or to the difference between primary and secondary affixes, the very old distinction in morphology that goes back to Indian linguists and is not per se controversial.

More pertinent to the discussion here, stratum 1 also contains irregular inflections; stratum 2 contains the regular inflectional processes. In this way a root like *sing* would undergo past tense formation on stratum 1. [sing + PAST] would then (still on stratum 1) presumably undergo the appropriate phonological rule; as *sing* is marked as a class III verb (like *shrink – shrank – shrunk*), the phonological ablaut rule would turn out the form *sang* marked for past tense. On each stratum, the appropriate phonological rules always apply before the lexical item is moved further to the next stratum; this is the rule of Strict Cyclicity (also called the Strict Cycle Condition).[5] The internal brackets are then erased, so that the next stratum has no access to the fact that *sang* contains the root *sing*. This is the rule of Bracket Erasure (or the Bracket Erasure Convention). *Sang* is still marked as being a verb and as being a past tense form, conventionally noted in this way: [sang]$_{V\ PAST}$. For this reason all regular (past tense) processes on stratum 2 cannot apply, preventing forms such as **singed* (because the rule does not have access to the root *sing* any longer) or double past tense forms like **sanged* (because *sang* is already marked for past tense). Equally, no further phonological processes apply. Once a lexeme has passed through stratum 2, it then leaves the lexical component and is 'ready' to be used in syntax.[6]

For *regular* past tense forms, the complementary picture applies: a root like *hunt* is not marked as undergoing an irregular process on stratum 1 and thus passes through stratum 1 unchanged, enters stratum 2 as [[hunt]+PAST] and there undergoes regular *-ed* suffixation. The appropriate phonological rule then applies to [hunted]$_{PAST}$, (namely that after /t/ and /d/, the past tense morpheme is pronounced as /ɪd/), resulting in the correct phonological

---

[5] I am aware that this is an oversimplification. Halle and Mohanan explicitly claim cyclic and non-cyclic strata, saying that in 'a cyclic stratum, we intend that the relevant phonological rules apply to every morphological constituent in the stratum … immediately after the application of each morphological process. After the phonological rules have applied, the result is again a potential input to morphology … In addition to cyclic strata there are noncyclic strata in which all the morphological processes apply en bloc followed by the phonological rules of that stratum' (Halle and Mohanan 1985: 66).

[6] Here, postlexical phonological rules may of course apply, but these are not the concern of morphology any longer and will therefore not be presented here in detail.

form /hʌntɪd/ and *hunted* can leave the lexicon to enter syntax. The same principles apply, ceteris paribus, to irregular vs. regular plural formation (e.g. *oxen* vs. *foxes*), comparative formation (*better* vs. *hotter*) and any other inflectional processes.

Katamba's two-stratum model makes some more claims, such that in general, more productive processes apply later than less productive ones; and semantically more regular processes also apply later than more irregular ones. In general, one can say that the criterion of affix ordering is the most important criterion in determining strata membership of individual affixes (and rules) (for severe criticism of the importance of affix ordering, see again Giegerich 1999).

In Katamba's model inflection and derivation are situated in one stratum together, so an important question for morphological theory is the order of processes *inside* the same stratum. In general, an *external* ordering can only be effected (by the linguist) by stratum ordering. Katamba therefore claims that inside a stratum, rules are intrinsically ordered:

> They apply following the general principle that where several rules can potentially apply in a derivation, the interaction between them that maximises the chances of each rule applying is what the theory dictates ... Every opportunity to apply should be given to each rule at the stratum where its input requirements are met ... if rule A feeds rule B, rule A must apply first ... If rules are in a bleeding rather than a feeding interaction [i.e. if rule A pre-empts the application of rule B and C, LA] ... the Elsewhere Condition comes in.
>
> (Katamba 1993: 126)

The Elsewhere Condition states that the rule applying to the most specific subset must apply first, and the most general rule only applies once all the more specific rules have already had a chance of applying. The most general rule can then simply be stated to apply 'elsewhere', hence the name. An example would be the regular past tense allomorphs, which, when ordered, provide a very neat schema:

Regular past tense <-ed> becomes:

(i)   /ɪd/ after /t/ or /d/
(ii) /t/ after voiceless consonants
(iii) /d/ elsewhere.

Rule ordering is a very efficient mechanism as it makes redundant (in this case):

(a) having to specify in (ii) that /t/ is precluded after /t/ (as this is already stated by the more specific rule in (i), which has already applied by the time rule (ii) applies);
(b) having to specify in (iii) that /d/ is similarly precluded after /d/, again because this case has already been covered in (i); and finally

(c) having to specify in (iii) that /d/ occurs after both voiced consonants and vowels, as these are what constitute the 'rest', i.e. the 'elsewhere' class.

Rule ordering in this way is thus very economical and results in a very elegant and reduced system.

The two-stratum model also explains the phenomenon of blocking, both inside a stratum (e.g. by the Elsewhere Condition) and across strata – it is, for example, generally held that the irregular past tense *sang* blocks the application of the general rule in stratum 2. Stratum ordering also mirrors productivity (if we assume that generality of application is equivalent to productivity), and the regular/irregular distinction also holds for semantics, such that the semantically more regular processes are ordered on a higher stratum, the semantically more idiosyncratic ones on a lower one.

One possible remaining question relates to homonyms. Why does *ring*1 ('ring a bell') undergo past tense formation on stratum 1 to *rang*, whereas *ring*2 (in the sense 'put a ring around') is regular and passes through stratum 1 unscathed? Katamba's answer has to do with conversion. He claims that the relatively rare verb-to-noun conversion is situated on stratum 1, being an irregular sort of process, but that the regular (and much more wide-spread) noun-to-verb conversion does not take place before stratum 2. In other words, the verb *to ring*2 only becomes a verb on stratum 2, namely through conversion from the noun *the ring*. This is the word as it is stored in the base stratum and as it enters stratum 1. Naturally, past tense forma-tion cannot apply to *ring* at this stage because it is still a noun. Once it has become a verb on stratum 2, only regular inflectional processes are available, hence the difference between irregular *sing – sang* and regular *ring – ringed* (or, indeed, between the irregular *ring – rang* (a bell, the phone) and regular *ring – ringed*). It has not yet been tested whether all apparent exceptions can be explained like this.

Perhaps the biggest advantage of the stratum model and no doubt one of its most attractive features is the fact that a wide range of observations in morphological theory can be subsumed under one general idea and can thus be connected. This no doubt results in an economical and elegant model – however, as McMahon comments, 'elegance, maximal generality and econ-omy are still considered, not as useful initial heuristics, but as paramount in determining the adequacy of phonological [and, presumably, morpho-logical, LA] analyses' (McMahon 2000: 7). Giegerich similarly points out that many features of these theories are the linguist's and not necessarily the speaker's (see Giegerich 1999: 80 et passim) – adequacy of the model is thus even internally not determined yet. In explanatory terms, it is also important to note that Lexical Phonology and Morphology does not make any specific claim to psychological reality. Particularly if one is interested not just in adequacy within the constraints and terms set up by a particular theory, but in functional or cognitive explanatory power, Lexical Phonology and Morphology has had little to offer as yet.

It is interesting to note, however, that the model of Lexical Phonology and Morphology, in this respect like Chomsky and Halle (1968), relies on rule-based mechanisms only. Very clearly, both *sang* and *hunted* are created by rules, the difference being that *sang* is created by a rule that applies far less generally than the *hunted* rule. The differences between strong and weak past tense forms are accounted for simply by affixation on different levels of the linguistic system (stratum 1 vs. stratum 2 affixation). In the extreme case, of course, this means that we would again have one rule for one verb form.[7] Katamba tries to account for subregularities in the strong verb domain by grouping strong verbs into ablaut classes, as we have seen (see the classification on page 5). As discussed there, however, this classification alone cannot account for the majority of strong verbs, e.g. identical verbs (*hit – hit – hit*), former weak verbs with a devoiced alveolar (*bend – bent – bent*), former weak verbs with additional vowel change (*mean – meant – meant*), true strong verbs with vowel series different from Katamba's seven classes (*choose – chose – chosen; break – broke – broken; take – took – taken,* etc.) and some others. As already mentioned, rules or sub-rules also cannot account for the obvious similarity between forms with different present tense vowel, as *choose – chose – chosen* and *break – broke – broken* above, as these same forms cannot be derived from the different present tense forms (without stipulating two rules). Halle and Mohanan, however, claim that their model handles all Modern English strong verbs except *go, make* and *stand* and only employs phonological rules to do so (see Halle and Mohanan 1985).

A further point is that it is not clear what the psychological claims in this model are. Based on Universal Grammar, it would seem that Lexical Phonology and Morphology would also have to be committed to innateness (see the discussion in Lightfoot 2006: 66–70). It is intuitively clear, however, that individual rules cannot be innate, as they are highly language-specific. Even the most general past tense rule ('add *–ed*') does not apply to any other language than English. (Although one might conceive of an even more abstract rule, e.g. 'Mark the past tense'; this is the solution some authors propose in Optimality Theory.) If rules are not innate, they have to be learnable, and here it is not clear whether the evidence supports a purely rule-based learning scenario (Halle and Mohanan 1985 are silent on this point).

Secondly, while Lexical Phonology and Morphology might fulfil abstract criteria like elegance, economy and perhaps symmetry, which may be desirable in a theory from a meta-theoretical point of view, it is by no means clear

---

[7] Whether this is really fundamentally different from claiming lexicon entries for individual verbs as in dual-route theories is debatable. This discussion is continued in Chapter 7.

that these are also criteria that would make a theoretical description psychologically plausible. A theory might describe the facts adequately[8] and yet not be psychologically adequate in that it may not tell us anything about the way the human brain processes this information, or why.

Like Chomsky and Halle (1968), Lexical Phonology and Morphology is also an expressly synchronic theory. Like its predecessor, Lexical Phonology and Morphology accounts for most diachronic processes by relegating them to stratum 1. Halle and Mohanan invent a battery of nine rules, most of them 'ablaut rules' to account for 'the inflexion of the approximately 200 English "strong" verbs' (Halle and Mohanan 1985: 104–14), but as these apply even to base forms (e.g. present tense *run* is derived from underlying /rɨn/, present tense *buy* is derived from underlying /bīx/), they have met with strong criticism even from within the generative camp, and their suggestions have mostly been abandoned again.[9] As Bybee comments:

Level-Ordering models this diachronic layering by recreating it in a synchronic grammar. This works fairly well for English where the deepest level is largely comprised of morphological patterns that entered English through the borrowing of French words, many of which were already morphologically complex and thus carried with them fossilized phonological processes that had occurred in French. Thus certain old phonological processes of French (like Velar Softening) as well as the older sound changes of English (like the Great Vowel Shift) affect words at this level and not at later levels, where the more productive, largely Germanic patterns are described. However, in other languages, which may not have this bifurcation in the lexicon, it is not so clear that rules are positioning so neatly on distinct levels. (Bybee 1996: 262)

It is no wonder then that, apart from internal inconsistencies and contradictions, Lexical Phonology and Morphology has been further developed in two ways: in psycholinguistic theories, first of all taking account of results from psycholinguistic experiments and trying to model more accurately the way the human brain works, and secondly in Optimality Theory, getting rid of serialization in favour of parallel processing. Both approaches will be presented next.

2.4   Optimality Theory

Optimality Theory is not expressly a morphological theory. Unlike the other theories exposed above and especially below, it has said little about

---

[8] And even this is disputed in the case of Lexical Phonology and Morphology; which is why it has been further developed into either psycholinguistic approaches or Optimality Theory.

[9] But for a more constrained account inside the framework of Lexical Phonology, cf. McMahon (2000: 129–39).

the past tense (yet), much less taken it as a test case, and it has not pre-sented any coherent answers yet in the weak verb–strong verb debate. On the other hand, Optimality Theory is so ubiquitous in phonology today that it is worth briefly exploring its potential for the past tense debate here; this section relies mostly on the introduction to 'mainstream' Optimality Theory by McCarthy (2002).

Optimality Theory, probably the most fashionable theory of formalists of the late 1990s, was established in 1993 as one of the reactions against level ordering in phonology (e.g. as in Lexical Phonology and Morphology). (It was only published more than a decade later as Prince and Smolensky 2004, but had been circulating in manuscript form and was later also made avail-able online.) While the stratum model relies on serial processing (such that the output of one process can then serve as the input to the next process), Optimality Theory is expressly a model of parallel processing.[10] Optimality Theory has only later been extended to cover syntax as well as language acquisition; it is striking that Optimality Theory as it is established today does not – or only very rarely – mention morphology (for a notable excep-tion, cf. the one overview article by Russell 1997). This may again in part be due to the fact that morphology for many theorists is not a separate module, but is subsumed under syntax on the one hand and phonology on the other (as in much generative work).[11] In Optimality Theory, therefore, phono-logical constraints often include morphological information.

The most important components of Optimality Theory are: GEN, univer-sal constraints, and EVAL. GEN (from Generate) produces all possible input candidates. This is effected by a stipulation termed 'richness of the base'. A finite number of constraints constrain the output of GEN. Constraints are ranked hierarchically, and are violable. Crucially, constraints are univer-sal, obeying the principles of Universal Grammar (and are thus presumably innate – although many authors are silent on this point), whereas constraint *ranking* is language-specific (or indeed grammar-specific, i.e. speaker-, dia-lect-, or even style-specific). The third component is EVAL (from Evaluate), which evaluates all possible candidates generated by the base against the constraint hierarchy by assigning violation marks. The candidate that incurs fewest violations of the highest-ranking constraints comes out as the opti-mal candidate and is therefore the candidate that we witness in a particular language.[12]

---

[10] Optimality Theory is therefore not 'generative' in the original meaning of the word, although it stands in personal as well as institutional inheritance to Generative Grammar, and is expressly formalist in theoretical outlook. Nevertheless, Optimality Theory contains clear functional elements and can indeed be regarded as a meeting ground for formal and functional approaches (Prince and Smolensky 2004).

[11] The debate is long-standing; for arguments why morphology cannot be reduced to phon-ology and syntax, see especially Aronoff (1994).

[12] In practical terms, of course, the procedure goes the other way around: the linguist observes the actually occurring form, which is by definition optimal, and tries to arrange

Constraints basically fall into two groups: faithfulness constraints (positing identity of input and output), and markedness constraints, antagonistically opposed to faithfulness.

Optimality Theory has developed a strict set of formal conventions, and in order to understand the conventional notation in tabular form a short introduction is necessary. In Optimality Theory tables (called OT tableaux), the candidate forms are entered into the first column; the next columns represent the constraints and their ordering. The highest-ranking constraint is entered furthest left, the lower-ranking constraints in the subsequent positions to the right. In the intersecting boxes (below the constraints and to the right of the candidates) the evaluation of each candidate in the light of each constraint is entered. If a candidate violates a constraint, one (or more) asterisks are entered in the respective field. If a candidate violates a high-ranking constraint crucially (i.e. where another candidate does not violate this constraint), this violation is fatal, removing the offending candidate from the competition, and this fatal violation is marked by an exclamation mark. Once a candidate is removed, other violations (or not) of lower-ranking constraints are not relevant any longer, and the cells are therefore shaded grey. Violation marks are simply compared across candidates, and the candidate with the fewest violations of the highest-ranking constraints comes out as the winner. The winning candidate is marked by a pointing hand (rarely an arrow is used instead).

In the hypothetical example shown in Table 2.1, constraint 1, the highest-ranking one, serves to eliminate candidate C from the competition. As C fatally violates constraint 1, it is not further considered in the lower constraints, even though it might actually do better there than any of the other candidates (cf. for example constraint 2). But because it has already violated constraint 1, the evaluation only proceeds for candidates A and B. For them, the next highest constraint is decisive: candidate B violates constraint 2 fatally, again taking it out of the race, leaving only candidate A as the winner. Even though candidate A fares much worse on constraint 3 (where it incurs three violation marks, vs. candidate B's zero, and candidate C's one), this is not taken into account by the evaluator.

This example shows how a candidate may come out as 'optimal' even though it clearly violates one or even several constraints. What counts is only that it is relatively 'better', i.e. incurs fewer violations than the other

the constraints in such an order that the actual form (as well as all other observed actual forms) is compatible with the constraint hierarchy. As Auer has correctly pointed out, the name Optimality Theory may in fact be a misnomer, as linguists in this framework do not pursue the question of what is optimal (Peter Auer, personal communication). Optimality Theory is also not concerned with the discovery of the one optimal linguistic system, or the one optimal language. The goal is instead the discovery of a consistent constraint hierarchy, which amounts to the writing of a complete grammar of a language – an honourable, if slightly different goal.

Table 2.1 *Example 1 OT tableau*

	Constraint 1	Constraint 2	Constraint 3	Constraint 4
☞Candidate A		*	***	
Candidate B		!**		*
Candidate C	!**		*	

Table 2.2 *Example 2 OT tableau*

	Constraint 2	Constraint 1	Constraint 3	Constraint 4
Candidate A	!*		****	
Candidate B	!**			*
☞Candidate C		**	*	

Table 2.3 *Example 3 OT tableau*

	Constraint 3	Constraint 2	Constraint 1	Constraint 4
Candidate A	!****	*		
☞Candidate B		**		*
Candidate C	!*		**	

candidates on the high-ranking constraints, not that it does not incur *any* violations on a particular constraint.

At the same time, this example demonstrates how a simple re-ranking of constraints would result in dramatically different forms coming out as optimal. A simple exchange of the order of constraints 1 and 2, for example, results in candidate C as the winner; an exchange of constraints 3 and 1 results in candidate B coming out as optimal, as shown in Tables 2.2 and 2.3.

These examples show the powerful technicalities of Optimality Theory. Simple re-ranking of constraints can result in radically different output, although exactly the same constraints are involved. It is clear, at least in principle, that the exponential number of possible ranking orderings may account for a very large number of different languages. Indeed, constraint ranking might be too powerful in this respect. Clearly, the comparatively small number of actual languages would have to be shown to use only a restricted subset of possible ranking orders.

There are several possible strategies to constrain constraint ranking, such that some constraints may be linked to others, etc. At the same time, however, proposals for new constraints are proliferating, making more and more unlikely an orderly, plausible set of universal constraints that can indeed be shown to be active in a wide variety of languages. McMahon, for example, deplores that 'there are currently so many candidate constraints which could be used and combined in so many different ways, that it is hard to see how we are to tell when we have found the right analysis. Many analyses therefore reduce to exercises in constraint invention, in the absence of any sensible limit on the form and number of constraints to be proposed' (McMahon 2003: 86).

While Optimality Theory can be shown to work well in phonology, with universal constraints like 'all syllables must have an onset', 'syllables must not have a coda', 'similar sounds must not occur next to each other', etc., it is not at all clear yet what universal *morphological* constraints would look like. Because of the stipulation that constraints have to be language universal, it would make little sense positing a constraint like 'for past tense: add *–ed*', because clearly this is language-specific; even for the Germanic languages this constraint could not hold. If we formulate a more general constraint (e.g. 'Express past tense on the verb'), then it is not clear how EVAL would distinguish between the possible form *knowed* and the actual form *knew*, as for both the past tense is clearly expressed. Other constraints would clearly have to come to the analyst's aid.

Indeed, the few Optimality Theory morphologists that have tried to investigate this topic seem to assume largely language-specific constraints. However, even once these are permitted, constraints like 'for past tense: add *–ed*' cannot do the complete work: it is clear that all strong verbs would violate this general constraint. A higher ranked constraint, somehow specific to strong verbs, would therefore have to be admitted.

Strong verbs are accounted for differently in Optimality Theory to date, no doubt mirroring the fact that Optimality Theory morphology is still very much a minority concern. Stemberger (2001), for example, posits constraints like[13] 'Express the past on the verb', 'Express the past on the auxiliary', or 'Express the past only once', which can be reasonably assumed to be universal (if differently ranked), and then adds the English-specific constraint '**Past(d)**', accounting for the default past tense (i.e. the weak verbs), whereas the host of irregular forms are constrained individually, e.g. by the constraint '**Past(sæŋ)**' (Stemberger 2001).

Russell on the other hand tries to make something of the observation that 'most irregular past tenses of English resemble regular past tenses at least to the extent that they end in an alveolar stop' (Russell 1997: 128). Nevertheless, he has to concede that 'it is not immediately clear what the best way is of making the irregular pasts of English look like [*feed – fed*, LA], while keeping the regular pasts from ever following suit' (Russell 1997: 128).

Burzio (2002), finally, as another of the few proponents of Optimality Theory morphology, stipulates a second kind of faithfulness condition: besides the 'classical' input-to-output faithfulness, he also considers output-to-output

---

[13] I paraphrase his constraints slightly here for intelligibility. My paraphrases are in single inverted commas, direct quotation of his constraints are in bold.

faithfulness constraints. This is a very interesting extension of Optimality Theory, as the theory is made to account for surface similarities of output forms as well. In fact, Burzio explicitly acknowledges the connectionist approach (see below) and proposes connectionist output-to-output links for strong verbs, but 'pure' constraint ordering for weak verbs.[14]

Stipulating language-specific constraints, however, leads Optimality Theory *ad absurdum*. In this way, constraints proliferate beyond measure – in the case of the English past tense, this would probably mean that up to 150 constraints would have to be posited for the 150 strong verb types (see Quirk et al.'s list in Appendix 1), resulting in astronomical and nonsensical ranking orders. Alternatively, these 150 constraints would be unranked, again resulting in a not very economical system. In addition, once the theoretical status of constraints as universal and (by extension) innate is given up, this leaves the constraints themselves unconstrained and ultimately unverifiable. If languages do not have to be compared and thus no counterexamples are possible, Optimality Theory morphology becomes, at most, nothing more than an elegant descriptive system, at worst vacuous and utterly circular.

Clearly, if one proposes language-specific constraints (other than just as a descriptive device), one would have to give up innateness; as language-specific constraints cannot possibly be innate, they would have to be learned or invented during language acquisition. This is in fact a minority position inside Optimality Theory, held by, e.g., Hayes (1996).

As Otto Jespersen has already said, 'no one has ever dreamed of doing a universal morphology' (Jespersen 1924: 52), and as Singh similarly points out, 'it [is] not possible to construct any very tightly restricted system of universal morphology' (Singh 2001).

On the basis of probably the most detailed investigation of inflectional systems to date, Wurzel says very specifically: 'die in einer gegebenen Sprache vorkommenden Marker gehören keinem universellen vorgegebenen Inventar von Markern an, morphologische Marker sind strikt einzelsprachlich. In diesem Sinne haben Flexionsklassen anders als ... phonologische Klassen keine universelle Basis' ([Morphological] markers occurring in a given language do not belong to a universally determined inventory of markers; morphological markers are strictly language-specific. In this sense, in contrast to phonological classes, inflectional classes have no universal basis) (Wurzel 1984: 71, my translation).

In summary, then, one can say that there are no coherent accounts of the past tense problem in Optimality Theory yet, probably due to inherent

---

[14] Different extensions or reconfigurations of 'classic' Optimality Theory have been proposed more recently, e.g. Bye in a conference paper proposes an additional component called 'morpholexical control', in which all output from EVAL is 'checked against language-specific declarative constraints', arguing that 'not all allomorphy is governed by phonotactic considerations', eventually conceding that 'allomorph distribution is beyond the pale of the Optimality Theory phonology' (Bye 2005).

difficulties, much less any predictions for non-standard systems, although there are very promising attempts to model intra-speaker variation in derived models such as stochastic Optimality Theory.

2.5   Stochastic Optimality Theory

Variation in 'classical' Optimality Theory is handled in the 'usual' generative way, in that speakers are assumed to possess multiple (rather than variable) grammars. In the case of Optimality Theory this means that speakers juggle between different constraint rankings. Variable output would thus really be code-switching or grammar-switching (cf. Anttila 2002 for phonological variation – by extension, the same should hold for morphological variation as well). It is clear that with the astronomical number of possible constraint rankings for a single grammar already, the possession of a multitude of constraint rankings becomes increasingly implausible (for sociolinguistic arguments why grammars must be variable, see Preston 2004).

For these and other reasons, Optimality Theory has been further developed to model variation explicitly. So-called stochastic Optimality Theory (Boersma and Hayes 2001) differs from standard Optimality Theory in that constraints are not ranked absolutely, but on a continuous scale. Constraints are positioned on the scale by their ranking value. The crucial point is that during 'evaluation time' (the moment of speaking) a random value is added to the ranking value. In this way, constraints that are sufficiently close to each other can sometimes overlap in their ranges: 'the grammar can produce variable outputs if some constraint rankings are close to each other' (Boersma and Hayes 2001). Assuming that the ranges of all constraints are equally wide, and that the ranges are normally distributed, in most cases the ranking order will be a >> b >> c. Sometimes, however, a and b can switch places, so that the ranking order is reversed to b >> a >> c. There is a gradual learning algorithm that, implemented on a computer, performs reasonably well. Starting from identical ranking values, on the basis of learning data the constraints are ordered and re-ordered (promoted and demoted). In this way, not only the learning data can be described, but also their quantitative preferences.

However, a similar caveat applies to stochastic Optimality Theory as to standard Optimality Theory: Optimality Theory presupposes (in most versions) that constraints are innate. All stochastic Optimality Theory does is show how the correct ranking of constraints can be performed during a learning stage. It does not show how language learners (computers or children) come to *acquire* the constraints in the first place. Boersma and Hayes do not mention this explicitly, but they say: 'if the language learner has access to an appropriate inventory of constraints, then a complete grammar can be derived' (2001: 45).

Baayen also notes that (stochastic) Optimality Theory is a 'memoryless system that presupposes that it is known beforehand which constraints might be relevant' (Baayen 2003: 257). The gradual learning algorithm discards exemplars after learning (this is the reason why Baayen calls it 'memoryless') – this may in fact be unnecessary, as the phonological form of the words has to be stored anyway.

However, in the absence of an Optimality Theory model for the English past tense (let alone non-standard systems of the past tense including variable ones), stochastic Optimality Theory, although an interesting starting point, is difficult to assess as a serious contender that would offer meaningful insights into this topic.

2.6 Psycholinguistic theories

It is in psycholinguistics where the English past tense has taken on the role of the guinea pig, 'fruit fly' or even 'single combatant' (Pinker 1999: 92) between rivalling theoretical approaches. The (English) past tense is seen to best exemplify the distinction between two fundamentally different psychological mechanisms, namely the creation by rules on the one hand, and word storage in the memory on the other hand – also described as the difference between rule learning and rote learning, or between syntax and the lexicon. So-called dual-route or dual-processing theories come closest to the traditional regular–irregular distinction, and can also be traced back to the generative stratum model, with which they are not wholly incompatible. (See also Hockett 1987.) (The rival connectionist approach is discussed in section 2.7.)

Dual-route theories, or words-and-rules theories in Pinker's more popular terms (cf. the title of his publications, e.g. Pinker 1998, 1999), claim that there is a very basic mental, psychological contrast between strong verbs like *sing – sang* and weak verbs like *hunt – hunted*. The past tense *sang* has to be listed in the lexicon (or, in more psycholinguistic terms, has to be stored in the memory), from where it is retrieved as such. Technically, *sang* can therefore be regarded as a stem. This means that irregular verbs have to be simply learned by rote and then remembered (according well with most second-language learners' experiences). This is facilitated by the fact that strong verbs tend to be highly frequent (although the causal connection probably goes the other way: strong verbs can keep their strong forms precisely because they have an extremely high token frequency, at a comparatively low type frequency).[15] Weak past tense forms like *hunted* on the other hand are created by the general rule 'add -*ed* to the base', and only the base has to be

---

[15] As mentioned above, Pinker has striking figures. In average conversational data, weak verbs (despite their incredibly high type frequency) only amount to 25 to 30 per cent of past tense tokens; see Pinker 1999: 227.

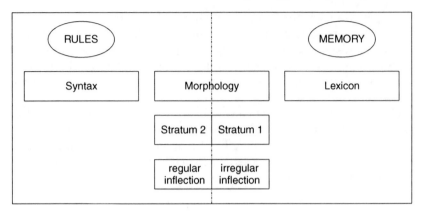

Figure 2.1 Dual-route models

stored in the memory. Past tense formation thus basically employs two very different processes, remembering (retrieving stored forms) on the one hand, and applying rules creatively on the other, and its theoretical interest derives precisely from straddling the boundary between two supposedly fundamental processes of human cognition.[16]

There is a host of experimental evidence that can be adduced in support of this claim (opponents adduce a second group of experiments that support diametrically opposed positions), in fact so much evidence that it has filled whole books (e.g. Pinker 1999 is almost exclusively concerned with the English past tense; Penke 2006 is a particularly good overview of psycholinguistic experiments in English and German). Dual-route theories can best be diagrammatically depicted as in Figure 2.1 by where they draw the boundary between the mental 'territory' where rule-governed behaviour dominates (syntax and regular inflection) and the territory where memory retrieval dominates (lexicon including irregular inflection).

Nevertheless, this position is probably too strong. As Pinker says, 'the story could end here were it not for a complicating factor. That factor is the existence of *patterns* among the irregular verbs ... these patterns are not just inert resemblances but are occasionally generalized by live human speakers ... the irregular forms are not just a set of arbitrary exceptions, memorized individually by rote, and therefore cannot simply be attributed to a lexicon of stored items, as in the word-rule theory' (Pinker 1998: 223–4 – emphasis original). Pinker's solution is a modification of word-and-rule theory by adding an associative component in the memory, probably quite similar to Bybee's associative network presented below: 'memory ... is not just a list

[16] As Bybee points out, rules and representations (i.e. 'words') may be equivalent logically (Bybee 1988: 121), but Pinker explicitly claims psycholinguistic reality for either procedure.

of unrelated slots, but is partly associative: features are linked to features (as in the connectionist pattern associators), as well as words being linked to words' (Pinker 1998: 225).

On the other side of the dividing line, Pinker has also recently conceded that rule-based forms do not have to depend exclusively on rule-production, but that the very frequent weak verbs may in fact also be stored in the memory:

> words-and-rules theory assumes that memory is constantly working alongside rules – that's how irregular verbs arise to begin with – and it would be a strange mental block indeed that would force the memory system to be amnesic for all the regular past-tense forms it hears ... The words-and-rules theory predicts only that people don't *depend* on stored past-tense forms, not that they are *incapable* of storing them. People use a rule to generate and judge past-tense forms when they need to, and if some regular forms have been stored in memory, they are available but not indispensable.
>
> (Pinker 1999: 137)

With these concessions, Pinker's position comes much closer to a model like Bybee's, possibly bridging the gap between dual-route and connectionist approaches (more on which below).

It could be argued that the stipulation of Lexical Phonology and Morphology (in the lexicon) that *sing* undergoes irregular past tense formation at stratum 1 is not so different after all from stipulating in the dual-route model that the past tense of *sing* is *sang* (in the memory), and thus dual-route theories and two-stratum models might after all be considered quite similar. The difference is that dual-route theories explicitly claim that they intend to model a psychologically real situation, and suggestively support their model with experimental evidence (such as reaction times, retrieval times, evidence from language acquisition and language loss, language disabilities, neurolinguistic evidence like brain scans, etc.; see Penke 2006). In particular, (token, not type) frequency, as we have seen in the quote by Pinker above, plays a pivotal role and is used to explain (1) why strong verbs are still strong; (2) why infrequent strong verbs tend to switch verb classes and become weak; (3) why new analogical extensions like *sneak – snuck* are possible; (4) why frequent weak verbs can be both stored and derived through a rule; and of course productivity; (5) why new or unknown verbs can immediately and uncontroversially be assigned a correct weak form (the 'wug' test, see Berko Gleason 1958).

Experimental evidence on the other hand does not play a role at all in Lexical Phonology and Morphology, perhaps because this kind of evidence ranges too clearly under performance; like all generative approaches, Lexical Phonology and Morphology is designed to model competence, not performance, which results in slight, but ultimately important differences between these two models.

Finally, however, the most important difference is that Lexical Phonology and Morphology considers only one mechanism, rules (if different kinds of them), that are responsible for the output of strong vs. weak verbs, whereas dual-route theories use two very different mechanisms.

In sum, especially with Pinker's concession above (p. 34–5), dual-route theories offer an intuitively plausible, psycholinguistically well-supported model of the (English) past tense forms. However, frequency effects and associative components seem to have been added to the model in a rather ad hoc manner in the light of overwhelming evidence from the connectionist camp, watering down the original dual-route theory considerably.[7] It is at least conceivable that in the light of non-standard data, dual-route theories would have to be altered further; it is also conceivable that Pinker's model is flexible enough to allow incorporation of results from non-standard data.

2.7   Connectionist approaches

In contrast to the dual-route model presented above, the connectionist approach can be termed a 'single-route' theory which only proposes one mechanism, rather than two, for the creation of past tense forms. In principle, single-route theories could rely either on rules alone, or on memory alone, but reliance on rules alone (as exemplified by Chomsky and Halle 1968) has come under serious attack by critics (especially in the aftermath of the publication of Halle and Mohanan 1985; for a more recent modified proposal, see McMahon 2000: 129–39). All other proponents of single-route theories can therefore be counted in the connectionist camp, relying on memory alone, and it is here that frequency plays an important role. Rules are seen not as constitutive, but as emergent properties of complex systems. This fact is of course very persuasive; as we know, all native speakers are able to apply highly complex (morphological or syntactic) rules seemingly effortlessly and accurately. However, even trained specialists (like students of linguistics, for example) have difficulties in making explicit apparently simple rules, e.g. the regular past tense allomorphs in past tense formation. It is clear that the vast majority of the population therefore do not possess these rules explicitly, even if they apply them practically without exception, effortlessly as well as faultlessly. In other words, simple observation makes clear that these kinds of rules have to be part of implicit or unconscious knowledge at best. If a model can be constructed in which rules emerge from the data input, and the system works 'as if it knew' the rule, then this would of course be a possible model for how the human brain may for example process past tense data during language learning.

---

[7] This does not need to be a real-world disadvantage, of course: eclectic theories might be able to model linguistic reality far better than theoretically pure or stringent models.

Connectionism is a cover term for several artificial neural networks, technically also called pattern associator models, and the term alone already shows that a strong claim about modelling the human brain is made. In connectionist models, there is no inherent difference between strong and weak past tense formation – this is clearly a minority position, if one considers how widespread dual-route assumptions are across different functional as well as formal frameworks. Contra dual-route theories, connectionists would hold that the striking differences that we do observe, e.g. between strong and weak past tense verbs, are mainly due to frequency.

Connectionism was first introduced by Rumelhart and McClelland (1986), but has been modified considerably since then. (For a more recent summary of the debate, cf. Daugherty and Seidenberg 1994; and especially Penke 2006.) Connectionists argue from facts concerning language acquisition. As is generally well known (if simplified), in learning strong verbs children typically start out by producing the correct strong verbs in a first stage. In a second stage, they typically over-generalize the (weak verb) regular rule, resulting in mistakes like *breaked*, *knowed*, whereas in a third stage the strong verbs are then applied correctly again. This U-shaped learning curve is generally interpreted as resulting from 'mimicking' (reproducing the correct parental input) in phase one, the discovery (or acquisition) of the weak-verb rule in phase two, hence its over-generalization to cases where it does not apply, and finally the correct distinction of rule-governed (=regular) weak verbs vs. lexicon listed (=irregular) strong verbs.

Problems with connectionist approaches have been pointed out most vociferously, in particular by Steven Pinker in innumerable publications (Pinker 1999; Pinker and Prince 1991, 1994), and this approach does probably have to be modified before it can be said to model past tense acquisition successfully. The most problematic case, and one where connectionist models differ most clearly from humans (even four-year-old humans), is the area where rules apply most clearly, namely the extension of past tense *–ed* to rare, novel or nonsense words (the 'wug' test, see again Berko Gleason 1958). Here, connectionist models do not consistently come up with the correct past tense forms, but, relying on memory alone, often bring up utter nonsense, based on superficial similarities.

In sum, it can be said that although connectionist approaches form a very interesting alternative to the usual conceptions of rules, as long as they fail the 'wug' test, they cannot be seriously upheld as a valid model of human morphology. Another inherent problem with connectionism is that its artificial neural networks are not really similar to actual human neurons; as neurolinguists have complained, 'the "artificial neurons" exhibit only a superficial similarity with their biological prototypes, and it is easy to show that they have properties which are in conflict with biology. Even the structure of a connectionist model as a whole shows only a superficial resemblance with structures of the cortex'.[18] On the other hand, as Baayen points out in defence, 'the interest [of the connectionist model] resides not in the precise form of its network architecture, which is biologically implausible. The value of their study is that, by showing that a network of very simple processing units can perform a linguistic mapping, they have provided a powerful scientific metaphor for how neurons in the brain might accomplish linguistic mappings' (Baayen 2003: 231). In this metaphorical way, then, connectionism offers very interesting insights into a possible modelling of seemingly rule-governed processes.

2.8   Network model

A different proposal is made by Bybee (1985, 1995); it is linked to connectionist frameworks by the fact that in her network model, rules also emerge from the association of forms, rather than being explicit. Bybee's model is probably the model where frequency plays the largest part. She proposes that words in the lexicon have a certain lexical strength, determined mainly by their token frequency. High token frequency facilitates retrieval and increases a word's autonomy: high frequency makes a word resistant to change and increases its semantic independence (i.e. opacity) (Bybee 1995: 428). In addition, words are linked to each other on the basis of phonological and semantic similarity (or identity). These links result in a superficial analysis of words into morphemes without having to specify an internal morphological structure in the lexicon (Bybee 1995: 428).

Lexical connections between words can be stronger or weaker, according to how many features they share. Recurrent sets of phonological and parallel semantic connections across several words constitute morphological relations. It is here of course that type frequency comes in ('across several words'). Thus the link of final /t/ or /d/ with the semantics 'past tense' across a range of words would be sufficient to constitute the morpheme PAST TENSE, which thus emerges from lexical connections without an explicit rule.

Strength of lexical connections and lexical strength are inversely related by stipulation: 'Words that have high token frequency have greater lexical autonomy and one reflection of this is that such words form weaker connections with other items' (Bybee 1995: 429). Although this might at first seem counterintuitive, the basic claim that highly frequent words can become semantically as well as phonologically autonomous is illustrated by a wide range of historical developments, as shown for example by the fact that suppletive forms only occur in high frequency paradigms. This claim in particular separates Bybee's network model from all other connectionist models.

---

[18] www.cortical-linguistics.de/telecrtlinfe.htm (last updated September 2003).

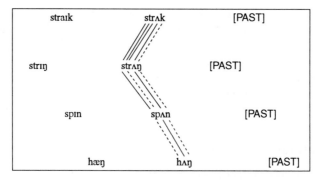

Figure 2.2 Product-oriented schema for past tense forms

According to Bybee, 'sets of words having similar patterns of semantic and phonological connections reinforce one another and create emergent generalisations describable as schemas' (Bybee 1995: 730). For example, similar past tense forms are linked by chains of similarity or indeed identity, as depicted in Figure 2.2 (based on Bybee 1985: 130; Bybee 1988: 135; Bybee 1995: 430, 1996: 250). Identical elements (phonemes in this case) are marked by uninterrupted lines, similar ones by dotted ones.

Bybee distinguishes source-oriented schemas that act like traditional rules (e.g. *wait – waited*) and can equally be described as operations that derive the output B from the input A, and product-oriented schemas, which have no equivalent in generative rules. For product-oriented schemas, such as the one illustrated in Figure 2.2 for a subclass of strong verbs, morphologically complex forms are linked to each other, based on family resemblances. The prime example for a product-oriented schema is the strong verb class that includes *string – strung – strung*. New members enter this class, i.e. the schema is extended to them, even though they do not have /ɪ/ in the present tense, e.g. *strike – struck* with /aɪ/ or American English *sneak – snuck* with /iː/. This verb class will be dealt with in much more detail in section 5.2.

It is surprising that in her work on inflectional paradigms, Bybee does not acknowledge the very similar work done by Wolfgang Wurzel, especially since she also deals with German noun and verb paradigms. Both empiricists come to very similar conclusions regarding inflectional systems and productivity, apparently independently of each other (also noted by Carstairs-McCarthy 1992: 244). In particular, through her analyses of frequency relations Bybee can supply the missing link in Wurzel's theory of how and why token and type frequencies behave so differently, and have such different effects on paradigms. Bybee's network model is thus compatible with natural morphology along the lines of Wurzel and can indeed expand it in interesting ways. Bybee's model has recently been implemented and formalized by Baayen (e.g. Baayen 2003 and references therein) as a spreading activation model with 'excellent predictive powers' (Baayen 2003: 249). It has to be said, however, that although the network model can account for the emergence of 'rules' and even morpheme structures in a psychologically plausible way, and incorporates type as well as token frequencies, it does not predict which patterns should be dominant in non-standard systems, or which directions should be taken in language change.

2.9 Natural morphology

2.9.1 Universal morphological naturalness

Naturalness has been defined in more technical terms first for phonology, in the Prague School of natural phonology (Trubetskoy, Jakobson, later taken up by Stampe (1979)). The German-Austrian 'school' of natural morphology has tried to extend this more technical notion of *naturalness* to morphology (see Dressler et al. 1987 for one of the rare English summaries of their thoughts; see also the summary in Carstairs-McCarthy 1992). Mayerthaler in particular has formalized his criteria of language-independent naturalness to a considerable degree (see Mayerthaler 1981, 1987). However, this group of German-speaking scholars has published mainly in German and has been little read and adopted in the non-German speaking rest of the world, so that their thoughts have so far not informed the general morphological (or indeed naturalness) debate much.[19] The school of morphological naturalness has so far not included non-standard varieties in its discussion. On the other hand, non-standard varieties are not principally excluded so that this theory should, in principle, be extendable to non-standard systems.

Wurzel, who has specialized in inflectional systems (Wurzel 1987, 1984), points out that developments that increase speaker or hearer economy in phonology are in fact counterproductive for morphology: 'phonologische Veränderungen – deren Motivation in einer besseren Anpassung der sprachlichen Formen an die Gegebenheiten der Artikulation und Perzeption besteht – wirken zu jeder Zeit störend und zerstörend auf die Morphologie ein' (phonological change – which is motivated by adapting linguistic forms to the circumstances of articulation and perception – is at any time disruptive and destructive for morphology) (Wurzel 1984: 190, my translation).

Nevertheless, Wurzel also claims that in morphology, naturalness is the overriding factor, and language change is always in the direction towards more naturalness. However, phonological and morphological naturalness are diametrically opposed, as phonological naturalness is motivated phonetically (by ease of articulation and ease of perception – where these are strong

[19] For example, in the Blackwell *Handbook of Morphology*, purportedly giving a comprehensive overview of the field, natural morphology is mentioned just once in a subclause in over 600 pages (Spencer and Zwicky 1998).

opposites!), whereas morphological naturalness is motivated semiotically (by an optimal symbolization of grammatical categories in linguistic forms). This of course results in permanent conflict between phonological naturalness and morphological naturalness: 'jede der beiden Typen von Natürlichkeit kann sich ... immer nur auf Kosten des jeweils anderen durchsetzen' (each of the two types of naturalness can only be satisfied to the detriment of the other) (Wurzel 1984: 30, my translation).

There are two kinds of morphological naturalness: one universal, investigated in depth by Mayerthaler, and one language-specific, described in detail for inflectional systems in particular by Wurzel.

Universal morphological naturalness is determined by features of iconicity, uniformity and transparency (Mayerthaler 1981, 1987) – features that are purportedly motivated extralinguistically (i.e. by general principles of human cognition). This means that, universally, an inflectional system is considered as being more natural if semantically unmarked categories are encoded with no formal marking,[20] and semantically marked categories are encoded by formal markers (i.e. if semantic markedness and formal marking coincide; Mayerthaler calls this 'constructional iconicity'). Mayerthaler draws up a scale of constructional iconicity, such that a form is (a) maximally iconic if it shows constructional iconicity expressed by the addition of a marker, e.g. *boy* – *boys* (the semantically marked plural is paralleled by an extra element on the form side); (b) less than maximally iconic if it shows constructional iconicity expressed by modulation and addition (e.g. for German umlaut plus an extra segment); (c) minimally iconic if it shows constructional iconicity expressed by modulation only (e.g. umlaut, ablaut, presumably changes in quantity etc.), e.g. *goose* – *geese*; (d) non-iconic if it shows no constructional iconicity, e.g. *sheep* – *sheep*; and (e) counter-iconic if there is formal asymmetry, but this does not correspond to the semantics, but is reversed, e.g. German *Elternteil* – *Eltern* or Welsh *pysgodyn* ('fish' singular) – *pysgod* ('fish' plural) (where the semantically marked plural is 'less' than the singular).[21]

Applied to English verb paradigms, this would result in the following scale:

(a) *maximally iconic* are weak verbs (the semantically marked meaning 'Past' corresponds to the formal addition of the segment <-ed>), e.g. *hunt* – *hunted*;
(b) *less than maximally iconic* are 'mixed' (weak–strong) verbs ('Past' meaning corresponds to the addition of <t>, but there is modulation as well), e.g. *keep* – *kept*;

---

[20] Semantically unmarked categories derive from the speaker's here and now, and thus encompass features like animate, personal, human, first person singular, active, present tense, indicative, etc.
[21] These are of course classic contexts for markedness reversals known from typology (cf. Tiersma 1982; Croft 1990: 66, 145; Haspelmath 2002: 243–4).

(c) *minimally iconic* are the typical strong verbs ('Past' meaning is indicated solely through modulation), e.g. *sing – sang*;

(d) *non-iconic* are verbs that are identical in present and past tense ('Past' meaning is not indicated formally), e.g. *hit – hit*;

(e) *counter-iconic* would be verbs that are formally marked in the present, but less marked in the past (no paradigm example from English, but perhaps the third person singular would be an example: it is marked by *–s* in the present, but not in the past tense: *hits – hit*).

In addition, Mayerthaler proposes the two principles of 'uniformity' and 'transparency', both relating to an ideal one-to-one correspondence of function and form: if one marker corresponds to one function (uniformity), and if the same function is consistently indicated by the same marker (transparency), a category is less marked than otherwise.

These universal features account for many general patterns. For English, for example, we can see that weak verbs are more natural on this scale than strong verbs, and indeed the type distribution supports the claims made by universal morphology: the group of maximally iconic weak verbs is much larger than the group of less iconic strong verbs.

In addition, Mayerthaler makes interesting (and testable) predictions about morphological change: morphological change should reduce markedness, i.e. either change a more marked form to a less marked one, or, if two competing forms exist, choose the less marked form over the more marked one. This principle neatly accounts for the fact that the (minimally iconic) strong verbs do in fact tend to become weak and join the maximally iconic class, a trend that can be observed in all the Germanic languages and that has been going on for the last two millennia. However, for many other phenomena, Mayerthaler's theory is too narrow. For example, two inflectional classes may be equally natural by Mayerthaler's criteria, but nevertheless speakers 'feel' that one is more 'normal' than the other, and indeed the less normal one may disappear through language change. In fact, there are instances of language change that constitute counterexamples to Mayerthaler's predictions, where an inflectional class or just a paradigm does not change towards a universally less marked form, as Wurzel has shown in much detail (see the section below). It is thus very clear that often languages have their own 'logic' and change counter to Mayerthaler's predictions.

2.9.2 Language-specific morphological naturalness

This is where language-specific naturalness comes in. Sometimes these two types of naturalness are distinguished by calling language-specific naturalness 'normal' (but as there is no practical noun form, I will retain the term *naturalness* here as well). In his detailed study of the German noun inflectional system, Wurzel (1984) has developed two language-internal (or 'system-dependent') criteria for what constitutes a 'natural' morphological system, namely the principle of system-congruity and the principle of class stability. As it is not immediately clear what is meant by these terms, a slightly more detailed exposition is in order here.

Wurzel claims that any inflectional system can be characterized by the following properties:

(a) its inventory of category structures and categories (e.g. number: singular, plural, dual; case: nominative, genitive, accusative, dative, instrumental, vocative)
(b) whether we find base form inflection or stem inflection (English *friend – friends* vs. Latin *amic-us – amic-i*)
(c) whether categories are symbolized separately or in combination (Swedish *kapten-er-s* 'captain'+plural+genitive vs. Russian *kapitan-ov* 'captain'+genitive plural)
(d) the number and manner of formal distinctions in the paradigm (Old High German NSg = ASg ≠ GSg ≠ DSg)[22]
(e) the types of markers involved in the respective category sets (affixes vs. ablaut, etc.)
(f) whether it has inflectional classes at all (German: yes, Turkish: no).

Those properties that are used either exclusively or predominantly in a system are the system-defining structural properties (SDSPs). The number and relative sizes of inflectional classes determine which properties are dominant. (It has to be noted here that it is type frequency, not token frequency that is decisive.) Once the system-defining structural properties are determined, one can then gauge any paradigm or inflectional class as to its degree of correspondence to the system-defining structural properties and determine its *system-congruity* (or appropriateness in the system, or system fit). System-congruity thus 'favours inflectional systems which are structured typologically in a uniform and systematic way with respect to the main parameters of the respective system' (Wurzel 1987: 92) detailed above. Consistency with the main parameters is thus an important criterion, and it is clear that these parameters can only be determined after a detailed language-specific analysis of a morphological system.

The second criterion of *class stability* favours inflectional classes that are independently motivated. Wurzel claims that morphological properties tend to be linked to extra-morphological properties. These can be either phonological properties (e.g. a word ending in −*a*) or semantic-syntactic ones (e.g. gender, stativity, animacy), or of course combinations of the two ('animal name ending in −*a*', etc.). Inflectional classes are structured by implications (e.g. Russian: if a word ends in −*a*, it will have /i/ in the GSg, /e/ in the

---

[22] The abbreviations relate to the four cases (nominative, accusative, genitive, dative singular) and whether these forms are identical (nominative and accusative) or not (all others).

DSg). However, it probably has to be noted that this criterion applies much more easily to noun classes (as in Wurzel's studies) than to verb classes. To my knowledge, inflectional verb classes have not been linked to semantic properties yet, although a link to phonological or syntactic ones is of course conceivable.[23]

This concept becomes interesting in the more difficult cases, for example when two (or more) inflectional classes compete for the same word. Two possible scenarios are imaginable: both classes could be equally strong, or one could be stronger than the other. This second case seems to be the rule in natural languages; equally strong classes are relatively rare. For unequal classes, Wurzel proposes type frequency as the determining criterion: 'von solchen Flexionsklassen ist jeweils diejenige normaler bzw. die normalste, die innerhalb des Flexionssystem deutlich quantitativ, d.h. nach Anzahl der ihr zugehörigen Wörter, überwiegt' (in such inflectional classes the more (respectively the most) normal class is the class which dominates the inflectional system quantitatively, i.e. through the number of words belonging to it) (Wurzel 1984: 127, my translation). Only if both (or more) classes have comparable type frequency do we get two (or more) equally normal or natural inflectional classes, and class membership of a word is arbitrary.

Stable inflectional classes are thus those classes that either have no competing classes, or that dominate their competing class. Unstable inflectional classes have a dominant complementary class, and stability-neutral classes have complementary classes with roughly the same type frequency. This leads to an interesting prediction about language change: 'Natürlicher morphologischer Wandel ist … dadurch gekennzeichnet, dass die Wörter von der weniger normalen zur normaleren Flexionsklasse übertreten; systembezogene Markiertheit wird durch Klassenwechsel abgebaut' (Natural morphological change is characterized by the fact that words switch from a less normal to a more normal inflectional class; system-internal markedness is reduced by class change) (Wurzel 1984: 78, my translation).

Morphologically 'normal' change, however, does not always mean a switch from one unstable class to the dominant, more natural one. Sometimes a more abstract structure is copied, for example the fact that nominative and accusative singular and plural are identical, even though distinct inflectional classes are maintained. Even in this more abstract way, Wurzel claims, inflectional systems change towards more stability: 'Das Flexionssystem ist auf diese Weise vereinheitlicht worden' (The inflectional system has been unified in this way) (Wurzel 1984: 79, my translation). Although Wurzel only mentions this possibility in passing, we will see that it is a very important mechanism of change for non-standard verbal systems.

---

[23] This is not to say that there are no semantic criteria for establishing word classes (clearly, aktionsart criteria can be and have been applied) – however, there do not seem to be inflectional reflexes of this, such that an inflectional system would group all durative verbs in one inflectional class, inchoative verbs in a morphologically different one, etc.

2.9.3 Criticism

Critical points that have been levelled against Wurzel's concept of morphological naturalness are that it is not clear what role Mayerthaler's concepts play if language-specific naturalness always wins anyway (see Harnisch 1988). Does it make sense to retain the notion of universal morphological naturalness in this case?

A second point of criticism is that Wurzel explicitly excludes token frequency as an explanatory mechanism (see Werner 1987, 1989, 1990). Werner has shown that very frequent forms, which tend to be highly irregular, run counter to Wurzel's criteria of naturalness, but make sense in Werner's own concept of 'system economy': according to Werner the function of morphology is the reduction or compression of information. This necessarily goes at the expense of iconicity and transparency, so that a 'worst case' scenario would be cases of suppletion. On the other hand, suppletion is a fact of probably every human language and thus deserves a principled explanation. Werner argues that suppletion is 'worth' the cognitive cost (e.g. in terms of system irregularity, rote learning instead of rule application, etc.) for the most frequent items (see Werner 1987, 1989, 1990). Dahl supports Werner's position with his concept of 'smart redundancy' which is found only with mature constructions: 'high frequency items more easily undergo reductive change' (Dahl 2004: 159).

2.9.4 Compatibility with other models

Natural morphology can be broadly classified as a dual-route model; Wurzel explicitly states that '"irregular" inflection forms like *feet* from *foot* appear ... in the lexicon representations of words; "regular" inflection forms like *hands* from *hand* are produced by general rules, and, since there is only one plural rule in English, this need not be explicitly entered in the lexicon representation of *hand*' (Wurzel 1990: 204). In analogy, this of course also extends to the past tense. However, in an interesting twist Wurzel differs from Pinker's perhaps overly simplistic categorization of verbs as either regular or irregular.[24] While in English, regular paradigms are usually designated 'unmarked', and irregular paradigms are considered 'marked', for other languages with a richer inflectional system this two-way distinction is not sufficient. Wurzel therefore proposes a subdistinction for regular (i.e. rule-formed) paradigms into unmarked vs. marked as illustrated in Figure 2.3 (after Wurzel 1990).

In this classification, irregular paradigms encompass in particular suppletive forms (for the English tense paradigms, only *be – was – been* and *go – went – gone*), whereas the strong verbs would be 'regular', i.e. could be

---

[24] This is perhaps related to the fact that Pinker works mainly on English, but Wurzel on German, where classification is of necessity more complex.

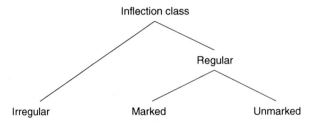

Figure 2.3 Inflection class classification (after Wurzel 1990)

created by a rule, but are 'marked' in comparison to the weak verbs. Weak verbs are a paradigm example of a 'regular unmarked' inflection class, i.e. they are the default that applies if no further specification is entered in the lexicon entry of a specific word. Strong verbs on the other hand would constitute (several) regular marked classes, again presumably falling into similar subgroups as in Katamba's classification (see page 5). (As mentioned before, unfortunately Wurzel has worked on German nouns, which complicates the analogy with English verb paradigms somewhat.)

As Bybee has pointed out, lexicon entries can be represented as a highly specific (idiosyncratic) rule, while rules on the other hand can also be modelled as generalizations over representations, so that the two mechanisms can be thought of as logically equivalent or isomorphic: 'I argue ... that the best exemplar of a rule and the best exemplar of a representation are two poles of a continuum, and that some rules have properties we associate with representations while some representations bear a resemblance to rules' (Bybee 1988: 121).

In contrast to Pinker's dual-route model, which cannot account for non-arbitrary resemblances among strong verbs, and Katamba's verb classes based only on some ablaut series that do not account for the majority of verb forms, in Wurzel's model the range of system-dependent structural properties can structure the range of verb paradigms in an illuminating and non-arbitrary way. Wurzel in particular can show that type frequency (the number of verb paradigms that belong to a certain inflectional class) has a major effect on the structure of an inflectional system and indeed on the direction of linguistic change.

2.10 Conclusion

What this overview has shown is that the English past tense, small and simple as it may seem, plays a prominent role in current morphological theoretical debates, and that there are several ways of accounting for the seemingly simple facts of its derivation. Table 2.4 gives a schematic

Table 2.4 *Schematic comparison of morphological theories*

Theory	Verb system	Strong verbs	Diachrony
Chomsky and Halle	No	–	–
Lexical Phonology and Morphology	Yes	No	–
Optimality Theory	No	–	–
Stochastic OT	No	–	–
Words-and-rules	Yes	No	–
Connectionism	No	–	–
Network model	Yes	Yes	No
☞Natural morphology	Yes	Yes	Yes

overview of the theories in order of treatment in this chapter, asking the question: does this theory account for the verbal system of present-day English? Only if it does will it make sense to consider the theory further in this investigation. The second question to be answered is, does this theory account for all strong verbs without exception (i.e. is it descriptively adequate)? Finally, can this theory integrate findings from diachrony (and perhaps even make interesting predictions for language change, or for non-standard systems)?

For the present investigation, it will be most important to be able to work with a model that has already proved itself in a very similar domain. None of the models has been tested explicitly on non-standard data (although Bybee can and does account for non-standard American strong verbs like *drag – drug* and *sneak – snuck*, as mentioned above, and Wurzel hints at some general vernacular or dialectal developments as his theory predicts them in the realm of German – mostly nominal – inflectional classes). We can combine Wurzel's insights with Bybee's psychologically plausible network model and regard the properties that Wurzel employs in his model as emergent, rather than as fixed lexicon entries. Nevertheless, it will be convenient to continue common linguistic terminology and to speak of paradigms, case, number, tense, etc. in the remainder of this book. It is important to remember, however, that I will not claim that native speakers necessarily have conscious knowledge of these categories. Instead, connectionist and network approaches have shown that these properties can be modelled as emergent; in particular, I will assume that they emerge from the system of lexical organization in the sense of Bybee (1988). In this way, Wurzel's framework can be made compatible with Bybee's ideas, and her product-oriented schemas, in particular, will be integrated into natural morphology when we discuss the English verbs in more detail. Natural morphology and Bybee's network model are also the only frameworks that can account for type, rather than token, frequency in a principled way.

In sum, if we extend natural morphology with the psycholinguistically plausible network model, we can link a model employing sophisticated linguistic terminology with possible low-level neural mechanisms, resulting in a highly empirical framework that has been extensively tested and which makes interesting predictions for inflectional systems, and which will therefore be employed in the remainder of this book.

3 Naturalness and the English past tense system

> The verbs that do not conform to the 'regular' pattern of adding – *(e)d* in past and participle are so divergent that it is hardly worth trying to classify them. (Strang 1970: 147)

3.1 General features of the English verb system

To recapitulate, we have seen that Wurzel characterizes inflectional systems with the help of the following properties:

(a) category structures and categories
(b) base vs. stem inflection
(c) separate or combined symbolization of categories
(d) formal distinctions in the paradigm
(e) types of markers
(f) existence of inflectional classes.

If we apply Wurzel's features to the system of English verb forms, we derive the following picture:

(a) Inventory of category structures and categories: for the super-category TENSE we find the following categories in English: PRESENT (or, more precisely, NON-PAST) vs. PAST; this contrast is the only one expressed synthetically (e.g. *want – wanted; ride – rode*). In addition, we have a compositional future form (*will ride*) which has grammaticalized to a considerable degree from its volitional origin and can thus properly be called a tense of English (e.g. *Tomorrow will be sunny*). We also find the PERFECT, as in all languages a category of unclear status, perhaps best situated between tense and aspect. The perfect is compositional and can combine with all three basic tenses, resulting in the PRESENT PERFECT, the PAST PERFECT and the FUTURE PERFECT (*have wanted, had wanted, will have wanted*).

Also relevant to the verb system is the super-category ASPECT with just two categories: SIMPLE and PROGRESSIVE. Again, the PROGRESSIVE in

English is compositional and in principle can combine with any tense above (*is riding, was riding, will be riding; has been ri*ding, *had been riding, will have been riding*), although there are semantic restrictions.

A third super-category expressed in English is VOICE, with only two categories: ACTIVE and PASSIVE. The PASSIVE is also expressed compositionally and can be combined with any verb in any tense and aspect where this is semantically permitted, although in particular the combination of the progressive and passive becomes progressively more anomalous (*is wanted, was wanted, will be wanted; has been wanted, had been wanted, will have been wanted; is being ridden, was being ridden, ?will be being ridden; ?has been being ridden; ?had been being ridden, ?will have been being ridden*).

Two final categories that are expressed on English verbs are PERSON and NUMBER. From a full person system in Germanic times, present-day English has only retained a morphological contrast between the third person singular and the rest, and this only in the present tense. This form therefore incorporates both the super-category PERSON (THIRD PERSON vs. NON-THIRD PERSON) and NUMBER (SINGULAR vs. PLURAL). All other persons (and numbers) are expressed analytically in the combination of a pronoun or full noun phrase and the verb. Although morphologically English verbs thus only have two forms in the present tense (*wants – want*), systematically we find three persons and two numbers, with a considerable amount of syncretism: *I want, you want, he/she/it wants, we want, you want, they want; the boy wants, the boys want.*

(b) English is characterized by the fact that we generally find base form inflection.[1] English has no (infinitive) endings that could be substituted by tense, voice or person endings.

(c) English categories as a rule are symbolized separately, in fact analytically, although the third person singular (present tense) *–s* combines all three categories: PERSON, NUMBER and TENSE.

(d) Formal distinctions in paradigms are very few and have already been detailed above; for person and number, only the third person singular is distinct in the present tense: 3SG ≠ 1SG = 2SG = 1PL = 2PL = 3PL.[2] In addition, typical verb paradigms follow the pattern *want – wanted – wanted* with identity of past tense and past participle, while present tense and past tense forms are formally distinct: PRES ≠ PAST = PPL.

(e) In verbal paradigms, the typical markers employed are affixes (*want – wants, want – wanted*), but in the sizeable group of strong verbs, vowel

---

[1] The only exception seem to be loanwords with inherited stem plurals, e.g. *ind-ex, ind-ices; dat-um, dat-a.* Not surprisingly, these show a strong tendency towards base-form plurals (*indexes, data* used as singular). To my knowledge, in verbs no stem inflection occurs.

[2] This pattern is only valid for the main verbs. Auxiliary verbs are characterized by the fact that they have no third person singular *–s*. The primary verbs *be, have* and *do* pattern with the main verbs morphologically even when used as auxiliaries.

changes also occur, either instead of or sometimes in addition to affixes (e.g. *keep – kept, ride – rode – ridden*).

(f) Finally, English has inflectional classes, if only very few in the verb class system.

3.2 Dominant features

Following this overview, we can now determine the dominant properties of the English verb system. The *dominant verb class* is clearly (by sheer type frequency) the class of weak verbs, and its structural properties therefore determine the dominant properties of the English verb system. In particular, this means that the *dominant past tense marker* is the affix <-ed> with its three phonologically determined allomorphs /t/, /d/ and /ɪd/. In addition, the *dominant pattern* for verbs is a morphological distinction of present and past tense forms, while past and past participle are identical, i.e. the pattern PRES ≠ PAST = PPL. The few inflectional classes in the verb system that have remained from the elaborate Old English system are characterized mainly by the fact that they are diminishing more or less rapidly, and that in particular extra-morphological motivation (constituting class stability) is today not discernible any longer, except very marginally for some subclasses.

On the basis of these language-specific properties, we can now predict some paths of change towards more naturalness in the verb system: (a) a change of a strong verb to a weak one, i.e. into the dominant verb class; this is the most radical change conceivable; (b) a verb taking over the dominant past tense marker <-ed>, without becoming a weak verb altogether; (c) a verb taking over a dominant strong verb marker; and finally (d) a more abstract change in that a verb paradigm takes over the dominant pattern PRES ≠ PAST = PPL.

For these cases, we can clearly say that changes in this direction are changes towards a more natural system ((a) also in the sense of Mayerthaler's universal naturalness, all others only in the sense of Wurzel's language-specific naturalness). It is interesting to note that while options (a), (c) and (d) are attested in non-standard dialects (albeit with varying frequencies), option (b), e.g. the double marking of a strong past tense form with the dominant past tense marker <-ed>, is conspicuously rare. Forms like *gaved*, *stunged*, *wroted*, etc. are attested in older dialect descriptions (see especially Wright 1905: 284), but seem to be practically non-existent today.

Whether English strong verbs can be grouped in a non-arbitrary and illuminating way synchronically will be explored in the next section.

3.3 Standard English verb classes

As already discussed above in section 1.3.3, the present-day English verb classes in this book are primarily divided following the abstract principle of identity or non-identity of forms across a paradigm, as also hinted at in Quirk et al. (1985), and implemented in Nielsen (1985) and Hansen and Nielsen (1986), because in this way we can determine their stability with regard to Wurzel's criteria detailed above. Although Esser claims 'diese [sc. Nielsens Einteilung] richtet sich jedoch nur nach der Gleichheit oder Verschiedenheit von Infinitiv, Präteritum und Partizip und stellt daher keine eigentliche synchrone Systematik dar' (Nielsen's division only takes into account the identity or non-identity of infinitive, preterite and participle and thus does not constitute a proper synchronic classification) (Esser 1988: 26, my translation), it is in fact this abstract identity that is the best predictor of linguistic change, and that can best explain the various patterns encountered in nonstandard verbal paradigms.

Inside the verb classes, I will further subdivide verbs according to the following formal criteria:[3]

- Whether vowel change occurs, and how often. Just like for overall formal identity, five logical possibilities obtain: the vowel could be different for all three forms (V3: VPRES ≠ VPAST ≠ VPPL), it could be identical for two forms (V2a: VPRES ≠ VPAST = VPPL; V2b: VPRES = VPAST ≠ VPPL; or V2c: VPRES = VPPL ≠ VPAST), or it could be identical across all three forms (V1: VPRES = VPAST = VPPL).
- Whether /d/ or /t/ is added for past tense and past participle, or whether a distinct marking is effected that results in a past tense and past participle in /d/ or /t/ (i.e. devoicing of a stem in /d/ to /t/, or changing of a final consonant to /d/ or /t/).
- Whether the participle ends in <-en>.

These criteria are not completely independent of verb class affiliation. For example, identical forms (verb class 5) imply identical vowels, but not the other way around: there are verbs that are formally distinct, e.g. by devoicing, but may nevertheless have identical vowels, e.g. *send – sent – sent*. Identity of forms of course also precludes the other two criteria (<-en>-participle and devoicing). A complete list of all standard English verbs and their assignation to modern verb classes can be found in Appendix 1.

3.3.1   *Verb class 1: PRES ≠ PAST ≠ PPL*[4]

The first verb class is characterized synchronically by the fact that all three forms are distinct (PRES ≠ PAST ≠ PPL). As mentioned above in section 1.3.3, fifty-nine or just over 35 per cent of strong verbs follow this pattern, and it is therefore one of the very frequent patterns of English verbs. Despite the fact

---

[3] See also Quirk et al. (1985: 104f.).
[4] To avoid confusion, my modern English verb classes have been numbered by Arabic numerals; Old English verb classes by Roman numerals.

that verb class 2 contains more verbs, the pattern of verb class 1 seems to be the prototypical strong verb pattern that comes to mind first and that is in fact usually cited (in introductory textbooks, etc.). Inside this verb class, we find several subdivisions.

3.3.1.1 VPRES ≠ VPAST ≠ VPPL

The first subclass of nine verbs (including *drink – drank – drunk* or *swim – swam – swum*) employs only vowel change to indicate tense distinctions. These verbs are very similar to verbs of class 2 (Bybee verbs), and historically alternative past tense forms (identical with the past participle) exist (*drink – drunk – drunk, swim – swum – swum*), making them a natural candidate for change. Also historically this is not surprising, as all verbs in both subclasses derive from the Old English verb class III,[5] making them a historically continuous class.

3.3.1.2 <-en>-participle

The second defining characteristic of verb class 1 (and found only in verb class 1, as well as in the marginal verb class 4) is a past participle in <-en>, e.g. *drive – drove – driven*. As Figure 3.1 shows, all possible vowel patterns can be combined with the past participle in <-en>, and constitute the remaining subclasses of verb class 1.

In twelve verbs, all three forms have different vowels (abbreviated V3, e.g. *write – wrote – written*). Except for the verb *fly*, all of these verbs can be traced back to Old English verb class I, and this subclass is thus again historically continuous.[6] In addition, the suppletive paradigms of BE and GO as well as DO follow this pattern.

Sixteen verbs have identical vowels in the past tense and the past participle (pattern V2a, e.g. *break – broke – broken*). This subclass is mainly constituted by verbs from Old English verb class IV (e.g. *swear – swore – sworn*), but also contains two words from verb class II (*choose – chose – chosen* and *freeze – froze – frozen*), two words from verb class V (*lie – lay – lain* and *tread – trod – trodden*) and three verbs that follow this pattern now due to Old and Middle English changes in the quantity (and later quality) of the vowel, e.g. *bite – bit – bitten*. This subclass is thus rather heterogeneous and does not have a clear historical affiliation, although verbs from verb class IV do dominate.

In the next subclass of thirteen verbs, vowels are identical in present tense and past participle (V2c: *fall – fell – fallen*). Historically, these verbs come from Old English verb classes V (e.g. *see – saw – seen*), VI (e.g. *take – took – taken*) and VII (*grow – grew – grown* but also *fall – fell – fallen* above) and

---

[5] The assignation of verbs to Old English verb classes follows Esser (1988) and Krygier (1994).

[6] *Fly – flew – flown* was historically a class II verb which later switched into verb class VII.

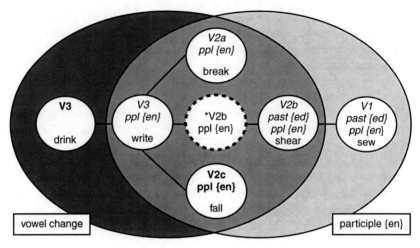

Figure 3.1 Internal structure of verb class 1

form still recognizably distinctive groups inside this subclass. Nevertheless, this large subclass of verb class 1 is remarkably stable and none of its verbs currently shows any sign of switching into the class of weak verbs.

A truly marginal subclass is constituted by only two verbs which have identical vowels in present and past tense (pattern V2b: *shear – sheared – shorn* and *swell – swelled – swollen*); for them, the past tense is in addition marked by the weak past tense marker <-ed>.[7] It is worth noting that in no other verb class does this vowel pattern occur (V<small>PRES</small> = V<small>PAST</small> ≠ V<small>PPL</small>), which makes it the least frequently used pattern of all vowel change patterns.

Finally, seven verbs have no vowel change, but add the weak marker <-ed> in the past tense and <-en> for the participle (V1: *saw – sawed – sawn*). All these verbs derive from Old English verb class VII, but many of them were originally weak before they switched into this Old English verb class (e.g. *sew – sewed – sewn*). It is therefore not surprising that these last two groups of verbs (with <-ed> in the past tense and <-en>-participles) all have alternative weak paradigms. Apart from the fact that many of them were originally weak, synchronically the only form that has to change to conform to the pattern of weak verbs is the participle, as the past tense is formed according to the regular pattern already (*swell – swelled – swollen* or *mow – mowed – mown*). The internal structure of verb class 1 can be diagrammatically depicted as in Figure 3.1.

Straight lines link subclasses in a chain of family resemblances (exactly one feature changes from subclass to subclass); the darker background joins

---

[7] Without this addition, these verbs would not be part of this verb class. The combination of V2b and participle in <-en> is therefore indicated by an asterisk and by a dotted outline in Figure 3.1 and is indeed not attested in English.

all subclasses exhibiting vowel change, the lighter background those subclasses with a participle in <-en>. A bold outline of a subclass indicates its
larger size (compared to the other subclasses), bold type indicates its stability, and italics its instability (members switching into the weak verb class).

As already indicated above, verb class 1 is not a stable class. Not only the
marginal subclasses, but also the strong subclasses with many members,
marked by a bold outline in Figure 3.1, are losing members to the class of
weak verbs. The only exception to this trend is the large subclass V2c with
past participle in <-en>, which is stable (e.g. *take – took – taken*), as well
as subclass V3 (e.g. *sing – sang – sung*) whose members, rather than becoming weak, have been fluctuating for most of their Modern English history
between verb class 1 and another strong verb class, verb class 2. The link
between these two subclasses will be explored further in section 5.2.

3.3.2   *Verb class 2: PRES ≠ PAST = PPL*

As mentioned before, verb class 2 conforms to the abstract pattern of weak
verbs in having identical past tense and past participle forms. In Wurzel's
terms, this verb class displays the dominant pattern and is therefore system-
congruous. For this reason not surprisingly, with eighty-one members (over 48
per cent) it is also the largest class of strong verbs. The pattern PRES ≠ PAST =
PPL is thus not only dominant overall (because it characterizes the large class
of weak verbs as opposed to the strong verbs), it is also dominant in the realm
of strong verbs (it is the single most frequent pattern that strong verbs follow,
although by a very narrow margin it is not found in the absolute majority of
strong verbs). Probably because of its size, this verb class as a whole is historically very heterogeneous. Although, as we have seen, at least one subclass acts
as a powerful attractor for strong verbs of class 1, verb class 2 is not altogether
stable in all its subclasses either. The subclasses are detailed below.

3.3.2.1   *VPRES ≠ VPAST = VPPL*

For thirty-six verbs, tense distinction is carried by vowel change alone. Past
tense and past participle are necessarily identical (given the verb class) and
the vowel change pattern is therefore always V2a (e.g. *hold – held – held* or
cling – clung – clung). They can be further divided into three groups, depending on further characteristics they have (or, indeed, the absence of them).

Bybee verbs
The first large subclass of verb class 2 is constituted by the fourteen verbs
like *cling – clung – clung* already mentioned, which I have provisionally
termed Bybee verbs. These serve as strong attractors to those verb class 1
verbs above which are formally very similar (V3 *drink – drank – drunk*), and
which are also historically related – as mentioned above, both subclasses
derive from Old English verb class III.

stem in /d/ or /t/

It is probably no coincidence that a large portion of verbs in verb class 2 which form their past tense and past participle only by vowel change (twenty-one or almost 60 per cent of the thirty-six words collected here) have base forms ending in an alveolar plosive already (e.g. *sit – sat – sat* or *slide – slid – slid*), so that the past tense forms look *as if* they carried an affix as well. Nevertheless, some members of this subclass are switching into the weak verb class, e.g. *speed – sped – sped, light – lit – lit* and *abide – abode – abode*. Historically, verbs in this subclass come from a range of Old English verb classes, in particular verb class III (e.g. *find – found – found*), verb class V (e.g. *sit – sat – sat*), and verbs which fell into this pattern through quantitative and qualitative changes (e.g. *meet – met – met*). Although two other Old English verb classes are represented here, this is due to just one basic lexeme each with a range of derivational forms, i.e. *stand – stood – stood* from verb class VI and *hold – held – held* from verb class VII. Nevertheless, even this subclass is still relatively heterogeneous historically.

Two verbs belong to neither of these two central groups (e.g. *heave – hove – hove* and *shine – shone – shone*), and perhaps predictably both are candidates for change and tend to switch into the weak verb class.

Vowel change + affix

Twenty-nine verbs use both vowel change and an affix to indicate tense distinctions. Again, these verbs fall into several subclasses. The largest of them, containing sixteen verbs, has an affix /t/ (e.g. *bereave – bereft – bereft*). It is extremely homogeneous historically, as all verbs derive from quantitative (and qualitative) changes.

A smaller class of six verbs add /d/ in addition to vowel change (e.g. *flee – fled – fled*); these derive from quantitative changes (e.g. *flee – fled – fled*) and from umlauting verbs, where the I-umlaut of the present tense eventually led to the qualitative differences observed today (only *sell – sold – sold* and *tell – told – told*, from *selljan* and *telljan* respectively).

Another small group of seven verbs in addition also have a consonant change (e.g. *bring – brought – brought*), in all seven cases resulting from the loss of /x/ which originally resulted from the phonological process of spirantization of /k/ or /g/ before /t/, with concomitant loss of a preceding /n/ or /ŋ/ as in *bring* (for more details, see section 1.3.1). This is therefore another homogeneous group historically, as all seven verbs can be traced back to these (rück-)umlauting verbs (the one exception, *catch – caught – caught*, was formed analogically later in Middle English times – more on *catch* in section 4.4.4).

All three subclasses are losing marginal members to the weak verb class, e.g. *cleave – cleft – cleft; shoe – shod – shod* and *beseech – besought – besought*. In cases where verbs switch to the weak verb class, they often leave only a distinction between a (formerly participial) adjective with the older irregular form (with vowel change and/or without a regular allomorph), and the past tense and past participle proper with the regular form which follows the allomorphy rules, cf. *a cleft palate* or *cleft structures* vs. *Protoxins which are cleaved by enzymes* (BNC).

3.3.2.2 No vowel change

Fifteen verbs have no vowel change; for six verbs, past tense and past participle are effected by devoicing (*bend – bent – bent*) today. Historically, they derive from the apocope of the dental suffix, i.e. they were originally weak verbs. Five out of these six verbs conform to the same schema; they all end in /-end/ in the present tense, /-ent/ in the past tense and past participle (*bend, lend, spend, send* and *rend*)[8] and in this way constitute one of the few subclasses that are extra-morphologically (in this case phonologically) motivated in the sense of Wurzel and should therefore be stable. Indeed they show no sign of switching into the weak verb class.

For seven verbs, the tense distinction is effected by the addition of the affix /t/[9] only (*burn – burnt – burnt*). What differentiates them from regular weak verb affixation is the obligatory voicelessness of the affix – according to the allomorphy rules of the *regular* past tense allomorphs, after voiced sounds the allomorph should of course be /d/. This voiceless (and non-syllabic) /t/ seems to have arisen through analogy; Esser claims that these seven verbs were formed in analogy with apocopated forms like *bend – bent – bent* above (Esser 1988: 36). The OED states for all of them that the regular form in <-ed> is in fact the older form, but the forms in <-t> are the more usual 'today' (i.e. at the end of the nineteenth century) (see e.g. OED: s.v. *burn* v.). However, for all of these verbs parallel forms in <-t> and <-ed> are attested since at least the seventeenth century, and this variability seems to have survived into standard English today (e.g. *burn – burned – burned* next to *burn – burnt – burnt*). In these characteristics then (historical provenance and present-day variable behaviour), these seven verbs form a very homogeneous subgroup.

Finally, two verbs (*have* and *make*) *substitute* their final consonant by /d/. Historically, *have* and *make* are irregular weak forms, and the fused forms can be traced back to a regular allomorph which, probably because of their high token frequency, merged with the stem consonant. Today, *have* and *make* still belong to the most frequent words absolutely. Even 'as a transitive main verb, *have* is as common as the most frequent lexical verbs in English' (Biber et al. 1999: 429), as figures from the Longman Corpus support, while *make* is one of the most frequent lexical verbs, taking rank 7 in

---

[8] The only exception is *build – built – built*.
[9] Again by definition, and in contrast to the vowel change subclass above, affix /d/ is never added, as this would result in a regular weak verb form.

their list of the most common lexical verbs (Biber et al. 1999: 373).[10] Probably
because of their very high token frequency, these two verbs show no sign of
regularizing.

Confusing as this list may seem, we can again summarize verb class membership in this verb class 2 with the help of family resemblances. In Figure
3.2 the three central subclasses are indicated by bolder outlines. Each subclass
to the right can be described by the change of one feature, linking it to the
subclass on its left, but not necessarily directly to the central members. The
first central feature, vowel change, is again marked by a darker background.
The second central feature is more diverse, but the results from these diverse
operations are always the same. Whether by 'coincidence' (a stem ending in
/t/ or /d/), by adding an affix or changing the final consonant to /t/ or /d/,
the past tense and past participle always end in /d/ or /t/ respectively. This
is then the second characterizing feature of verb class 2, and it is marked by a
lighter background in Figure 3.2. Figure 3.2 shows that these two characteristics exhaustively describe verb class 2. It also makes clear that only one small
link is missing to link this class to the regular weak class of verbs. It is thus
also graphically obvious that class membership might be gradient, and that
whole verb classes might be linked by family resemblances.

Figure 3.2 shows very clearly that the only stable subclasses in verb class 2
are the Bybee verbs, conforming to a product-oriented schema, and the two
peripheral subclasses, one in <-ent>, the other containing the high-frequency
items *have* and *made*. Of these subclasses, only the Bybee verbs are actually
gaining new members, namely from verb class 1. Verb class 2 as a whole, despite being the largest class, is thus also not particularly stable, but is losing
members in particular in the direction of the dominant weak verb class.

3.3.3   *Verb class 3: PRES = PPL ≠ PAST*

The remaining three verb classes have no internal structure and are much
smaller in comparison to the two first classes. Class 3 verbs have identical
present tense and past participle forms; this is a rare pattern and is only
found with two verbs, *come* and *run* (V2c: *come – came – come*). Their historical development is detailed in Chapter 6. Both verbs tend to change into
verb class 5 in non-standard systems as Chapter 6 will show, but are stable
in the standard.

3.3.4   *Verb class 4: PRES = PAST ≠ PPL*

This smallest of all verb classes consists of just one verb, *beat* (*beat – beat –
beaten*) and is thus truly marginal. *Beat* is the only survivor of the Old English

---

[10] See also the older figures from Francis and Kučera (1982: 465), where *have* takes rank 9,
      make rank 39.

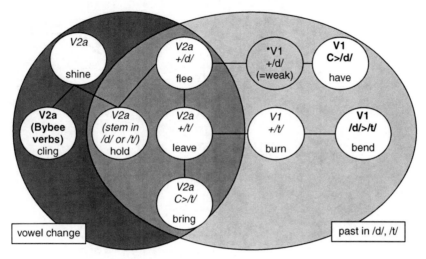

Figure 3.2 Internal structure of verb class 2

class of reduplicating verbs. According to Quirk et al. (1985), *beat* tends to level past tense and past participle (*beat – beat – beat*) and thus tends to switch into the larger class 5, with which it shares its feature of a stem ending in /t/.

3.3.5   Verb class 5: PRES = PAST = PPL

The non-iconic verb class 5 contains the surprisingly high number of twenty-four verbs. As already pointed out in Chapter 1, it is probably no coincidence that all verbs in this class end in /t/ or /d/ and thus look as if they contain an affix. In this, they also of course resemble the one central subclass of verb class 2 – we have seen there that a stem ending in /d/ or /t/ is a criterion that at least for a subclass may preclude the application of vowel change. While in verb class 2, some (if minimal) difference between present and past tense forms is effected through voicing contrasts, verb class 5 has completely identical forms (*hit – hit – hit*). The similarity could again be depicted by a chain of family resemblances, linking verb class 2 and verb class 5.

3.3.6   Summary

Figure 3.3 graphically links subclasses across verb classes. All links across verb classes are indicated by a bold line. It becomes apparent that indeed all verb classes can be linked by way of family resemblances, and that the weak verbs in particular are very well integrated into the system, as the many linking lines (at least four) indicate. Despite what many theories claim, then, one might argue that the difference between weak and strong verbs is gradual, rather than categorical.

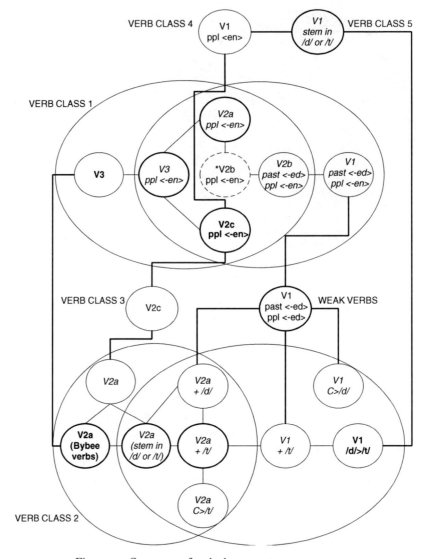

Figure 3.3 Summary of verb class structures

In particular, we can see that verb class 3 (*come – came – come*) in the middle of the diagram can be linked to the subclass V2a with <-en>-participle
(*fall – fell – fallen*) from verb class 1 above it, from which it differs only in
the affix of the participle, and to subclass V2a of verb class 2 below it (*hold –
held – held*), from which it differs in the vowel of the participle.

Verb class 4 (*beat – beat – beaten*) can be linked to verb class 1 below it
in several ways, only one of which is indicated in Figure 3.3 for the sake of

simplicity. It is linked to subclass V2c with participle <-en> (*fall – fell – fallen*), from which it differs only in the vowel of the past tense, but it could equally well be linked to subclass V1 with past tense <-ed> and past participle <-en> (*sow – sowed – sown*), from which it differs only in the past tense affix.

Finally, verb class 5 (*hit – hit – hit*) is on the one hand linked to verb class 4 (*beat – beat – beaten*), from which it differs in the past participle affix, and to verb class 2, especially to subclass V2a with a stem in /d/ or /t/ (*slide – slid – slid*), with which it shares the important characteristic of a stem ending in /d/ or /t/, although the vowel change is different, and subclass V1 (with a change from /d/ to /t/) (*lend – lent – lent*), which differs only in voicing.

3.4   The central characteristics

We have seen that most strong verb classes, with the exception of verb classes 4 and 5, make use of at least some vowel changes. In a similar investigation, Esser also comes to this conclusion: 'insgesamt gesehen ist der Vokalwechsel auch das wichtigste strukturelle Element der heutigen unregelmäßigen Verben' (generally speaking, vowel change is still the most important structural element of the irregular verbs today) (Esser 1988: 44). The second most important criterion, surprisingly, are forms ending in /t/, relevant in particular in word class 2 and a constituting criterion for word class 5. The third important criterion finally is a participle in <-en>, shared by (parts of) verb class 1 and class 4, and found across just under a third of all irregular verbs today (see again Esser 1988: 44).

The relationship between features is thus not implicational (e.g. 'if a verb has a participle in <-en>, it also has vowel change'), but all logical possibilities obtain. Relations can therefore best be depicted with the help of family resemblances, as Figure 3.4 shows.

3.5   Non-standard verb paradigms as test cases

The following case studies of individual non-standard past tense verbs are intended as test cases, testing the hypothesis that non-standard verb paradigms can be considered more normal or more natural in the technical sense of Wurzel detailed above. The verbs have been chosen as illustrations of some very general trends that can be observed for English non-standard systems, rather than freak occurrences. Faced with the long history of English and the striking changes that the verb paradigms, in particular, have undergone, several logical possibilities are attested and will be investigated in more detail. These are in particular: (a) new non-standard weak verbs, (b) new non-standard strong verbs, and (c) different non-standard strong verbs.

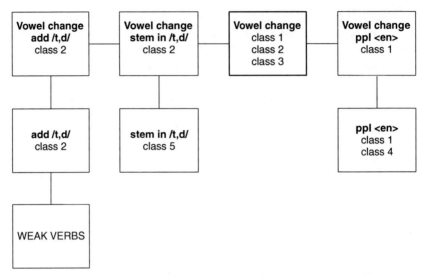

Figure 3.4 Features and class membership

3.5.1 New non-standard weak verbs

Some verbs that are (still) strong in the standard today have developed further in the non-standard system and changed conjugation class into the weak verb class (e.g. *sellt*, *knowed* vs. standard English (StE) *sold*, *knew*). This development is usually employed to illustrate the 'unnatural' tendency of a codified standard to preserve a conservative stage of the language and to inhibit, or decelerate, the rate of natural change, in this case the change from strong to weak verbs. Mayerthaler's general framework (1981, 1987) predicts that weak verbs are more natural than strong verbs, and that linguistic change should be in the direction of the weak verb class (see section 2.9.1). My analysis of the English verbal system in this chapter also suggests that weak verbs are the 'default' verb class, and we have seen that almost all competing strong verb classes do in fact lose members to the weak verbs. For the – by now almost commonplace – idea that dialects simply exhibit more natural processes, see a first explication for phonology in Kroch (1978).

3.5.2 New non-standard strong verbs

The reverse case, verbs that are weak in the standard but (newly) strong in non-standard systems, is little attested (though frequently quoted), at least for British English, and seems to be a relatively new development that is mainly found in American English (e.g. *snuck*, *drug* for StE *sneaked*, *dragged*). Where it does occur, these new strong forms can only be formed according to one very productive strong verb pattern (so-called Bybee verbs).[11] For lack of examples, these new formations will not be discussed in detail for British English, but the reader is referred to the work of Bybee (Bybee 1985; Bybee and Slobin 1982), Hogg (1998) and Murray (1998).

3.5.3   Different non-standard strong verbs

Some verbs are strong in both the standard and non-standard systems, but have different strong forms. This constitutes the most interesting group, as they run counter to Mayerthaler's universal prediction, and seem explicable in Wurzel's framework only if we permit some modifications, taking into account class membership, etc. From an initial overview, it seems to be the case for (British) English that standard and non-standard systems are not so much different in their strong verb–weak verb distinction, but in individual paradigms. In other words, StE strong verbs are in most cases also strong in non-standard systems, but have different forms. Two important subregularities can be distinguished: (1) three-part paradigms of the standard that only have two parts in non-standard systems, and (2) two-part standard paradigms that only have one form in non-standard systems.

3.5.3.1   Two- instead of three-part paradigms

Some three-part paradigms of the standard are simplified to two-part paradigms in non-standard systems (e.g. *drink* – ***drunk*** – *drunk* vs. StE *drink* – *drank* – *drunk*); this seems to be particularly frequent for verbs of a particular phonological shape and I have called this group Bybee verbs, as Joan Bybee has worked extensively on this phenomenon. The functional principle illustrated by these Bybee verbs is analogy – both on a concrete level, namely the phonological shape, the 'prototypical past tense marker' /ʌ/ that serves as the attractor to other similar verb paradigms – and more abstractly: by levelling the past tense–past participle distinction, these strong class 1 verbs in effect become class 2 verbs, conforming to the prototypical weak verb pattern and thus, abstractly, become more similar to the much bigger group of weak verbs, which also do not distinguish simple past and past participle (e.g. *love* – *loved* – *loved*). In other words, the structural principle PRES ≠ PAST = PPL is extended from the weak verbs and from a dominant pattern of strong verbs to this class of strong verbs, bringing it into line with one of the system-defining structural properties of English verbs.

However, there is a minority pattern that apparently results in a non-functional system, and this is exemplified by StE *eat* – *ate* – *eaten* which in many non-standard systems becomes *eat* – *eat* – *eaten*. Although there

[11] Campbell (1998: 94) also cites non-standard *arrive* – *arrove* and *squeeze* – *squoze* as instances of analogical extensions but indicates no sources for these forms (although they are probably derived from Wright's *Dialect Grammar*, see Wright 1905: 281ff.). Neither form is documented in FRED.

StE	Verb class	Non StE	Verb class	Chapter
strong		→ weak		4
– *sell, sold, sold*	class 2	– *sell, sellt, sellt*	weak	
– *know, knew, known*	class 1	– *know, knowed, knowed*	weak	
3 forms		→ 2 forms		5
– *drink, drank, drunk*	class 1	– *drink, drunk, drunk*	class 2	
– *do, did, done*	class 1	– *do, done, done*	class 2	
– *eat, ate, eaten*	class 1	– *eat, eat, eaten*	class 4	
2 forms		→ 1 form		6
– *come, came, come*	class 3	– *come, come, come*	class 5	
– *run, ran, run*	class 3	– *run, run, run*	class 5	

Figure 3.5 Pervasive patterns in non-standard tense paradigms

is also a development from three to two forms in this paradigm, the past tense here is identical to the *present* tense, not the past participle (as was the case for *drink – drunk – drunk*). Here, verb class 1 is losing members to the unlikely target class 4 (which in standard English consists of just the one verb *beat*). How widespread this non-iconic pattern is will be investigated for the paradigms *eat* and *give* in section 5.5.

Finally, *do* constitutes a separate case, although it also belongs with these verb paradigms: it is a three-part paradigm in the standard (StE *do – did – done*) and thus belongs to verb class 1, which is levelled to a two-part-paradigm in non-standard systems, entering verb class 2 with the expected levelling of past tense and past participle to *do – done – done*, again showing the pervasive power of the pattern PRES $\neq$ PAST = PPL.. However, this levelling goes together with a functional split in those dialects that feature this development, in that *do – did* is preserved for the auxiliary,[12] whereas levelling to *do – done – done* only occurs for main verb uses of *do*. This illustrates succinctly the phenomenon variously called re-functionalization, re-morphologization or exaptation (Lass 1990) of a morphological difference, and *do* will be discussed in detail in section 5.4.

---

[12] There is no participle form for the auxiliary, as the auxiliary *do* can by definition not occur in any tense that would require the past participle.

3.5.3.2 One- instead of two-part paradigms

A change from two- to one-part paradigms is never found with class 2 verbs (e.g. *hold – held – held*), but only in class 3. Both verb paradigms of this class are levelled to one form in non-standard systems, e.g. *come – **come** – come* (vs. StE *come – came – come*) and *run – **run** – run* (vs. StE *run – ran – run*). In other words, (the complete) class 3 switches, not to weak verbs, as would be predicted by Mayerthaler, but to the much less natural class 5. While the actual developments towards these simplified paradigms are characterized by historical coincidences, the strong stance they have today in non-standard paradigms is obviously not hindered by being morphologically non-iconic in almost all persons. Clearly here speaker economy wins out over hearer economy, as especially identical present and past tense forms are not very helpful, and therefore functionally less than optimal. Whether this pattern can be explained in the framework of natural morphology will be explored in Chapter 6.

3.5.4 Summary

It is in roughly this order that exemplary strategies will be discussed in the following case studies. As a summary, the pervasive patterns of non-standard tense paradigms can be listed as in Figure 3.5.

Whether there are sizeable numbers of counterexamples to these patterns will be discussed in the respective chapters.

4 *Sellt* and *knowed*: non-standard weak verbs

Jedes Wort has seine Geschichte und lebt sein eigenes Leben.
(Every word has its own history and lives its own life.)
(Grimm 1819: xiv, my translation)

4.1 Introduction

As already mentioned in section 1.1, weak verbs can very generally be considered a common Germanic innovation, although perhaps as many as 2 per cent may have come down from Indo-European, as West (2001: 54) points out. It is generally agreed that the class of strong verbs inherited from Indo-European, mainly characterized by ablaut in the Germanic languages, has been steadily diminishing in all Germanic languages, as verbs have been switching verb classes from strong to weak.

In terms of universal natural morphology, a switch of verbs from strong to weak constitutes a natural development (see section 2.9.1), and is one of the few predictions on verb classes that can be derived from Mayerthaler (1981, 1988). Strong verbs are either minimally iconic, if the meaning 'Past' is indicated solely through modulation (e.g. *sing – sang*), or they are less than maximally iconic, if the meaning 'Past' is indicated by the addition of a segment, but through modulation as well (e.g. *keep – kept*). Weak verbs on the other hand are always maximally iconic (the semantically marked meaning 'Past' corresponds to the formal addition of the segment <-ed>, e.g. *hunt – hunted*). The predicted direction of change in Mayerthaler's universal natural morphology is towards the maximally iconic form, as iconic (and transparent and uniform) forms are the least marked: 'Any change leading from what is more marked to what is less marked is a natural change' (Mayerthaler 1987: 51). In fact, Mayerthaler draws up an equation for strong and weak verbs in Germanic language, explicitly stating that 'for any given t [sc. time] there is a medium class shift: "strong verb → weak verb"' (Mayerthaler 1987: 38).

As Krygier (1994) has shown, although some strong verbs already shifted to the weak verb category in Old English, this development really gathered momentum in Middle English, in particular during the fourteenth century

(Krygier 1994: 194). Incipient standardization towards Early Modern English seems to have slowed down the shift again, essentially 'fossilizing some verbs as shifted, and others as strong, or irregular' (Krygier 1994: 232, see also 245). One might therefore expect that this development, even if halted or slowed down to imperceptible speed by standardization, may have continued in the dialects, or in general non-standard speech.

We do indeed find some non-standard weak past tense forms in dialect systems, as this chapter will show. However, although in British dialects the trend to regularize strong past tense forms certainly continues, this strategy is by no means frequent enough to claim that it constitutes a dominant option in non-standard verb systems. In addition, whereas in the standard only truly marginal and infrequent verbs seem to be switching verb classes from strong to weak, in non-standard English some very high frequency words are affected (as *sell* and *know* in the chapter title indicate). A look at individual verb forms will show that often individual histories are indeed responsible for the behaviour of non-standard verbs, supporting the commonplace dialectological wisdom that indeed 'every word has its own history' (see the quotation by Jacob Grimm above). On the other hand, certain words seem to form clusters, and these larger patterns can be explained by functional considerations, relativizing Grimm's dictum somewhat.

Unfortunately, very little systematic work has been done on weak non-standard verb paradigms so far, so that there is little previous work to draw on. The most comprehensive list of non-standard weak verbs is probably still found in Wright's *English Dialect Grammar* (Wright 1905: 285–7). Based on historical verb classes, Wright distinguishes two groups: old strong verbs which have acquired weak preterites (his §427), and verbs which have remained weak in the preterite (his §428) (i.e. where the standard must have developed a new strong form). Both groups are roughly equal in size in his overview and contain between sixty and seventy verbs. Of the total of 130 verbs or so, however, many non-standard weak forms are marked 'obsolete' even in Wright's times (i.e. more than a century ago). The regional affiliations given are in many cases sporadic and do not lend themselves to a depiction in map form. In addition, Wright's list is only of qualitative value in that no conclusions can be drawn on the actual frequencies of usage of these forms (except perhaps on the obsolete ones). Nevertheless, his list is useful as a starting point, as well as a reverse control: almost all verbs that are frequent enough to appear in FRED in a non-standard weak form are also already documented in Wright (1905).

More modern material on the other hand is largely lacking. Even in the otherwise often highly scrupulous SED only a rather unsystematic array of questions is concerned with verb paradigms in general. Only a small range of verb paradigms were elicited by questionnaire items (in particular, *find – found – found, put – put – put, come – came – come, break – broke – broken, make – (has) made, take – took – taken, grow – grew* and *rode*). Perhaps these verbs were expected to be weak in some dialects, but they do not constitute a coherent group, nor are the eliciting questions coherent in themselves: for some verbs, all three principal forms were elicited, for others just one. In particular, the potentially interesting past tense *made* is missing, likewise the very frequent (and interesting) paradigm of *run*, etc. Where appropriate, therefore, material from the SED (especially the Basic Material) will be consulted to elucidate possible historical dialectal developments. Unfortunately, this will not be possible for the majority of verb forms discussed in this chapter (or indeed in this book).

As Wright's distinction already indicates, most of the verbs in this chapter can be traced back to Old English verbs. The dominance of Germanic verb stems is of course not surprising, as weak forms can only be called non-standard if a strong counterpart exists. As strong verbs are typically (but not in all cases) inherited from Indo-European, most of the verbs discussed in this chapter occurred in Old English already. Nevertheless, it is interesting to distinguish Wright's two categories: on the one hand, verbs that were originally strong, i.e. where the standard has continued to use the strong form, but the non-standard systems were innovative and have created a newer, weak form; on the other hand, verbs that were historically weak, i.e. where the standard was innovative and has created a new strong form, whereas the non-standard systems are more conservative and have continued the older, weak form. Finally, a third category is conceivable, namely where forms were variable from a very early time onwards. Whether this exists shall be investigated with the help of data from FRED.

4.2   Data from FRED: what to count?

If we look at data from FRED, we do in fact encounter quite a wide range of verbs with weak past tense (and past participle) forms that have strong counterparts in the standard. For most verbs, however, this is a rather sporadic phenomenon, and for this reason quantification is inherently difficult. Because absolute numbers are so low, it makes little sense to give percentages (e.g. *knowed* calculated in relation to standard *knew*), although this is technically of course possible. I have only resorted to these kinds of token percentages where they can in fact be given a meaningful interpretation, in particular in the analyses of individual verbs. For totals especially, however, freak occurrences of otherwise very frequent verbs would distort the overall impression considerably, and the overview as well as the regional comparisons therefore do not rely on token percentages.

A different theoretical possibility would be a count of types, rather than tokens. This, however, is only a theoretical possibility and does not seem feasible in practical research. One would need a count for each dialect area of how many different – strong! – verbs are employed, in order to provide a ratio of how many of them display a non-standard weak form. Unfortunately, it is not possible (in an untagged and unlemmatized corpus like the provisional FRED) to find strong verb forms manually, so a type quantification is not realistic.

The only remaining sensible possibility is a normalized word count, that is, a calculation of the number of non-standard weak verb forms in relation to the overall number of words, if we want to get regionally comparative results. This method makes some implicit assumptions: it assumes that the ratio of strong to weak verbs is roughly similar across dialect areas, and that the ratio of verb forms to other word classes is also roughly similar. If we accept these assumptions, one can simply calculate the actual regularized (non-standard) weak past tense forms in relation to the number of words per dialect area in a relatively straightforward way. In particular, I searched all words ending in –*ed* or –'*d* per dialect area and manually excluded all standard English forms. Although time consuming, this method ensures that unexpected weak past tense forms (e.g. forms not recorded so far in the dialect literature) are included in the count. (Unfortunately, the reverse search for unexpected strong verbs is not quite as easy.[1])

4.3 Regional comparison

The overall word count figures, the basis for the following calculations, are detailed in Table 4.1 (column two headed 'words total', see also section 1.4). The number 100,000 was chosen for normalization as the usual measure of occurrences per running text in accordance with much work in frequency studies, resulting in the Mossé-coefficient or M-coefficient (abbreviated M-co in Table 4.1). The Mossé-coefficient simply indicates the normalized word count, i.e. the occurrence of weak verbs per 100,000 words of running text.

The normalized figures (see also Figure 4.1) already confirm that for a frequent variable like the past tense, the phenomenon of non-standard weak verb forms is a relatively rare feature – especially considering that in these figures, several lexemes are added together. There is no particularly notice-able regional distribution; Scotland ranges slightly above the average, per-haps expectedly: after all, one of the two verbs of the chapter title, *sellt*,[2] that comes to mind spontaneously when thinking about non-standard weak past tense forms, is as good as a shibboleth of Scottish and northern speech, whose geographical distance from the purported origin of the standard, the

---

[1] I did search for all common strong verb endings (e.g. *oke, *ose/*oze, *ole, *ove, *ore, *ew, *ook, etc.), as well as the list of strong verbs mentioned in Wright, but no counterexamples turned up in FRED (i.e. non-standard strong verbs that are weak in the standard). The thirty-six non-standard strong verbs with weak standard counterparts in Wright's substan-tial list (1905: 281–4) thus seem thoroughly outdated.

[2] The provisional corpus has *selled* in all cases. Since it is highly unlikely that the form *selled* is in fact used by these northern speakers instead of the devoiced *sellt* (and *tellt*) (Joan Beal, personal communication, 27 May 2006), I am using the dialectal form here.

Table 4.1 *Non-standard weak verbs per dialect area (normalized)*

	Words total	Weak verbs	M-co
Scotland	339,917	67	19.7
South East	652,871	118	18.1
Midlands	358,318	52	14.5
South West	569,969	71	12.5
North	432,214	24	5.6
Wales	89,018	1	1.1
Total	2,442,307	333	Ø 13.6

Ø = average.

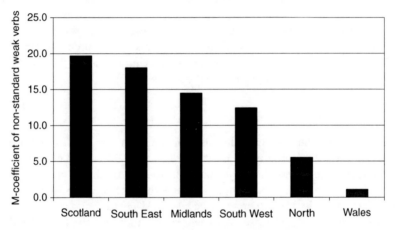

Figure 4.1 Non-standard weak verbs per dialect area (normalized)

South East of England, may already suggest considerable linguistic distance as well. For the same reason, it may be slightly unexpected that the North ranges below the national average. The North is in fact the only area that is consistently different from the others statistically. If one compares regions by chi square, the North is significantly different from all other dialect areas, except for Wales, and is thus the least integrated dialect area in this respect.[3] However, the overall figures mask some striking individual differences between verbs, which are worth investigating in more detail.

4.4   Individual verbs

For this reason, the individual verbs are cross-tabulated by dialect area in Table 4.2. Verbs that occur only once are found at the bottom of the table. Dialect areas are grouped roughly in North-to-South order.

---

[3] With df=1.

Table 4.2　*Individual weak verbs per dialect area*

	Scotland	North	Midlands	South East	South West	Wales	Sum
knowed		4	11	49	23		87
gaed	30						30
runned				20	10		30
telled, tellt	21	3	2				26
blowed			9	11	4		24
catched	2	3	5	6	5		21
seed		1	9	1	9		20
drawed			6	8	1	1	16
selled, sellt	6	9					15
gi'ed, gived	7			2	5		14
throwed			2	9	2		13
growed		3		5	3		11
bursted		2		4			6
busted		1		3	1		5
heared		1			4		5
comed			1		2		3
teached		1	1				2
digged	1						1
drinked					1		1
keeped		1					1
maked		1					1
shined					1		1
Total	67	24	52	118	71	1	333

This table is a good illustration of a recurrent pattern in language variation and language change, pointed out by Kretzschmar, who designates this pattern the 'asymptotic curve', or 'A-curve' for short (Kretzschmar 2002; Kretzschmar and Tamasi 2003). As Kretzschmar stresses, 'what we find consistently is that there is a wide range of possible realizations [of a variant] … Within the range [of realizations] there tend to be one or two common values and a large number of infrequent values' (Kretzschmar 2002: 100; see also Kretzschmar and Tamasi 2003: 378). While general trends often only hold for the high frequency items, the asymptotic curve helps account for the incidental or sporadic occurrences as well. In times of language change, these may either be relic forms, or highly advanced forms. In case of stable variation, these infrequent forms do perhaps not merit individual discussion, but it is expected that they will be there. Even if the following discussion therefore only concentrates on the more frequent items, the A-curve helps us remember in a methodical way that these rarer verbs are of course always present and can indeed be accounted for in the model. The distribution of non-standard weak past tense verbs is depicted in Figure 4.2.

Figure 4.2 also shows graphically that the most frequent verb, *knowed*, is really exceptionally frequent. For a closer investigation of the

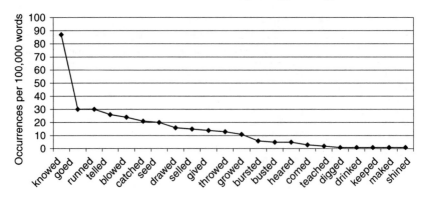

Figure 4.2 A-curve for non-standard weak verbs

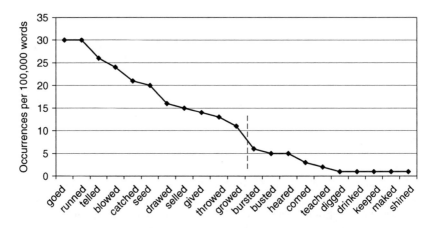

Figure 4.3 A-curve for non-standard weak verbs excluding *knowed*

distribution of the remaining verbs, *knowed* has therefore been excluded from Figure 4.3. As this allows more precise scaling, the more or less arbitrary break-off point from the more frequent verbs (more than ten occurrences) to the rather sporadic ones (six or fewer occurrences), i.e. between *growed* and *bursted*, also becomes intuitively apparent. (It is marked by a dotted line in Figure 4.3.)

There are some striking regional distributions in the more frequent verbs, as well as some systematic peculiarities that are worth discussing in more detail in the following sections, and for these purposes only those verbs that occur more than ten times in the corpus as a non-standard weak past tense form will be considered. Verbs will be discussed roughly in North-to-South order, with regionally specific features examined before more general ones.

4.4.1   Northern features

4.4.1.1   Past tense gaed *and* gi'ed

As is apparent from Table 4.2, four verb forms are clear northern features ('northern' comprising the North of England as well as Scotland): *gaed*, *tellt*, *sellt* and *gi'ed*. Two of these are restricted to Scotland and thus constitute clear Scotticisms: *gaed* and *gi'ed*, and it is with these two forms that this overview begins.

(1) Oh, you did get an occasional lad that *gaed* to the kirk. (PER 003) (Perthshire, Scottish Lowlands)

(2) We was gonna get married 'cause I *gi'ed* the lassie the seventy-odd pound I'd saved, ye see. (PER 001) (Perthshire, Scottish Lowlands)

Gaed [*goed*] is used exclusively in Scotland, and is indeed the historically attested, 'regular' Scots past tense form of *go*. Historically, a weak form of *go* is difficult to attest, as *go* itself had a defective paradigm. Wright also groups *go* in his first group, i.e. old strong verbs which have acquired weak preterites (Wright 1905: 285). In Old English, the past tense was regularly *éode*, a suppletive form of still not quite resolved ancestry. *Éode* developed regularly into Middle English (ME) *ede, yede, yode* (forms that are still attested as dialectal forms for Scotland, the 'North Country' and Derby in Wright (1905: 285)), until it was substituted by another suppletive form, *went*, originally the past tense of *wend*, at least in the South (OED: s.v. *go* v.). In Scotland, *gaed* seems to have been a new formation that succeeded ME *yede* from the fifteenth century onwards, so that southern *went* was never introduced into the dialect system.[4] The use of *gaed* in Scotland therefore constitutes a proper retention of a Middle English or Early Modern English form.

Gi'ed, as the past tense of *give*, is similarly characteristic of Scots today – the lack of the labiodental fricative is peculiar to Scots and still occurs reasonably frequently also in other lexemes (*deil* for *devil*, *neir* for *never*, etc.). However, *gi'ed* has a comparatively shorter history than the form *gaed* and is only recorded from the eighteenth century onwards (OED: s.v. *give* v.). A strong Scottish form *gae* (<*gave*) was in use in the eighteenth century, but is not recorded in FRED today.

4.4.1.2   Past tense tellt *and* sellt

(3) And he *tellt* me to do homework. (FRED ELN 012) (East Lothian, Scottish Lowlands)

---

[4] *Went* does occur frequently both in the Scottish Lowlands and in the Highlands and Hebrides in FRED, however, with no significant difference between the two areas. This is a good indication that in present-day Scottish English, southern forms are increasingly influential, and that the language represented in FRED is not 'pure' Scots (for the continuum between Scottish standard English and Scots, see most recently Miller 2004).

(4) They *tellt* us, there's the boss coming around. (FRED NBL 003)
    (Northumberland, North)
(5) The Corporation *tellt* him he couldn't do this and couldn't do that.
    (FRED WAR 001) (Warwickshire, Midlands)
(6) We *sellt* two calves at Kendal for three and sixpence each. (FRED WES
    008) (Westmoreland, North)
(7) She *sellt* ... eh ... clothes pegs ... (FRED INV 001) (Inverness-shire,
    Scottish Highlands)

As mentioned before, *tellt* and *sellt*[5] are shibboleths of northern English,
and the data from FRED confirm that these non-standard past tense verb
forms occur not only in Scotland but also in the North of England; *tellt* is
even recorded in the Midlands, as example (5) illustrates. This northern and
Midlands distribution can be traced back to Wright, who notes *selled/sellt* for
Scotland, the North Country more generally, Yorkshire [6], and Lancashire
[5] more specifically, but also Derby [8], Nottinghamshire [9], Lincolnshire
[10], Rutland [14], Berkshire [33] and even East Anglia; the distribution for
telled/tellt is slightly more extended and includes in addition Leicestershire
[13], Northamptonshire [18], southern Worcestershire [16], Shropshire
[11], Herefordshire [15], southern Pembrokeshire, Gloucestershire [24],
Oxfordshire [25], Huntingdonshire [19], and the South West, as indicated
in Map 4.1.

Although the present-day distribution seems to be much reduced geographically, it is still the case that *tellt* is more widespread than *sellt*; this
distribution can be traced back to the older dialect situation holding around
Wright's time.

Tellt and *sellt* in particular can in fact be traced back to the respective Old
English forms, where both verbs were weak verbs, if irregular ones. Again,
this is supported by Wright's classification of both *tell* and *sell* as 'verbs
which have remained weak in the preterite' (Wright 1905: 286–7). *Tellt* and
sellt are thus clear cases where a historically attested form is retained in some
dialects.

The Old English (OE) forms of *tell* were *tellan, tealde, geteald*, with 'alternation between a mutated and an unmutated vowel' (Ekwall 1980: 114), but
clearly weak through the addition of the dental suffix. OE Anglian sources on
the other hand have a strong(er) form *talde, getald* (in the Vespasian Psalter),
which might have been the source for the strong forms *táld, told* we find
in Middle English. Apparently, *tealde* remained in early Middle English in
southern [!] dialects; the OED claims that northern *tellt* is a later formation

---

[5] As mentioned before, I am not concerned here with the difference between the forms with
final devoicing, *tellt* and *sellt*, and those with the regular past tense allomorph (*telled, selled*),
although the exclusive presence of *selled* in the corpus may be a transcription error in the
preliminary version of FRED (Joan Beal, personal communication). This does not significantly change my argument, and I will simply treat these two forms together.

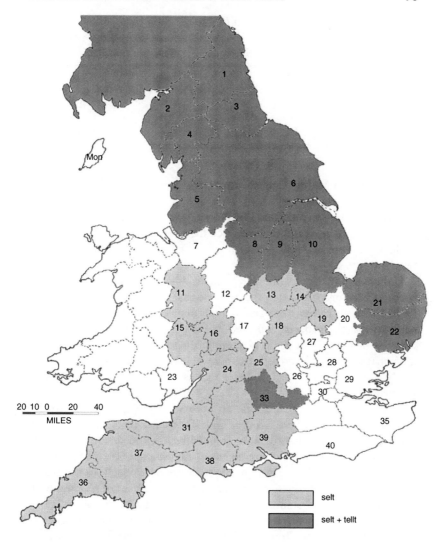

Map 4.1 Past tense *sellt* and *tellt* in the EDD

(OED s.v. *tell* v.). However, this claim contradicts their own careful charting of the forms through history, as past tense forms *tellde*, *telde*, *teld*, *tellid*, etc. are recorded from the fifteenth century onwards, and have clear precursors in the Old English forms. Nevertheless, it may well have been the case that the development of *tell* was influenced by the very similar *sell*.

The history of *sell* is parallel to *tell*: the Old English forms recorded were *sellan*, *sealde*, *seald*, but parallel strong forms are recorded from Old English onwards (*salde* in the Lindisfarne Gospels, ca. 950, *solde* from Middle

Table 4.3 *Relative frequencies of* tellt *in FRED*

	tellt	*told*	Sum	% *tellt*
Scotland (Lowlands)	21	27	48	43.8
North	4	55	59	6.8
Midlands	2	138	140	1.4
Total	27	220	247	Ø 10.9

English), and in Middle English, strong and weak forms existed side by side (OED: s.v. *sell* v.).

It is interesting to note that Old Norse only had a weak form of this verb (ON *selja, selda, seld*) and this may well have contributed to the continuation of the weak form *sellt* (and, by analogy, *tellt*), especially in the North and in Scotland.

Unfortunately, this is one of the many interesting verb paradigms that have not been investigated in the SED, so that we cannot compare data from FRED with an earlier finer grid of informants. Nevertheless, from a comparison with the material collected in Wright (1905) it seems that *tellt* and *sellt* may be recessive features geographically today. From the data in FRED it is apparent that *tellt* and *sellt* are today notable dialect features of Scots and the North of England only. Table 4.3 gives the relative frequencies for *tell* from FRED.

In Scotland, as expected, all 21 occurrences of *tellt* come from the Lowlands, the area where Scots is and was traditionally spoken. Standard English *told* is used slightly more frequently at 27 occurrences. This gives the non-standard form a text frequency of almost 44 per cent, and makes *tellt* a very pervasive dialect feature of Scottish English indeed. In the North of England, in contrast, the four non-standard occurrences of *tellt* are dwarfed by 55 occurrences of standard English *told*, giving a percentage of under 7 per cent; a highly significant difference.[6] While forms like *tellt* might therefore still be part of the traditional dialect system in the North of England, they are clearly dominated by their standard English counterpart, and will probably soon be noticeable only as 'quaint' or 'rustic'.

Non-standard *sellt* is by no means as frequent as *tellt*, and, as noted above, also regionally more restricted. Table 4.4 gives the relative frequencies for this verb.

As a comparison with *tellt* above shows, relative frequencies in Scotland are not as high as for *tellt*; however, this difference is not statistically significant.[7] Conversely, *sellt* is slightly more frequent in the North than *tellt* (but

---

[6] At p<0.001. Computed for a 2×2 table with df=1.
[7] Computed for a 2×2 table with df=1.

Table 4.4 *Relative frequencies of* sellt *in FRED*

	sellt	*sold*	Sum	*% sellt*
Scotland (Lowlands)	5	16	21	23.8
North	9	51	60	15.0
Midlands	0	57	57	0.0
Total	14	124	138	Ø 10.1

again this difference is not statistically significant), while it is non-existent in the Midlands. Overall, however, both words seem well established in both Scotland and the North of England, whereas in the Midlands this weak past tense form seems condemned to obsolescence.

4.4.2 Southern features

4.4.2.1 Past tense runned

(8) There was a little pipe what *runned* down the deck. (FRED SFK 028) (Suffolk, South East)

(9) We *runned* up a bill, just in the teens of pounds. (FRED CON 009) (Cornwall, South West)

Despite the fact that northern forms like *sellt* or *tellt* immediately come to mind when one thinks about non-standard weak verb forms, comparatively more non-standard weak verb forms are restricted to the South of England. Perhaps one of the most interesting is *runned*. As we shall see, *run* has another very frequent non-standard past tense, namely *run* (see section 6.2). This 'levelled' past tense *run* (which makes the past tense identical to the present tense and the past participle) occurs across Britain, but is also particularly frequent in the South with a text frequency of 66.7 per cent. As we have seen, levelling of present and past tense forms is non-iconic and therefore not optimal in functional terms, and it is therefore not surprising to see that in an area where the present and past tenses of *run* are in fact identical in the majority of cases, a new distinct past tense form is occurring, namely the weak form *runned*. *Runned* is comparatively frequent for a non-standard weak verb (in fact, it is the second most frequent non-standard weak form in Table 4.2), but completely restricted regionally to the South, where it seems to be well established.

Although the *English Dialect Grammar* does not mention *runned* (as one of only two of the non-standard weak verbs of Table 4.2 that are not mentioned in Wright's list), the much more detailed *English Dialect Dictionary* under the entry *run* does list some weak forms, namely for Nottinghamshire [9], Lincolnshire [10], southern Wales, Berkshire [33], Norfolk [21], Somerset [31], Devon [37], Cornwall [36], as well as a weak form with r-metathesis for west Somerset [31] (*urned*) (Wright 1898–1905: s.v. *run*). Historically, then, perhaps the distribution of *runned* was a little more widespread. On the other hand, Wright does not (and indeed cannot) distinguish sporadic from frequent uses, so that the question of pervasiveness cannot be resolved.

Historically, there are some attestations of a weak past tense form for *run* since at least Middle English. As the word *run* was often found with r-metathesis (as the infinitive forms *irnan*, *urnen*, *ærnan*, etc. indicate, which still survived in the South West at least until Wright's time, see above), the attested forms may look a little disorderly. A weak metathesized form is attested roughly one hundred years earlier than one without metathesis, namely throughout the thirteenth century (the OED cites *ærnde*, *arnde*, *h(e)arnde*, *arnede*, *hern(e)de*, *ernde* as well as *ornd*, and no doubt there are a range of other variants). A form without metathesis develops around 1300 (the OED has *rende*, *rennede* and *rennyd*), but notably here the vowel is clearly different from the form *runned* we encounter today. (For the complicated history of this seemingly simple verb, see section 6.2; but for the moment compare it to its two German cognates *rinnen* and *rennen* for vowel differences.) The form *runned* as we find it today is cited for the sixteenth century, and then again as dialectal for the nineteenth century (OED: s.v. *run* v.) and would therefore be a candidate for a relatively new formation. Perhaps on the basis of continuing parallel strong and weak forms throughout Middle English, the syncretism of present and past tense forms of *run* in the English South seems to have supported the creation or, more precisely, the re-establishment of the corresponding weak form *runned* in this area, to counter the non-optimal situation encountered in the paradigm *run – run – run*. The non-standard weak form *runned* can therefore be analysed as the re-emergence of a historically attested form, perhaps in order to remedy a functionally non-optimal situation.

4.4.2.2 Past tense gived

(10) He said, Let me have your hand, so I *gived* me hand. (FRED SOM 032) (Somerset, South West)

(11) Couple of the girls *gived* me away. (FRED LND 005) (London, South East)

Perhaps something similar can be said about *gived*, which is also restricted to the South (Scots has a separate, but parallel, development to *gi'ed*; see section 4.4.1.1 above). Again, this is a paradigm that is typically and more frequently levelled in the South, where the dominant non-standard pattern is *give – give – given* (see section 5.5.3), not *give – gived – gived*. But similarly to *run* above, the non-functional pattern *give – give – given* (again with identical forms in past and present tense) has given rise to the development of a regularized counterpart in *gived*, parallel to *run – runned – runned* above. As the non-iconic *give – give – given* is again restricted to the South, it is therefore not surprising to find the regularized *gived* exclusively in the South as well.

Historically, the verb *ʒiefan* in Old English was a strong verb, with the past tense forms *ʒeaf* in the singular and *ʒéafon* in the plural; the past participle was *ʒiefen*. The initial velar consonant we find today seems to be due to Scandinavian influence, otherwise the form today should have developed an initial /j/. The OED records a weak past tense form *gived* for the eighteenth century onwards, i.e. relatively late – like *runned* above this therefore seems to be a genuine new formation, perhaps in reaction to the levelled past tense *give* in the South.

4.4.2.3   *Past tense* knowed, growed, blowed *and* throwed

(12) I *knowed* where I could get thruppence for them. (FRED KEN 003) (Kent, South East)

(13) They *growed* vegetables. (FRED NTT 005) (Nottinghamshire, Midlands)

(14) What stuff we *growed* we could take home. (FRED WIL 001) (Wiltshire, South West)

(15) Me and my father *blowed* the Dale organ between us for forty years. (FRED SAL 018) (Shropshire, Midlands)

(16) Somebody *throwed* a apple and hit a bloke in the face with it. (FRED KEN 003) (Kent, South East)

(17) We *drawed* our money each week. (FRED KEN 003) (Kent, South East)

Knowed, growed, blowed and *throwed*, as well as *drawed*, are regularized past tense forms that are used in place of StE past tense forms in <-ew> (*knew*, *grew*, *blew*, *threw* and *drew*). In Old English, *grow, blow* and *throw* (together with *know*) belonged to the mixed verb class VII (the 'leftover' class) and formed a small subregularity there even in Old English times. All were strong verbs, and their forms are given below. *Draw* belonged to a different verb class and is dealt with in the next section.

The historical paradigm of *know* in Old English (OE) consisted of the forms *cnáwan – cnéow – cnáwen*; this is the verb with the earliest weak past tense form attested, namely *cnawed* from the fourteenth century onwards. *Knowed* is by far the most frequent non-standard verb form today, as we have seen in Table 4.2, and it is also spread furthest regionally, so that today it is present practically throughout Britain. For this reason, *knowed* will be discussed in section 4.4.4.1 (on general features) in more detail, although of course it belongs with the other words of this class.

The Old English paradigm of *grow* was *grówan – gréow – grówen*. For *grow*, the first weak forms are attested in the OED from the fifteenth century onwards (forms like *growide, grouuede*), about a century later than for *know* above. Nevertheless, this relatively early date means that for Early Modern

English, parallel forms of *grow* (weak and strong) must have existed side by side. Interestingly, cognates of *grow* are weak in all Germanic languages where they have survived (cf. Dutch, Danish or Swedish), but the Danelaw area has no occurrences of a weak past tense *growed* – this seems to be one of the few lexemes where Scandinavian influence on its morphological shape probably has to be ruled out.

Moving to the history of *blow*: OE *bláwan* was also a strong verb (cf. past tense *bléow*, past participle *bláwen*), but from late Middle English times some weak forms are attested (*blowide*, from the fifteenth century, *blowd* in the eighteenth century). Finally, the history of *throw*: OE *þráwan* belonged to the same strong verb class with the past tense *þréow* and the past participle *þráwen*. First weak forms here are not attested before the seventeenth century.

In general, the unusual Modern English past tense form in these four verbs in /u:/ stems from the OE diphthong <éo> which developed into ME <íu>, <iú>, Early Modern English and present-day English /u:/, and for all verbs, parallel weak forms are attested at least since the seventeenth century, i.e. since Early Modern English.

Today, weak past tense forms for these four verbs are restricted to the South and the Midlands. The similarity in form very much suggests some kind of systemic pressure. In Quirk et al. (1985: 109) *know, grow, blow* and *throw* constitute their own verb class, which only consists of these four members (their verb class 4Ba). In my classification, they belong to the prototypical strong verb class 1, together with *draw* (subclass <-en>, vowel pattern 2c). As we have already seen, *knowed* is one of the most frequent non-standard weak verbs, and may well have served as the model for an alternative to these unusual past tense forms in /u:/.[8] *Knowed, growed, blowed* and *throwed* in turn may have served as the attractor for the similar past tense form *drew* /dru:/. In fact, *draw* is sometimes classified as the only member of another, closely related, verb class (class 4Bd, Quirk et al. 1985: 110), and there are only two other verbs with a past tense in /u:/ today in standard English: the verb *fly – flew*, which shows no signs of regularization and, perhaps because of its different present tense form, does not seem to be affected by any kind of systemic pressure from the other past tense forms in /u:/, and the (now marginal) verb *slay – slew* which is mainly found in historical texts, again with a very different present tense stem.[9]

---

[8] In fact, *know* is one of the most frequent verbs overall. In Francis and Kučera's list, *know* is the eleventh most frequent strong verb, and is the sixty-third most frequent word (!) overall (Francis and Kučera 1982: 465).

[9] In at least some traditional dialects, however, the situation looks quite different. Peter Trudgill reports that in traditional East Anglian dialects, past tense forms in /u:/ seem to have constituted an attractor for other verbs, attracting such forms as *thew* (past tense of *thaw*), *snew* (past tense of *snow*), or even *ew* (past tense of *owe*) and *mew* (past tense of *mow*). Thus the East Anglian saying: *First it blew, then it snew and then it thew*, or *he ew me one pound* (Trudgill, personal communication 29/30 April 2005). Only some of these verbs

4.4.2.4 *Historical dialect data*

The EDD has only two entries for past tense *growed*, namely from north-ern Lincolnshire [10] and Warwickshire [17], i.e. the Midlands. (However, no other forms are given, so that we cannot know whether this is meant to imply that all other counties employed the standard *grew*, or whether a non-standard form of *grow* was simply not mentioned.) For *throwed*, there is some more material available. Four of the forms given as the past tense are clearly weak, if with different vowel qualities, namely *thraowed*, *thrawed*, *thro'd* and *throwed*. They are attested for south Worcestershire [16], Berwick, Northumberland [1], Devon [37], Cornwall [36], west Yorkshire [6], south Cheshire [7], south Staffordshire [12], Warwickshire [17], Shropshire [11], and Surrey [34]. Despite the range of counties this list only makes a rather patchy map, without a discernible regional distribution, as there are sim-ply too many white areas. Again, Wright does not systematically distinguish sporadic occurrences from more widespread ones. For this reason, it is more useful to turn to the SED, where the grid of informants is much more finely meshed.

Grow is the only verb of this group where data were systematically col-lected in the SED (in question IX.3.9, referring to potatoes): *Last year it was astonishing how quickly they* ——. Collecting all responses from the Basic Material (Orton and Halliday 1962–64; Orton and Barry 1969–71; Orton and Tilling 1969–71; Orton and Wakelin 1967–68), one can see that only the North and the North Midlands as well as East Anglia are really excluded from the geographical spread of *growed*, as Map 4.2 shows, or rather, that occurrences of *growed* are merely sporadic there. Informants employing *growed* are marked by a grey dot in Map 4.2.

It is clear that the comparatively early regularization of *grow* in late Middle English must have permitted this verb form to spread relatively far, and the general South and Midlands distribution of *growed* that we have found in FRED can be roughly confirmed for the older SED material as depicted in Map 4.2. The group of words *know*, *grow*, *blow* and *throw* thus constitute a subregularity, or proper verb class, not only in the standard, but also when we consider non-standard verb forms in English dialects. The time frame over which the individual weak forms are attested (between the fourteenth century for *knowed* and the seventeenth century for the latest of these forms, *throwed*) suggests that the later forms may have been modelled on the earlier ones, in particular on *knowed*, in order to avoid the highly unusual past tense phoneme /u:/. It is interesting to note that this non-standard development does indeed seem to be motivated by this kind of functional consideration. Whereas in standard English, the infrequent verbs, in particular, tend to switch into the weak verb class, in the case of *know*, etc. it is also pockets (or 'niches'

have an attested strong past tense form historically, notably *snow* (cf. OED entries for these words).

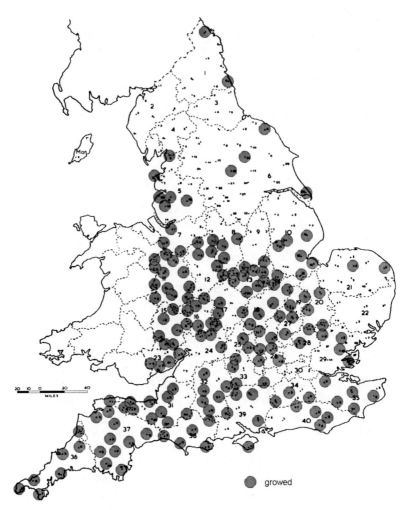

Map 4.2 Past tense *growed* in the SED (Basic Material)

in the sense of Dahl 2004: 78) of highly frequent words that are affected in non-standard varieties.[10]

4.4.2.5 *Past tense* drawed

The history of *draw* is quite different from *know*, *grow*, *blow* and *throw* above: it belonged to OE class VI with the forms *dragan – dróȝ – dragen*. The <g> caused a different development from the rest of this class (cf. *shake – shook – shaken* or

---

[10] *Know*, *grow* and *draw* are among the top 50 strong verbs in Francis and Kučera's frequency list; *throw* and *blow* still make it into the top 100 (Francis and Kučera 1982: 465–88).

swear – swore – sworn), namely to /ɣ/ and then to /w/, similarly in the past tense, which regularly became *drow*. The reason why today we find *drew* rather than *ˈdrow* seems to be that this past tense form was already substituted, apparently already by analogy with *blow – blew* and *grow – grew*, and thus became *drew* in the fourteenth to fifteenth centuries, apparently first in the North (OED: s.v. *draw* v.). First weak forms are attested occasionally from the sixteenth century onwards. As the *know* (sub)class seems to have been a powerful attractor for *draw* already for the strong form, it is not unreasonable to assume the same kind of analogy for the non-standard weak form *drawed* as well. After all, in the whole of the English past tense system, the only other past tense forms in *-ew* (/uː/) would be the very rare *slay – slew*, as well as the reasonably frequent *fly – flew* (*flew* occurs 25 times in FRED, with no weak forms attested).

4.4.2.6   *Relative frequencies*

Finally, it has to be mentioned that for these four verbs, the shift into the weak verb paradigm is a highly frequent phenomenon and anything but marginal, as a look at the relative frequencies shows. Relative frequencies are calculated as percentages of the non-standard weak form (e.g. *drawed*) in relation to the sum of weak and (standard) strong form (e.g. non-standard *drawed* plus StE *drew*). Percentages are given in Tables 4.5 to 4.8.

Tables 4.5 to 4.8 show large individual differences, both between verbs and between dialect areas, but overall the most striking figures are the averages (in the last respective rows). In the case of *drawed*, this non-standard verb form is used in almost 50 per cent of all cases – as the individual figures show, the regional average is much higher in all cases except the South West, which influences the overall average with its comparatively low figure of just one occurrence of *drawed* (vs. fifteen of *drew*). *Blowed* still has an average of almost 40 per cent, a very high figure for a non-standard feature. While here the South West and the South East pattern very similarly (at around 30 per cent), it is the figure from the Midlands that significantly changes the average, as here *blowed* is used in almost 70 per cent of all cases. For *throwed*, figures are comparatively equal around the average of 22 per cent, while for *growed* all three dialect areas which feature this word are quite different. (Incidentally this seems mainly due to a different emphasis in the interviews; the predominantly agricultural informants in the South West talk about growing crops, fruit, etc. much more than informants in the other interviews.) Nevertheless, the figure of 6.7 per cent, the lowest figure of this collection, is the only one that could be called marginal. In general, however, the relative as well as the absolute figures confirm that for this group of words, non-standard regularization proceeds through the relatively frequent words, and is not in all cases a marginal phenomenon, but can indeed constitute the majority option at least for some speakers.

Table 4.5 *Relative frequencies of* drawed *in FRED*

	drawed	*drew*	Sum	*% drawed*
Midlands	6	2	8	75
South East	8	10	18	44.4
South West	1	15	16	16.7
Wales	1	1	2	50
Total	16	18	34	Ø 47.1

Table 4.6 *Relative frequencies of* blowed *in FRED*

	blowed	*blew*	Sum	*% blowed*
Midlands	9	4	13	69.2
South East	11	24	35	31.4
South West	4	10	14	28.6
Total	24	38	62	Ø 38.7

Table 4.7 *Relative frequencies of* throwed *in FRED*

	throwed	*threw*	Sum	*% throwed*
Midlands	2	7	9	22.2
South East	9	29	38	23.7
South West	2	10	12	16.7
Total	13	46	59	Ø 22.0

Table 4.8 *Relative frequencies of* growed *in FRED*

	growed	*grew*	Sum	*% growed*
Midlands	3	14	17	17.6
South East	5	11	16	31.3
South West	3	42	45	6.7
Total	11	67	78	Ø 14.1

4.4.3   *Western feature*

4.4.3.1   *Past tense* seed

(18) I *seed* another lady carrying a big heavy bag. (FRED SAL 018) (Shropshire, Midlands)

(19) Wi' a rifle he were one of the best shots I ever *seed*, never get outside a Bull. (FRED WIL 001) (Wiltshire, South West)

A weak past tense of *see* (StE *see – saw – seen*) is the only feature that seems particularly frequent in the Midlands and the South West in FRED, while occurrences in the South East and in the North are sporadic at best. *See* is more frequently levelled to *seen* in the past tense, especially in the West Midlands and across the South East, as section 5.3 will show, while another non-standard past tense form, past tense *see*, occurs almost exclusively in the South East.

In the SED, fortunately, past tense forms of *see* were elicited (in question VIII.2.5: *Our cousin Jim from Canada actually came to see us three times, but unfortunately I never once ... him.*), and in these older data, surprisingly *seed* is the favoured response. Nevertheless, a clear regional distribution is already visible in this material, as Map 4.3 shows."

Concentrating on the grey dots for the moment (past tense *seen* will be discussed in section 5.3, past tense *see* in section 5.5.4), Map 4.3 shows that in the older material from the SED, past tense *seed* is very clearly preferred in the western parts of the country. The South West uses *seed* almost exclusively, and so do the West Midlands (except for the southern part, in particular Worcestershire [16] and Warwickshire [17]). *Seed* also extends into the North, especially the central North (i.e. Yorkshire [6] and Lancashire [5]). The distribution of *seen* and *see* need not concern us at this stage. Outside of this relatively well-defined area, occurrences of *seed* are sporadic at best, or are variable with *seen* (e.g. in the South East: in Kent [35] and Sussex [40]).

According to the OED, *see* from Old English times onwards was a strong verb (OE *séon – seah – sáwon/sǽʒon – ʒe-sewen*). Although a wide range of variant forms are attested through the centuries, all of them are strong. Weak forms of *see* are not attested before the nineteenth century (OED: s.v. *see* v.) and thus seem to be truly innovatory.

As the map from the SED material has shown, *seed* seems to have been restricted to the west of the country at least since the beginning of the twentieth century. The data from FRED support this regional differentiation. Although *see* is a relatively frequent verb, it is not meaningless to compare the non-standard weak form with its standard counterpart numerically, as Table 4.9 shows.

While the figures for *seed* are surprisingly similar across those dialect areas where they occur, they are dwarfed by the competing non-standard form *seen*. In the Midlands especially, non-standard *seen* is in fact the dominant form in FRED, used in over 50 per cent of all cases. In the South West, *seen* is also the favoured non-standard form over *seed*, but as *seen* 'only' amounts to just over 26 per cent, *seed* seems to have a slightly stronger hold here. The regional restriction, and the fact that non-standard *seed* is a new form that is clearly only a minority option, suggest that past tense *seed* is already on its

---

" A sample map including all county numbers and a list of all counties can be found in Appendix 2.

Table 4.9 *Relative frequencies of* seed *in FRED*

	seed	*seen*	*saw*	*see*	Sum	*% seed*
Midlands	9	91	81	6	187	4.8
South West	9	37	84	9	139	6.5
Total	18	128	165	15	326	Ø 5.5

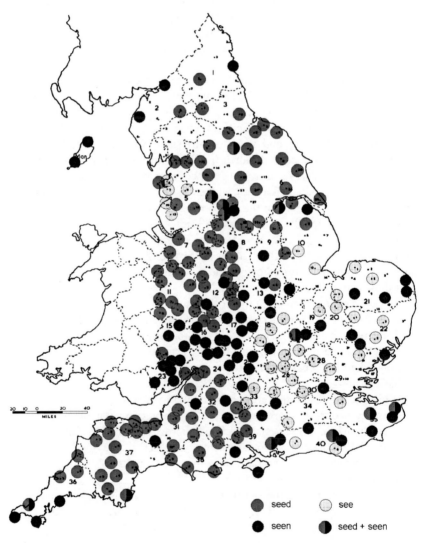

Map 4.3 Past tense *seed*, *seen* and *see* in the SED (Basic Material)

way out again. For a fuller picture, also taking into account the other dialect areas and especially the other non-standard variants, see section 5.3.

4.4.4   *General features*

4.4.4.1   *Past tense* knowed

(20) We never *knowed* what it was to go out and buy a cake. (FRED LAN 004) (Lancashire, North)
(21) And in those days it was what we called, Everybody *knowed* everybody. Everybody was willing to help everybody. (FRED SAL 027) (Shropshire, Midlands)
(22) I never *knowed* that man work from that day till when he passed away. (FRED MDX 001) (Middlesex, South East)
(23) Old Draper, see, I *knowed* he. I 'spect you did. (FRED WIL 010) (Wiltshire, South West)

Knowed is by far the most frequent of these non-standard weak verbs, and the most widespread, as examples (20) to (23) indicate. It is not found in Scotland for the only reason that *know* is a typically English verb; the Scottish equivalent is *ken*, deriving from Old English *cennan*, which died out in English perhaps around 1500 (OED: s.v. *ken* v.1). While *know* in England took over the territory of *cennan*, the reverse must have happened in Scotland, where *ken* is used in all places instead of *know* today. Today then these two verbs seem to be in perfectly complementary regional distribution in Great Britain.

Weak forms of *know* can be traced back to early Middle English, where they occur sporadically next to the more usual strong past tense form *knew*. However, regularized forms of *know* must at all times have been rather marginal. Thus, in the Helsinki corpus there are no attestations of *cnawed* or *knowed/knowede* (or spelling variants), whereas the strong forms are well documented from Old English onwards (i.e. *cneow, knewe, knew*). Present-day non-standard past tense *knowed* can therefore be regarded as a retention of a minority option which has survived, equally as a minority option, in the dialects.

Compared to the other four similar words of this word class above (*drawed, blowed, growed* and *throwed*), the highly frequent *know* is regularized much less frequently, as Table 4.10 indicates.

Figures for the individual dialect areas are quite similar and cluster around the average of 7.7 per cent, with the North being the only exception. In fact, *knowed* in the North is the only case of these five words where a regularized form can be said to be truly marginal, and it is also the only dialect area that is statistically significantly different from the three other areas.[12] Nevertheless, it is also clear that the average of *know* with below 8 per cent is

---

[12] Computed for a 4×2 table at df=3, p<0.001.

Table 4.10 *Relative frequencies of* knowed *in FRED*

	knowed	knew	Sum	% knowed
North	4	257	261	1.5
Midlands	11	161	172	6.4
South East	49	383	432	11.3
South West	23	249	272	8.5
Total	87	1,050	1,137	Ø 7.7

Table 4.11 *Relative and absolute frequencies of* know, *etc. in FRED*

	nStE	StE	Sum	% nStE form
draw	16	18	34	47.1
blow	24	38	62	38.7
throw	13	46	59	22.0
grow	11	67	78	14.1
know	87	1,050	1,137	7.7

nStE = non-standard English.

significantly different from the higher averages of the other lexemes, where even the comparatively infrequent *growed* is almost twice as frequent. Even the figures from the South East, which employs *knowed* more frequently than the other dialect areas, are below any of the figures for non-standard weak *drawed*, *blowed*, *growed* and *throwed*.

No doubt token frequency plays a part in the explanation of this discrepancy, as Table 4.11 displays.

Knew seems to resist the pressure of all its similar co-verbs to become *knowed* merely by the fact that it occurs so very frequently – in fact, *knew* is the fourteenth most frequent past tense form e.g. in the BNC overall, and thus disproportionately more frequent than *grew*, *drew*, *threw*, and *blew* taken together.[13] At least for this little subgroup of verbs, then, weak forms are the more frequent in relative terms, the less frequent a verb is absolutely.[14] Whether all non-standard verbs follow this regularization trend will be discussed at the end of this chapter.

---

[13] Retrieved from Mark Davies' VIEW program (Variation in English Words and Phrases), http://view.byu.edu/ (31 March 2005). The other four verbs are ranked at 82, 84, 118 and 250 respectively and are thus still relatively frequent, perhaps with the exception of *blew*.

[14] A statistical analysis confirms this. Over all verbs, differences are statistically significant (at df=4, p<0.001). If we compare individual lexemes in pairs, *draw* and *blow* are sufficiently similar, as are *throw* and *grow* (both comparisons at df=2, p<1, not significant). Between all other pairs of lexemes, differences are statistically highly significant.

4.4.4.2 *Past tense* catched

(24) I waited and waited and eh, I *catched* him one day. (FRED LAN 010)
(Lancashire, North)
(25) I rushed in at him, and *catched* hold of one front leg and one back leg.
(FRED KEN 002) (Kent, South East)

The weak past tense *catched* is the second verb form next to *knowed* that is very widespread and shows practically no regional limitation. It is the only word in our collection that does not derive from an Old English verb. Instead, *catch* is a word of Romance origin which is documented for English from the thirteenth century onwards. *Catch* underwent a curious shift in meaning in English, which is relevant here because it affected the morphology of its paradigm as well. The original meaning must have been more similar to 'chase', whereas the present-day meaning 'catch' was expressed by Old English *læccean*, Middle English *lacchen*, *lachen*. This shift in meaning from a process to the end result of the process is not surprising in itself and can easily be subsumed under metonymic changes. What is interesting is that these two words quickly became synonymous, and the forms of *lachen* seem to have acted as the model for the paradigm of *catch* as well, as we find *cahte* (> *caught*) parallel to *lahte* next to the regular and expected *catched* (OED s.v. *catch* v.). Although the OED claims that *caught* only superseded *catched* in literary language 'during the present century' (which I take to refer to the nineteenth century), and Ekwall similarly notes that 'the form *catched* was still used by good writers in the 18th century' (Ekwall 1980: 116), a look at the Helsinki corpus tells a slightly different story. Here, the only examples of *catched*[15] come from the period Early Modern English 2 (i.e. 1570–1640), while strong forms[16] are recorded for Middle English 3 (1350–1420) and for all periods of Early Modern English (1500–1710) at a very steady rate. Nevertheless, as this only mirrors literary language, it is not surprising that *catched* may have survived in spoken language and is still regularly encountered in the traditional dialects.

At the end of the nineteenth century, Wright records not a single instance of *caught* or related forms in his *English Dialect Dictionary* (Wright 1898–1905: s.v. *catch* v. I.2) except *caucht* in Scotland. Data from the SED similarly show that *catched* is used practically everywhere, as Map 4.4 indicates – there are very few white areas on the map, and many of these indeed result from the fact that, sometimes, a question was not answered, or the question was not put in the course of an interview.

---

[15] I use this form in the text to include the enormous range of weak verb forms as listed in the OED, e.g. *catched, cached, katched, cacchid, cacchit, cacht, catch'd* and *catcht.*

[16] Including e.g. *cahhte, cahte, cauhte, caȝte, kaȝte, cauȝte, kauȝte, caȝt, kaȝt, cauȝt, kauȝt, cawght, caghte, kaghte, caute, caght, kaght, kaught, coght, cought, caughte.*

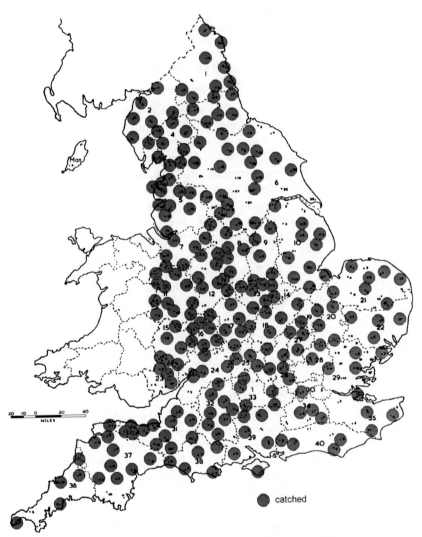

Map 4.4 Past tense *catched* in the SED (Basic Material)

Although the data are a little distorted by the fact that the North has a different word for 'catch', namely *to cop* (*copped*, *copped*), even for the North, *caught* is a very rare exception and most informants supply the form *catched*.

The situation has changed dramatically for the later material collected in FRED. Here, the traditional dialect form *catched* has become more marginal, as Table 4.12 shows.

Although the non-standard form *catched* really represents the expected past tense (considering that *catch* is a Middle English loan word), today it is

Table 4.12 *Relative frequencies of* catched *in FRED*

	catched	caught	Sum	% catched
Midlands	5	13	18	27.8
Scotland	2	10	12	16.7
North	3	16	19	15.8
South West	5	43	48	10.4
South East	6	52	58	10.3
Wales	0	12	12	0.0
Isle of Man	0	1	1	0.0
Total	21	147	168	Ø 12.5

very much a minority option in most dialect areas even for traditional dialect speakers. It is still strongest in the Midlands, followed by Scotland and the North.

4.5   Verb classes

As already mentioned in Chapter 3, what is striking about non-standard weak verbs is the fact that relatively high frequency verbs are affected, as well as marginal or infrequently used strong verbs which tend to become weak. If we look at verb class affiliation, this fact also becomes visible. In verb class 1, those subclasses that are affected by loss into the weak verb class in the standard (the two rightmost subclasses, see Figure 3.1) are not affected by non-standard verb class switches (or at least this cannot be shown on the basis of the material from FRED). Instead, it is two stable subclasses where we find (at least sporadic) regularization. Thus *go* features vowel change 3 and a past participle in <-en>, and *blow, know, throw, grow, draw*, as well as *give* and *see*, have a past participle in <-en> and vowel change 2c in the standard. In fact, these seven verbs account for a quarter of all members of this subclass, which is thus seriously depleted through regularization in non-standard systems. The two subclasses of verb class 1 are indicated by bold lines in Figure 4.4; arrows indicate that from these subclasses, verbs regularly appear in the weak form in non-standard systems.

Verb class 2 on the other hand is left relatively untouched by non-standard switches into the weak verb class. Those verbs that do change, however, tend to be high frequency items. *Sell* and *tell*, for example, belong to the subclass V2a with added /d/, which in standard English is at present only losing the very marginal *shoe – shod – shod* (no doubt due to extralinguistic changes; the number of horses being shod or shoed must have decreased dramatically over the last 100 years or so). The only other member of verb class 2 discussed in this chapter is *catch*, again a central member of subclass V2a with added consonant change and added /t/, while the only standard English member leaving this

VERB CLASS 1

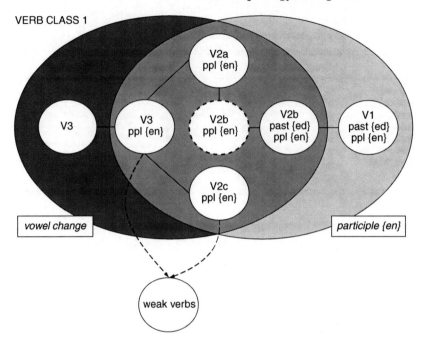

Figure 4.4 Verb class 1 affected by non-standard weak forms

class is *beseech – besought – besought*. Finally, *run* of course belongs to verb class 3 and indeed constitutes one half of it, and we have seen that the more usual path of change in non-standard verb systems is not towards the weak verbs, but into verb class 5 with three identical forms (see also of course section 6.2).

4.6 Statistical models

A statistical analysis can help to show whether the trend in non-standard systems to regularize strong verbs into weak verbs is the same as in the standard, or not. A process of regularization would presume that the infrequent and marginal strong verbs (like *shoe* or *beseech*) are regularized first, or more frequently, while verbs with a very high token frequency can preserve their irregularities (in this case, their strong form) for longer, and more easily. As we have seen, many frequent strong verbs are in fact affected by becoming weak in non-standard dialects of English, so this question is by no means a trivial one.

For the sake of this statistical analysis, I have taken all verbs that have *any* non-standard weak form, i.e. the complete list from Table 4.2, and searched all their strong verb occurrences in order to calculate relative and absolute frequencies (where this had not already featured in the preceding analysis of individual lexemes). The results are displayed in Table 4.13. Verbs have been

Table 4.13 *Relative and absolute frequencies of all non-standard weak verbs in FRED*

	nStE	StE	Sum	% nStE form
busted	5	0	5	100.0
shined	1	7	8	12.5
bursted	6	15	21	28.6
digged	1	24	25	4.0
drawed	16	18	34	47.1
drinked	1	36	37	2.7
throwed	13	46	59	22.0
blowed	24	38	62	38.7
teached	2	64	66	3.0
growed	11	67	78	14.1
gived	14	129	143	9.8
seed	20	128	148	13.5
catched	21	147	168	12.5
runned	30	203	233	12.9
tellt	26	220	246	10.6
heared	5	350	355	1.4
sellt	15	427	442	3.4
keeped	1	905	906	0.1
knowed	87	1,050	1,137	7.7
comed	3	1,161	1,164	0.3
maked	1	2,000	2,001	0.0
goed	30	10,000	10,030	0.3
Total	333	16,890	17,223	Ø 1.9

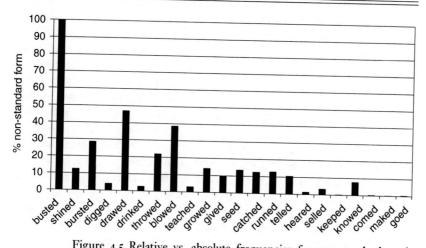

Figure 4.5 Relative vs. absolute frequencies for non-standard weak verbs in FRED

ordered according to their absolute frequencies (column 'sum') in increasing order, with *bust* the least frequent verb and *go* the most frequent one.

If we display the relative frequency in relation to the absolute ones graphically, we get the diagram shown in Figure 4.5. Intuitively, we can see what

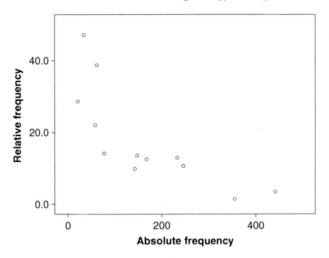

Figure 4.6 Scatterplot of relative vs. absolute frequencies of
non-standard weak verbs

looks like a correlation: the more frequent a verb is (in absolute terms), i.e.
the further to the right in this graph it appears, the less frequently it is 'regularized', i.e. the less frequently it has non-standard weak forms. To test this
statistically, though, we have to make certain adjustments. A first analysis[17]
suggests that the four most frequent verbs are really unusually frequent, and
so as not to distort the overall analysis, these four outliers (*know*, *come*, *make*
and *go*) should be excluded from the subsequent analysis. On the other hand,
statistical tests (like chi square) need minimum frequencies of at least five, so
all verbs with cells lower than five were also excluded. As the scatterplot in
Figure 4.6, carried out on the remaining verbs, shows, the distribution does
not look random, but resembles a curve (basically, any asymptotic curve as
described by Kretzschmar 2002; Kretzschmar and Tamasi 2003).

On these data, a curve estimation was run in the statistical software
package SPSS. This estimation confirmed intuitions and the scatterplot;
three (only minimally different) curves fitted in a highly significant way (at
$p < 0.001$), as Figure 4.7 shows.[18]

The link between absolute and relative frequencies is thus not random,
but these two frequencies are linked in a systematic way: the more frequent
a verb is overall, the less frequently it occurs with a non-standard weak verb
form. Ultimately, then, the statistical analysis confirms that weak verb forms
in British dialects follow the same very general pattern of regularization as
in standard English.

[17] E.g. the 'Explore' function in SPSS.
[18] The curves are the compound curve, the logistic curve and the exponential curve, all
highly significant with Sig=0.000 with df=10 and F=35.80.

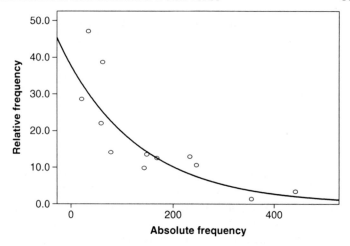

Figure 4.7 Curve estimation on relative vs. absolute frequencies of non-standard weak verbs

4.7 Comparison with COLT

To get an impression of the present-day situation of non-standard weak verbs for at least a subgroup of speakers, namely London teenagers, the corpus COLT was investigated for all weak verb forms as well. As the corpus comprises just under half a million words, it is roughly comparable to data from the South East collected in FRED.[19] Recall that in the FRED data, 118 non-standard weak verb forms were found for the South East, which had a Mossé-coefficient of 18.1. If weak verb forms were still a stable feature of non-standard dialects, we would expect around eighty-four non-standard weak verb forms in the data from COLT (18.1*462,455/100,000).[20] What we find instead is exactly one non-standard occurrence, displayed in example (26) below.[21]

---

[19] Although the genre is of course quite different; as noted in Chapter 1, FRED comprises mainly oral history material and is perhaps therefore more skewed towards past tense contexts, whereas COLT consists solely of spontaneous everyday conversations, where past tense contexts are probably much rarer. In addition, COLT is socially balanced, whereas FRED only contains traditional dialect speakers, which further reduces the overall incidence of non-standard forms for COLT. These differences do not affect most of my analyses, which are based on relative rather than absolute frequencies, with the exception of the weak past tense forms. As these are calculated in relation to absolute number of words, we would expect much lower frequencies in COLT (but not the very low ones we do in fact find).

[20] 652,871 = number of words in FRED South East, 462,455 = number of words in COLT (WordSmith count excluding all brackets).

[21] COLT was searched for all forms ending in *ed and/or *'d.

(26) They were like standing there, I thought they were looking, I *shined* the torch on them and they still was there. (COLT b136501) (Westminster, Inner London)

At least in data from COLT, then, employing non-standard weak verbs is not one of the majority strategies that can be said to characterize the system of verb forms today.

4.8 Summary

We have seen in this chapter that non-standard weak forms of individual strong verbs can only be explained by recourse to their histories. Nevertheless, it would be stressing individualities too strongly if we only maintained that 'every verb has its own history'. As we have seen in the individual analyses, there are some more general trends. Like regularization in the standard, non-standard weak forms are formed in particular from less frequent verbs, but interestingly we also find weak forms of very frequent verbs – which in addition come from subclasses that are stable in standard English. In most cases, these non-standard weak forms can be traced back historically to weak forms that must have existed side by side with the respective strong forms, in extreme cases to forms (like *tellt* or *sellt*) that are attested since Old English times. For much of the history of the English language, weak and strong forms for the same verb must indeed have been variable – a variability that was lost during standardization when the strong form was chosen over the weak form to represent the verb in literary language. This long-standing variability has apparently persisted in non-standard systems only, and here mainly in the traditional dialects.[22]

In these traditional dialects, system-internal regularities on the other hand can be shown to have exerted significant influence as well. The formally similar verbs *blow*, *grow*, *throw* and *know* seem to have influenced each other, as well as exerted considerable force on *draw*. The only newer forms like *runned* and *gived* seem to be dependent on other, more widely available non-standard strategies. They are alternative non-standard forms to paradigms that level in particular the present tense–past tense distinction (to *run – run – run* and *give – give – given* respectively). In functional terms, establishing (or re-establishing) weak forms for the past tense in these cases repairs the non-optimal levelled paradigm.

While overall, then, non-standard weak forms can be described as following the same natural trend of strong verbs switching into the dominant class of weak verbs, as predicted by Mayerthaler and Wurzel, system-internal clusters of weak verbs illustrate that this trend also reacts to functional considerations: it is particularly strong when analogy plays a role (*blow*, *grow*,

---

[22] As Görlach points out, 'many weak forms recorded in ME did not establish themselves' (Görlach 1996: 163), but this statement seems to refer – tacitly – to the standard only.

throw, *know*), and is also strengthened when other, non-functional past tense forms are remedied (as in the case of *run*, *give*). In both cases, these system-internal developments do not run counter to universal natural predictions. Instead, system-internal forces seem to be able to strengthen or accelerate a natural trend.

In summary, however, it has to be stressed that using a weak past tense form for a verb that is strong in the standard is a comparatively rare strategy even in the traditional dialects (in FRED it applies to no more than 20 verb types – recall that there are around 170 strong verbs in English today) and even for those verbs that are affected, in general it is a minority option. This runs counter to predictions from most theories: weak verbs as the default verbal category should be a powerful attractor, and traditional dialects might be surmised to be less constrained to react to this attraction by switching verb classes. As we have seen, this is by and large not the case in traditional dialects. If the influential (trendsetting) group of London teenagers is anything to go by, non-standard weak past tense forms are even rarer in the non-standard today, and it seems unlikely that they will spread to become part of a supralocal non-standard. This does not mean, however, that non-standard systems behave much more like the standard. Instead, non-standard verb systems make extensive use of other non-standard strategies, as the following chapters will demonstrate.

5   *Drunk, seen, done* and *eat*: two-part paradigms instead of three-part paradigms

> There are not in English so many as a Hundred Verbs ... which have a distinct and different form for the Past Time Active and the Participle Perfect or Passive. The General bent and turn of the language is towards the other form, which makes the Past Time and Participle the same. This general inclination and tendency of the language, seems to have given occasion to the introducing of a very great Corruption; by which the Form of the Past Time is confounded with that of the Participle in these Verbs, few in proportion, which have them quite different from another. This confusion prevails greatly in common discourse. (Lowth 1762: 85–6)

5.1   Introduction

In this chapter, a range of seemingly quite different verbs will be discussed. They have in common that they are non-standard strong verbs with paradigms consisting of just two forms, while their standard English counterparts consists of three forms, e.g. *drink – drunk – drunk* vs. StE *drink – drank – drunk*; *see – seen – seen* vs. StE *see – saw – seen*; *do – done – done* vs. StE *do – did – done* and *eat – eat – eaten* vs. StE *eat – ate – eaten*. Two of these example paradigms are part of larger patterns: *drink – drunk – drunk* is what I will term a 'Bybee' verb, and there are a host of other verbs behaving like *drunk*, as section 5.2 will show. *Eat – eat – eaten* has two other verbs behaving similarly, namely *give – give – given* and *see – see – seen*, and they are discussed together towards the end of this chapter in section 5.5. *See – seen – seen* and *do – done – done* on the other hand are idiosyncratic paradigms, but in some respects more similar to the 'Bybee' verbs than to *eat – eat – eaten*, and are therefore treated in sections 5.3 and 5.4 respectively.

5.2   'Bybee' verbs

In a series of articles, Joan Bybee and co-writers have expanded on the notion that in the English past tense system, there seems to be a semi-productive strong verb paradigm which can still attract new members; this is the pattern *string – strung – strung*. This newly productive pattern has grown since Middle English; it is structured in terms of family resemblances (each member resembling the central, prototypical member *string – strung* phonologically more or less; cf. Figure 5.12 and Figure 5.16 at the end of this chapter). They have in common that they form their past tense as well as the past participle with <u>, prototypically pronounced /ʌ/ in the South of England and /ʊ/ in the North.[1] The complete schema for the past tense forms is given in (1):[2]

(1) $[C (C) (C) \land \{\text{velar/nasal}\}]_{\text{past}}$

It is important in this respect to make clear that this schema is product-oriented. It is not a rule that derives a past tense form from its respective present tense stem, but a schema that only applies to the 'end' product, i.e. the past tense form itself. (This distinction will become important once we move away from the prototypical Bybee verbs in section 5.4 and Chapter 6).

Because she has worked so extensively on this phenomenon, I will call these verbs 'Bybee' verbs.[3] In Bybee's network model (see section 2.8), a chain of connected past tense forms is depicted as in Figure 5.1,[4] giving rise to the schema in (1) through relations of graded similarity as a kind of epiphenomenon.

This figure is of course a highly simplified diagram which only concentrates on the connections between some individual past tense forms. Not depicted, for example, are the connections between the present and the past tense forms (but cf. Bybee 1995: 431) that constitute the paradigm for each individual word, or the connections between past tense forms other than neighbouring ones in this diagram, etc. Dotted lines indicate non-identity, unbroken lines identity of phonemes.

For our purposes, this group of verbs belongs to verb class 2, and in fact constitutes one of the few stable subclasses there (see section 3.3.2). As already mentioned there, Bybee verbs seem to act as a strong attractor for verb class 1 words in the non-standard systems, in particular the subclass of verbs that used to belong to the same Old English word class III as *string – strung – strung*, etc., i.e. verbs like *drink – drank – drunk*. In non-standard dialects, these class 1 verbs (e.g. StE *drink – drank – drunk*) show a very strong trend towards merging with verb class 2, e.g. substituting the StE past tense *drank* by *drunk*, resulting in the partially levelled paradigm *drink – **drunk** – drunk*, as noted by Bybee herself. Indeed, the few new strong verbs, especially in American English, *sneak – snuck* or *drag – drug*, follow the same past tense

---

[1] Although there are intermediate, especially 'fudged' forms between these extremes (cf. Swann et al. 2004: 29–30 s.v. *border dialect*; Chambers and Trudgill 1998: 110–13).
[2] See Bybee (1995: 431).
[3] I would like to thank Joan Bybee for allowing me to do so.
[4] From Bybee (1985: 130). See also Bybee (1995: 431).

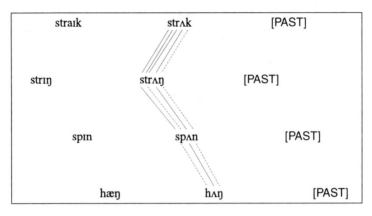

Figure 5.1 Past tense, Bybee verbs[5]

pattern (see Hogg 1998; Murray 1998). Bybee even claims that 'the sequence [ʌ] plus final velar and/or nasal is the marker for Past Tense in these verbs' (Bybee 1985: 130). Non-standard 'levelling' in verbs like *drink* is so ubiquitous that Chambers includes it as one of his 'vernacular roots' (Chambers 1995: 242), later calling it a 'vernacular primitive' (Chambers 2003: 255) or even a 'vernacular universal' (Chambers 2004: 129).[6]

In the case of past tense *drunk*, we can observe two principles at work: there is internal analogy, as *drunk* like *sunk* follows the prototypical Bybee verb pattern quite closely: the past tense is signalled by /ʌ/ plus a nasal velar plus a velar. There is in addition more abstract analogy: by not distinguishing between past tense and past participle (in contrast to the standard *drink – drank – drunk*), non-standard *drink – drunk – drunk* conforms to the system-defining pattern PRES ≠ PAST = PPL and has thus a higher system congruency overall. As Wurzel has pointed out, inflectional systems can be stabilized in this way, without words changing word classes completely into the dominant class of weak verbs.

The first part of this chapter investigates how strong an attractor Bybee verbs really are, for the first time quantifying these sporadic occurrences. From Quirk et al.'s comprehensive list, the following verbs qualify for investigation (in alphabetical order): *begin – began – begun, drink – drank – drunk, ring – rang – rung, shrink – shrank – shrunk, sing – sang – sung, sink – sank – sunk, spring – sprang – sprung, stink – stank – stunk*, and *swim – swam – swum*. It is clear that even in a large corpus like FRED, not all of these verbs will appear equally frequently. Only the five most frequent ones are therefore investigated

---

[5] Again based on Bybee (1985: 130; 1988: 135; 1995: 430; 1996: 250).
[6] However, it has recently been shown that Chambers' list of vernacular 'universals' is heavily biased towards pervasive features of non-standard American English, not taking much account of other dialect regions and certainly not of other languages; see Kortmann and Szmrecsanyi (2004).

in detail here. They are (in order of descending frequency): *begin, sing, drink, ring* and *sink*.

5.2.1 History

The verb series of *drink* and co. are characterized by the fact that they belonged to the Old English verb class III, together with the larger group of what became 'Bybee' verbs (*spin, win, slink, cling, sting, wring* …). All had vowel gradation between singular and plural past tense forms, cf. *drincan – dranc, druncon – druncen* or *spinnan – span, spunnon – spunnen*. Typically, the past tense singular (preterite I)[7] had forms in <a>, which was the source for the present-day standard English form (e.g. *drank*), while the plural (preterite II) and, in this verb class, also the past participle, had forms in <u>, variously spelled <o> since Middle English times in so-called *minim*-environments (before <m, n, v>, etc.; cf. similarly *son, love*).

Since Middle English, Bybee verbs have attracted other strong or indeed weak verbs (see Esser 1988: 27–8), which already speaks for their status as a stable subclass. For example, *dig – dug – dug* only entered the English language in Middle English times, but became a strong verb – unusually for loan words; *hang – hung – hung* belonged to different Old English verb classes: the transitive verb *hon – heng, hengon – hangen* was part of strong verb class VII, but the intransitive *hangian* was weak (there may also have been yet other precursors, e.g. causative *henjan* from Old Norse); all these forms merged and the resulting verb paradigm *hang* entered the Bybee verb class between the thirteenth and fifteenth centuries. *Fling, stick, strike* and *string* were also not originally part of the class of Bybee verbs. *Strike* was an Old English class I verb which switched verb classes during Middle English; *fling* and *string* (like *dig*) only entered the English language in Middle English times and became part of Bybee verbs; and *stick* was also an Old English weak verb (for individual histories, see the OED: s.v. *dig, fling, hang, stick, strike, string*).

As Wyld pointed out, levelling of the past tense forms (to just one form used for the past tense irrespective of person distinctions) proceeded differently regionally. In the North, typically the preterite I stem was chosen as the past tense marker (Wyld has coined the term 'northern preterite' for this phenomenon; see Wyld 1927: 268). Görlach also notes this kind of levelling (inside the past tense) for Scots: 'in some contrast to English, Scots almost invariably chose the former singular as the base form for the preterite – where there was a choice' (Görlach 1996: 168–9; the choice only existed for those paradigms that had different preterite I and II stems). In the West, on

---

[7] I use the terms past tense singular and preterite I (as well as past tense plural and preterite II) interchangeably. This is a simplification, as the preterite I stem was used in the formation of the first and third person singular only; the second person singular was derived from the preterite II stem. However, this simplification does not affect my argument.

the other hand, the 'western preterite' used the past participle vowel to level the past tense paradigm (Wyld 1927: 268); according to Lass, 'this begins to appear as a minority variant in the fourteenth century, and stabilizes for many verbs only in the period EB3 [i.e. 1640–1710] and later' (Lass 1994: 88, based on the Helsinki corpus).

Although Wyld claims that 'the dialects of the S[ou]th. and Midlands preserve, on the whole, the distinction between the Singular and Plural of the Pret[erite], where this existed in O.E., with fair completeness during the whole M.E. and into the Modern Period' (Wyld 1927: 268–9), both the northern and the western patterns seem to have spread geographically across the country, and became either dominant in different verbs, or indeed in direct competition. With standardization and concomitant codification of verb paradigms in Early Modern English, the former coherent verb class IIIa was thus essentially split between those verbs displaying the western preterite (our first group of verbs, or Bybee verbs proper, e.g. *string – strung – strung*) and those following the northern preterite pattern, resulting in a three-part paradigm today (*drink – drank – drunk*). Not surprisingly, therefore, past tense forms were variable between <a> and <u> for a long time after the Old English number distinction broke down in the past tense.

It has to be borne in mind that for all verbs of the Old English verb class III, the preterite II vowel was identical to the past participle vowel. This has led to some confusing statements in the literature on the source of non-standard simple past forms. Wyld for one argues that the decisive influence must have come from the past participle:

The new M.E. forms might therefore at first sight be derived from the Pret[erite] Pl[ural] type, and some writers explain them in this way, but ... the Pret[erite] Pl[ural] type is the least permanent of the various forms of the Strong Verbs, and never survives in Mod[ern] Engl[ish] unless it be the type also of the Past Participle. While therefore the Pl[ural] may have helped to fix its type in the Pret[erite] Sing[ular], it seems probable that the main influence was exerted by the P[ast] P[articiple] (Wyld 1927: 269).

Ekwall similarly states that 'In ModE ... the part[iciple] often influenced the form of the pret[erite] ... or even took over the function of the pret.[erite], as in *sung* (pret[erite]) for *sang* after the part[iciple] *sung*' (Ekwall 1980: 99). However, the 1980 editor Ward qualifies Ekwall's statement in a footnote, pointing out correctly that 'preterites like *sung* ... derive as much from the ME pret[erite] pl[ural] as from the part[iciple]; for in these verbs the pret[erite] pl[ural] and the part[iciple] have the same stem' (Ekwall 1980: 99 note 31). Ekwall himself points out that at least since the sixteenth century, past tense forms varied between <a> and <u>. 'In the 18th century it looked as though the *a*-forms would be completely displaced ... In the 19th century a reaction set in, and today the *a*-form is in some verbs the only one ... or is at least the usual form' (Ekwall 1980: 104). Although synchronically we might be tempted to claim that the participle *drunk* is used for the past tense today in non-standard verb paradigms, we have to bear in mind the history and acknowledge that past tense *drunk* is a legitimate descendant of the preterite II vowel, i.e. the plural form *druncon*. This derivation should in fact be preferred, as in other verb classes where past tense form and past participle are distinct, the past participle form (e.g. forms in <-en>) is not usually chosen for the past tense function.

In the next sections, I will investigate the historical development of the five more frequent verbs by looking at the historical Helsinki and ARCHER corpora, which cover the time span of interest for this phenomenon from Middle English to present-day English adequately. Contemporary prescriptive grammars have of course also commented on these verb paradigms, but as Oldireva's study (1999) has shown, these comments should be used qualitatively: apparently, they do not mirror actual quantitative differences faithfully – those verb forms commented on the most are not necessarily those that are in fact employed most frequently (Oldireva 1999).

5.2.1.1 Past tense forms of begin

(2) I remember one day when I was at school, the stag hunters come through there, I don't know where they come from, but all of a sudden they *begun* to scatter about there, these here ladies and gentlemen and gentlemen in their red coats, and the old horses all plastered up with mud. (FRED KEN 004) (Kent, South East)

(3) The price o' coal *begun* t' come a little dearer. (FRED SFK 020) (Suffolk, South East)

Begin can be traced back to Old English times, although according to the OED it was very rare then; the more usual word was *onginnan* in the sense of 'begin, start something' (OED: s.v. *begin* VI). While the present tense stem has not undergone much change apart from losing the final syllable (*beginnan* > *begin*), the past tense forms are very interesting for our purposes and exemplary for the whole group of verbs. The OED states that

As in other verbs having grammatical vowel change in the pa[st] tense, there was an early tendency to level the forms of the 1–3 sing. *began*, and of the 2 sing. *begunne*, pl. *begunnon*, which has resulted in the establishment of *began* as the standard form; but an alternative from the old plural *begun* has also come down to the present day (OED: s.v. *begin* VI. 'Present day' refers to the end of the nineteenth century).

Thus for Old English we find the following forms: *began* in the past tense singular, *bigunnon* or *begunnon* in the past tense plural. In other words, the two different Old English past tense stems already laid the foundation for variation we can still observe today. Since the fifteenth century some singular past tense forms in <o> and <u> are recorded (e.g. *begon(ne)*, *bygon(ne)*), and *begun* with its present-day spelling appears in the seventeenth century. At the same time, the plural past tense forms show some variable forms in <a>: in the fifteenth century *bigann(e)*

Table 5.1 *Diachronic development of past tense* began *vs.* begun *(Helsinki, ARCHER)*

	Period	*begun*	*began*	Sum	*% begun*
Helsinki	1250–1350	3	1	4	75.0
	1350–1420	3	11	14	21.4
	1420–1500	3	16	19	15.8
	1500–1570	0	40	40	0.0
	1570–1640	0	42	42	0.0
	1640–1710	1	22	23	4.3
ARCHER	1650–1700	6	43	49	12.2
	1700–1750	4	48	52	7.7
	1750–1800	2	41	43	4.7
	1800–1850	0	44	44	0.0
	1850–1900	2	55	57	3.5
	1900–1950	0	21	21	0.0
	1950–	0	53	53	0.0

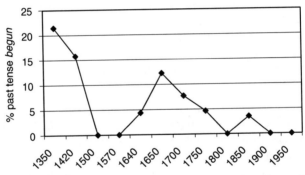

Figure 5.2 Diachronic development of past tense *begun* (Helsinki, ARCHER)

or *began(ne)* are recorded, in the seventeenth century also *bygane*. Levelling thus appears to have worked in both directions. Nevertheless, the singular stem seems to have 'won out', as it became the basis for the levelled plural forms (*began*) which later became the standard, while the plural stem was the basis for the levelled singular forms (*begun*) which were then relegated to non-standard speech. (The participle remained relatively unaffected, although, as Lass has pointed out, there were at least five different forms available in late Middle English; see Lass 1994: 92.)

Began and *begun* are frequent enough to trace their development through the centuries for which corpora are available. In the Helsinki corpus, past tense *begun* is practically never more than a minority option, as a look at the absolute frequencies shows (Table 5.1).

As Table 5.1 shows, figures for past tense *begun* are dwarfed by *began*, which is the majority option by far from 1350 onwards. *Begun* remains a minority option until the nineteenth century, with absolute figures never higher than six (in the late seventeenth century) throughout the periods covered by ARCHER. Today, there is no variation between *began* and *begun* permissible in the standard, as Figure 5.2 shows. Because figures in the first period (1250–1350) are so low in absolute terms, the possibly distorting 75 per cent has been excluded from the diagram in Figure 5.2.[8]

5.2.1.2   *Past tense forms of* drink

(4) There's eh these elderberry flowers, mash them and drink them, they didn't taste very nice but they used to, eh, stop inflammation from setting in and eh, there used to be well eh that lad of mine what eh got killed on back of a motorbike when he had measles I bathed his (trunc) ey- (/trunc) he *drunk* it and bathed his eyes in it, because he had them very bad they had them all in his eyes you know they're liable to blind you, eh in them the measles was very bad in them days, and ehm bathed his eyes in it and he *drank* it and everything (FRED NTT 006) (Nottinghamshire, Midlands)

(5) And ehm, she had all her little mates round there [in the pub]; so eh, she'd trip round there and then come back oh, well, well-canned. But she only *drunk* ale – nothing else. (FRED LND 003) (London, South East)

The history of *drink* is slightly different – although, belonging to the same verb class as *begin*, the vowel change between singular and plural was of course the same in Old English, cf. the paradigm *drincan – dranc, druncon – druncen*. However, as the OED notes, by the thirteenth century in northern texts, by the fifteenth century more generally, past tense forms were levelled to *drank* for singular and plural. *Drank* even spread to the participle, possibly to avoid the connotations of the adjective *drunk* (see the OED: 'prob[ably] to avoid the inebriate associations of drunk', OED: s.v. *drink* vi). In the sixteenth century past tense *drunk* reappears, either through levelling with the participle or from (southern) dialects which retained the original difference, and is 'occasional' to the nineteenth century (OED: s.v. *drink* vi).

Data from the Helsinki corpus and from ARCHER, however, do not support Ekwall's and the OED's impression of this variation. In the Helsinki corpus, there is only a single incidence of *drunk* used in the past tense outside of Old English, and this is indeed from the period 1570–1640. Otherwise,

---

[8]   In comparing these figures it has to be borne in mind that the sub-periods are a little different from each other; in the Helsinki corpus, a period covers seventy years after 1350, while ARCHER is divided into equal fifty-year periods. This does not affect the overall development, of course, only the scale of the figure. Of course all spelling variants were searched, especially for the earlier periods.

Table 5.2 *Diachronic development of past tense* sank *vs.* sunk *(ARCHER)*

Period	*sunk*	*sank*	Sum	*% sunk*
1700–1750	8	0	8	100.0
1750–1800	1	0	1	100.0
1800–1850	7	2	9	77.8
1850–1900	2	4	6	33.3
1900–1950	0	3	3	0.0
1950–1990	0	2	2	0.0

however, at least since 1250 *drank*[9] is categorical. The data from ARCHER are similar, in that there is only a single occurrence of past tense *drunk* from the period 1700–1750, otherwise *drank* is the categorical past tense form in forty-one cases. In standard English, then, past tense *drunk* seems to have been truly a marginal, 'occasional' occurrence.

5.2.1.3   Past tense forms of sink

(6) Now the Ocean people had the selling rights of that pit see, and the Powell Duffryn *sunk* it see, that is what happened. (FRED GLA 002) (Glamorgan, Wales)

(7) They got in it, and then they picked him up, with the barge, and, 'course, the yacht *sunk*. (FRED KEN 006) (Kent, South East)

The verb *sink* behaves quite differently from *drink*, although it belonged to the same Old English verb class III; its paradigm in Old English was *sincan – sanc*, *suncon – suncen*. As the OED states, however, 'the use of *sunk* as the pa[st] tense has been extremely common. Johnson (1755) says "pret. *I sunk*, anciently *sank*"' (OED: s.v. *sink* v.). This distribution (the reverse of the situation today) must have changed during the nineteenth century towards a variable one, as the OED entry still notes both *sank* and *sunk* as acceptable past tense forms (i.e. at the end of the nineteenth century). Today only *sank* is the acceptable past tense form of *sink* (cf. a modern prescriptive dictionary like *The Macmillan English Dictionary for Advanced Learners* (MED): s.v. *sink* v.).

Again, data from the Helsinki corpus are sparse; there is a single instance of *sank* after Old English, namely from the period 1500–1570. Data from ARCHER on the other hand show the demise of *sunk* very nicely. Although the figures are comparatively low, the percentages show a clear development (see Table 5.2 and Figure 5.3).

Whereas for *drink*, past tense occurrences of *drunk* were rare at best in the historical corpora investigated, past tense *sunk* in ARCHER was obligatory before and up to 1750, according well with Dr Johnson's observation

---

[9] This includes all its spelling variants (*dranc, drancke, dranke*, etc.). The same of course goes for *drunk* and for all other verbs investigated in the historical corpora.

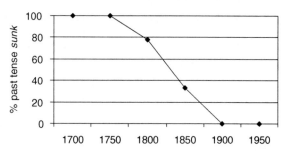

Figure 5.3 The demise of past tense *sunk* (ARCHER)

from 1755. It declines in use in an inverted S-curve until 1900, where *sank* becomes obligatory.

5.2.1.4 Past tense forms of sing

(8) I heard a Gospel group singing. They *sung* The Rugged Cross, and they *sung* some more, more hymns. (FRED LAN 006) (Lancashire, North)

Like *drink*, *sink* and *begin*, the past tense of *sing* differed between the singular stem in <a> and the plural stem in <o>/<u>, but unlike *sink*, at least since the fifteenth century both forms seem to have been equally acceptable as the past tense. The OED notes the following forms: *sang, sange, song, songe, soong* (OED: s.v. *sing* vi), and from the seventeenth century onwards also *sung* and *sunge* (OED: s.v. *sing* vi), and even in its headword notes both past tense forms *sang* and *sung* without discrimination. At least until the end of the nineteenth century, then, *sung* must have been acceptable as the simple past tense. In fact, the OED states that '*sung* was the usual form of the pa[st] tense in the 17th and 18th cent[urie]s, and is given by Smart in 1836 with the remark "Sang ... is less in use". Recent usage, however, has mainly been in favour of *sang*' (OED: s.v. *sing* vi).

Unfortunately, *sing* is a comparatively infrequent verb both in the Helsinki corpus and in ARCHER, and this development is therefore difficult to corroborate by solid figures. For example, regarding the seventeenth century, data from the Helsinki corpus have no occurrences of either *sung* or *sang*; for the eighteenth century, ARCHER has just one occurrence of *sang*, and one of *sung*. The nineteenth century on the other hand does indeed show a dominance of *sang* (ten occurrences) as opposed to just three instances of *sung*. However, we do not really have reason to doubt the acute observing powers of Smart or indeed of the OED compilers. A retention of past tense *sung* in historical dialects would therefore be more than justified on historical grounds, if *sung* was still fully acceptable in the standard as late as the nineteenth century.

Table 5.3 *Diachronic development of past tense* rang *vs.* rung
(Helsinki, ARCHER)

	Period	*rung*	*rang*
Helsinki	1250–1350	0	0
	1350–1420	2	0
	1420–1500	0	0
	1500–1570	0	0
	1640–1710	1	0
ARCHER	1700–1750	1	0
	1750–1800	1	0
	1800–1850	0	1
	1850–1900	0	2
	1900–1950	0	5
	1950–	0	9

5.2.1.5   Past tense forms of ring

(9) He run in and *rung* the bell twice, stopped the trucks. (FRED GLA 005) (Glamorgan, Wales)

(10) I *rung* him up and told him. (FRED NTT 003) (Nottinghamshire, Midlands)

Ring is the only one of these verbs where weak forms are historically attested. As the OED notes, *ring* was 'properly a weak v[er]b, the strong forms (which appear very early) being prob[ably] due to the influence of *sing*' (OED: s.v. *ring* v2). 'Very early' in this case means the fourteenth century, so not before Middle English times. Again, the past tense forms were variable in Middle English; the OED cites *rang(e)* besides *rong*, *ronge* and *rongen* and *rungen*, *rung* and *roong* for singular as well as plural forms, however, without commenting on their distribution. *Ring* is used only rarely in the Helsinki corpus, as Table 5.3 and Figure 5.4 indicate, so that quantification is again not overly reliable. There are no occurrences of past tense *rang* in either Middle English or Early Modern English, but three of *rung*. The early trend of using *rung* rather than *rang* continues in ARCHER, where the eighteenth century equally only has two occurrences of *rung*, none of *rang*. This situation changes with the nineteenth and twentieth centuries, where past tense *rung* disappears completely and *rang* is used instead. Finally, *rang* becomes much more frequent in absolute terms over the twentieth century (no doubt due to extralinguistic change, as *ringing* could now be applied not only to church bells, but also to electric door bells and of course the telephone). Nevertheless, these figures have to be treated with caution as they are so very low in most subperiods.

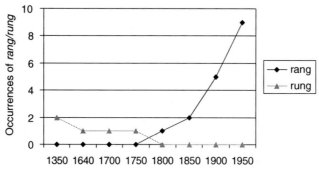

Figure 5.4 Diachronic development of past tense *rung* vs. *rang* (Helsinki, ARCHER)

5.2.2   Historical dialects

Strikingly, none of the new Bybee verbs is documented in either the EDD (Wright 1898–1905) or the SED. For the EDD, in particular, this might attest to their status as still variable in the standard at the end of the nineteenth century. In the *English Dialect Grammar* (Wright 1905), Wright indeed notes forms in /u/ or /ɐ/, i.e. our forms in <u>,[10] for *begin* (*begun*) in Yorkshire [6], Cheshire [7], Shropshire [11] and Berkshire [33]; for *drink* (*drunk*) in addition also in Cumberland [2], for *ring* (*rung*) in Shropshire [11], for *sing* (*sung*) again in Yorkshire [6], Cheshire [7] and Shropshire [11], for *sink* (*sunk*) and *spring* (*sprung*) in Shropshire [11], for *stink* (*stunk*) in Shropshire [11], and for *swim* (*swum*) in Cheshire [7], Shropshire [11] and East Anglia. (There is no entry for *shrink*.) This looks like a regional distribution favouring the northern Midlands and the North (with the exception of Berkshire [33] and East Anglia only), although there are again some problems with Wright's list. It does not record for the remaining counties whether this feature really does not occur, or whether the informants simply failed to notice it, or to comment on it. This is all the more problematic as *sink* and *sing* were still variable even in the standard when Wright collected his data. Also, of course, we cannot know from Wright's list how frequent the non-standard forms were, either in absolute or in relative terms. As mentioned above, unfortunately no comparable data from the SED are available, so that we cannot really chart the progress of these non-standard forms or their regional distribution through the last century.

[10] I concentrate on the variation between <u> and <a> forms here. There are some other marginal forms like *song* in western Wiltshire or *swom* in Yorkshire which will not be discussed here (but see Wright 1905: 281–4).

Table 5.4 *New 'Bybee' verbs in FRED*

	nStE	StE	Sum	% nStE form
sink	26	14	40	65.0
drink	18	18	36	50.0
ring	20	25	45	44.4
sing	16	26	42	38.1
begin	11	44	55	20.0
Total	91	127	218	Ø 41.7

Ø = average.

5.2.3 *Data from FRED*

5.2.3.1 *Verbs*

If we now turn to the dialectal data, grouped by verbs, the following occurrences as in Table 5.4 can be documented.

In contrast to the historical data, where the forms in <u> were almost always in the minority, figures from FRED show that these non-standard forms are highly frequent, in fact they are used in around or over 40 per cent of all cases for most verbs; for *sink* and *drink*, they are even the dominant option.

The only notable exception is *begin*; in fact, *begin* is the only verb of this group that behaves significantly differently from the other four verbs.[11] *Begin* is also exceptional in its phonological form, in that it is the only verb in this group with two syllables, and ending in a simple nasal; in addition, it is the only verb with strikingly different semantics: it is the only verb with a clear aspectual meaning (it is ingressive, i.e. indicating the start of an action), resulting also in syntactic differences (in the majority of cases, it is used as a concatenative verb, i.e. followed by other verb forms[12]). It is thus in several respects furthest removed from the prototype, and its slightly marginal status might also explain its significantly different behaviour in terms of relative non-standard frequencies.

5.2.3.2 *Singular vs. plural?*

Today there is no correlation of the morphological form with the distinction singular–plural; although it might be a reasonable speculation to hypothesize

---

[11] Overall differences are significant at df=4, p<0.001. Pairwise comparisons of all verbs show that only the comparison with *begin* yields significant differences, for all verbs (df=2, with p between 0.05 and 0.001).

[12] In FRED, past tense *begun/began* is followed by the *to*-infinitive in forty-three cases, by the *-ing* form in three, and the bare infinitive in one case. (The remaining occurrences are either truncated, the end of the utterance, or are followed by a prepositional phrase, usually with *with*, e.g. *they began with school dinners* (FRED YKS 008) (Yorkshire, North).) I would like to thank Björn Wiemers for helpfully mentioning verbal aspect at the right moment.

Table 5.5 *Singular referents of Bybee verbs*

% singular	StE <a>	nStE <u>	Difference
'ideal'	100	0	
drink	72.2	44.4	27.8
begin	48.8	41.7	7.1
sink	28.6	42.3	−13.7
ring	60.0	85.0	−25.0
sing	46.2	81.3	−35.1

that the formal distinction of Old English preterite I vs. preterite II stems might still carry a reflex today. If that was the case, we would expect the singular to tend towards the preterite I stems in <a> (i.e. the present-day standard forms), the plural towards the preterite II stems in <u> (i.e. the non-standard forms). However, this is not observable for any of the verbs investigated, as the figures in Table 5.5 show. The ideal distribution would indicate that the (non-standard) forms in <u> have no singular referents, while the (standard) forms in <a> only have singular referents (the two figures do not necessarily add up to 100, though: it is conceivable that all discourse concerning the verb x would have only singular referents. Rather, the difference between the actual figures and 100 indicates the complementary amount of plural referents, e.g. 27.8 for *drunk*, etc.). The last column 'difference' indicates the difference between the two preceding columns by subtracting the percentages in <u> from the percentages in <a>; thus skewing in favour of the <a> forms (the historically expected distribution) comes out as positive figures, skewing in the opposite direction as negative figures.

As Table 5.5 indicates, only *drank* vs. *drunk* and *began* vs. *begun* behave in the expected way: *drank* has far more singular referents than *drunk*, as might be expected from the Old English distinction, while the difference between *began* and *begun* is much smaller. For all other verbs, this trend is skewed in exactly the opposite direction. This opposite trend is strongest for *sing*, indicated by the large difference (over thirty-five percentage points), but is also quite noticeable for *ring* and *sink*. Despite appearances, however, none of these differences is statistically significant.[13] Whether the subject of a past tense form is in the singular or the plural, then, clearly does not determine today whether the form of the verb takes <a> or <u> for the past tense. This historical distinction seems to have given way to truly levelled forms in the dialects today.

5.2.3.3　*Regions*
The new Bybee verbs are not distributed evenly across regions, as Table 5.6 and Figure 5.5 indicate.

---

[13] Calculated for a 2×2 table in each case, with df=1.

Table 5.6 *The five most frequent Bybee verbs per dialect area in FRED*

	nStE	StE	Sum	% nStE
South East	42	20	62	67.7
Wales	5	5	10	50.0
Scotland	11	17	28	39.3
Midlands	12	19	31	38.7
North	12	26	38	31.6
South West	9	40	49	18.4
Total	91	127	218	Ø 41.7

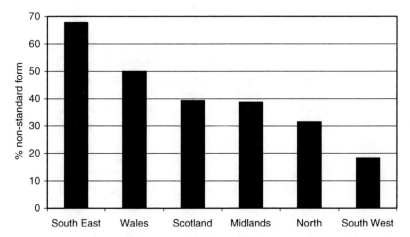

Figure 5.5   The five most frequent Bybee verbs per dialect area in FRED

The phenomenon of the new Bybee verbs shows a clear South-to-North cline, with the striking exception of the (typically very conservative) South West. In fact, the difference between the most advanced South East and the neighbouring South West is the greatest difference of all dialect areas.[14] Scotland and the Midlands pattern quite similarly around 40 per cent (absolute occurrences for Wales are comparatively lower than for all other

[14] Again, an overall comparison shows that the table contains significant differences at df=5, p<0.001. However, when we compare each lexeme with every other lexeme, the South East is significantly different from the other verbs in only four out of five cases (the direct comparison with Wales shows no significant difference), while the same is true for the South West at the other end (the direct comparison with the North shows no significant difference). This would argue for a gradient phenomenon.

dialect areas, and are therefore perhaps not as reliable), while the North patterns slightly below its two neighbours at just over 30 per cent – none of these differences is statistically significant, however.[15] While this is still a very high average, the difference to the South West is striking. The South West looks the most 'standard' for this feature with non-standard occurrences of *sunk*, *drunk*, etc. of under 20 per cent, far less than a third of the occurrences of the South East. It is conceivable, however, that also for this feature, the South West is indeed conservative, and that it preserves the reversed non-standard–standard situation of the eighteenth and nineteenth centuries mentioned above. If *sunk* was the acceptable past tense form then, and *sank* only became the standard during this time, the South West, in still using the former non-standard form *sank*, is actually employing the old non-standard form in almost 80 per cent of the cases – a very high percentage that accords well with the perception of the rural South West as a particularly 'dialectal' relic area where many historically attested features are still alive.[16]

What can certainly be stated is that the Middle English dialect situation is in no way reflected in the traditional dialect data today. While we might expect to see traces of Wyld's 'northern preterite' (levelling to <a> in the simple past, both singular and plural) dominant in the North, and traces of the 'western preterite' (levelling to <u> in the simple past, both singular and plural) dominant in the West, this cannot really be confirmed for the traditional dialects today. While the <u> forms are in fact comparatively rare in the North (which might be expected), they are even rarer in the South West, and only marginally more frequent in the Midlands. In fact, however, none of these differences is statistically significant.[17] In other words, the forms that in Middle English were restricted to certain dialect areas must have spread geographically relatively early on, as today there are no indications of this older regional differentiation. Instead, the general non-standard forms in <u> seem to have strengthened their hold, and are particularly strong in the South East.

5.2.4   Comparison with COLT

In data from COLT, these new Bybee verbs also occur, but comparatively infrequently. For this reason, it does not make much sense to look at the

---

[15] In pairwise comparisons, at df=1, with p<1.

[16] Some of this regional distribution is skewed by the fact that *begun* only appears in the South East (and, once, in Scotland), but standard English *began* occurs in practically all dialect regions, and is comparatively frequent. Calculating frequencies excluding *begun* results in only minor differences, however. Wales, Scotland, the North and the Midlands become slightly more similar, non-standard frequencies rise a few percentage points for all regions, but the basic difference between the South East and the seemingly less dialectal South West remains. For this reason I have chosen to present the more inclusive figures including *begun/began* here.

[17] At df=2, p>0.05.

Table 5.7 *New Bybee verbs in COLT*

	nStE form	StE	Sum	% nStE form
Social group 1 (higher)	1	12	13	7.7
Social group 2 (middle)	2	3	5	40.0
Social group 3 (lower)	8	4	12	66.7
Total	11	19	30	Ø 36.7

verbs individually; in almost all cases, occurrences are below five in the sub-categories, and only five verbs occur in the past tense (in either the standard or the non-standard form) at all (*begin*, *drink*, *ring*, *stink* and *sing*). When we take all five verbs together, however, the social patterning for the new Bybee verbs becomes clearly apparent, as Table 5.7 shows.

While the average seems considerably lower than the relative frequency for the Bybee verbs in the South East, this average clearly masks social differences. All FRED informants belong to the lower social groups and should thus be compared only to social group 3 in COLT. Indeed, frequencies for the lower social group (group 3) look very similar to the data from FRED for the South East as a whole, and in fact the difference is not statistically significant.[18] In the data from COLT we can also clearly see that although this non-standard feature is sharply stratified, the break-off point is not between social groups 2 and 3, but between the highest social group, where we find non-standard Bybee verbs at a very low rate, and social group 2, where non-standard Bybee verbs are also extremely frequent at around 40 per cent. In other words, we can see that non-standard Bybee verbs are still a very prominent feature of non-standard speech today, and that they seem to have gained social ground, having become a frequent feature also of middle–class speech (at least in the restricted sample of London teenagers in the 1990s).

Bybee verbs thus do not seem to have lost any of their attraction for other verbs, in stark contrast to the non-standard switch of verbs into the weak verb class – a process that is practically not observable in material from COLT today, as discussed in Chapter 4.

5.2.5   Cognitive explanation

As we have seen, all non-standard forms in this verb class can be traced back to historical forms. In particular, vowel gradation in the past tense in Old English verb class III between the singular in <a> and the plural in <u> is responsible for variable levelled forms, both in <a> and in <u>. While these forms were differently variable in the standard between the fifteenth and the nineteenth centuries (Lass 1994: 90 stresses the 'proliferative' character

---

[18] Calculated for a 2×2 table with df=1.

of these innovations), today variability is relegated to non-standard status. Levelled past tense forms in <a> became the standard, levelled forms in <u> became non-standard. It is clear, however, that this is not a 'new' development, contrary to what Esser (1988: 29) claims, but that variable forms have existed for the best part of the last 500 years or so.

However, historical continuity can only explain why these forms still exist, and how they came into existence. Historical continuity cannot account for the fact that these forms are highly frequent – in fact they are the dominant form for many verbs –, that they continue to be extremely popular, as data from COLT have shown, or why that should be the case. I have already hinted at some functional motivation throughout this chapter. Analogy seems to play a decisive role as this verb (sub)class switches in its entirety into the subclass of a different verb class. On a relatively concrete level, and again linked to the historical situation, the subclass of verb class I that only makes use of vowel change to indicate tense distinctions (e.g. *drink, sing, ring*) does look deceptively like verbs of verb class 2 (e.g. *shrink, spring, cling*) – this of course can be traced back to the fact that they did belong to the same Old English verb class once. Clearly, they are still felt by speakers today to be closely related.

On a more abstract level, we have seen that the *shrink* subclass is in fact one of the few stable inflectional classes inside verb class 2 (i.e. a class that is not losing marginal members to the weak verbs). On the one hand it is characterized by the global pattern PRES ≠ PAST = PPL that defines the whole verb class 2. Verb class I on the other hand is characterized by the fact that it contains only three-part-paradigms, i.e. the global pattern is PRES ≠ PAST ≠ PPL. By changing the past tense into a form identical to the past participle, the verbal paradigms of *drink, sing*, etc. now also conform to the pattern PRES ≠ PAST = PPL. As the reader will recall, this is the pattern not just of verb class 2, but of course also of the much larger class of weak verbs, and thus a system-defining structural property of English. This in itself is, however, obviously not enough to confer stability on the verb class, and it also does not explain why forms in <u> are chosen over those in <a>. (A levelled paradigm *drink – drank – drank* would of course fulfil the same formal criteria as a paradigm *drink – drunk – drunk*, but seems to have been marginal at all times at best.)

As noted before, in Dutch, strong verbs seem to be more stable than in other Germanic languages because they tend to have the same vowel in the preterite and the past participle (Durrell 2001: 13), and this applies in particular to cognates of *sing – sang – sung*. In Dutch, this group of verbs has been levelled even in the standard to *zingen – zong – gezongen* (cf. *beginnen – begon – begonnen; drinken – dronk – gedronken; zinken – zonk – gezonken*, etc.), and this strengthened verb class has in addition acted as an attractor for other verbs that have joined this class through analogical levelling. The same process basically seems to be at work in (non-standard) English as well. We have seen that the stable class of 'Bybee' verbs can be characterized by a product-oriented schema, in that all verbs conform to the phonotactic template given in (1), repeated here as (11):

(11) [C (C) (C) ∧ {velar/nasal}]$_{past}$

This template can be regarded as a 'marker' of this verbal subclass in Wurzel's sense. How the individual verbs conform to this schema is spelled out in Figures 5.6 to 5.10.

The subclass is stable through having this stable marker, in addition to following the majority pattern PRES ≠ PAST = PPL (which is one of the system-defining structural properties of the English verb system, after all).

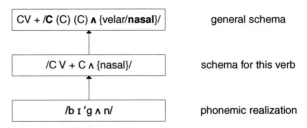

Figure 5.6 Schema for past tense *begun*

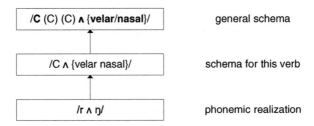

Figure 5.7 Schema for past tense *rung*

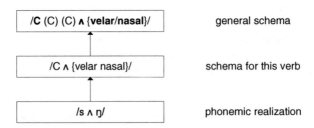

Figure 5.8 Schema for past tense *sung*

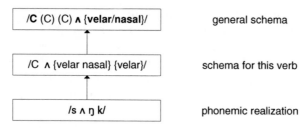

Figure 5.9 Schema for past tense *sunk*

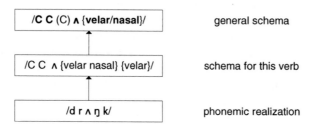

Figure 5.10 Schema for past tense *drunk*

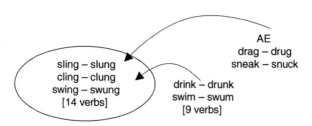

Figure 5.11 Stable word class as attractor

This stable marker makes this subclass highly attractive for other similar verbs, in particular, as we have seen, for those verbs that are historically related and still phonologically similar. (Other verbs are also attracted, as Figure 5.11 shows, in particular American English former weak verbs like *drag* or *sneak*; see Hogg (1998) and Murray (1998). For an extension of the diagram, see figures 6.8 and 6.12.)

While Figure 5.11 indicates a historical development (a group of core verbs attracts others), Figure 5.12 structures the verb class in terms of its proto-typical features. Verbs have been arranged in this two-dimensional matrix such that the more centrally a verb is situated, the more it resembles (or indeed constitutes) the prototype. The prototypical features are marked by a bold outline. These are, in particular, the initial consonant cluster /sCC/, and the final sequences /ʌŋk/ and /ʌŋ/. Features at the margin of the diagram have been arranged by degree of decreasing resemblance to the prototype, in such a way that each step away from the prototype equals the change in exactly one feature. This chaining also demonstrates the underlying family resemblances of this verb class. For example, moving up from the centre one step, the initial cluster /sC/ can be derived from the prototype /sCC/ by the deletion of one consonant, and is itself linked to verbs starting only with an /s/ by the deletion of a further consonant. Towards the bottom of the diagram, the prototype is linked to another chain of features by the deletion not of a consonant, but of the initial /s/, resulting in initial /CC/, which is further linked to verbs starting in just one consonant, /C/. The same principle holds for the horizontal x-axis.

A third dimension (presence or absence of <i> in the infinitive) is indicated by slanting lines for absence of <i>. The further away a verb is located from the central point of origin of this diagram, then, the less prototypical it is of this verb class. (The criteria have been adapted from Bybee and Moder (1983).) Note that the double occurrence of /rɪŋ – rʌŋ/ is not an oversight, but indicates *wring – wrung* (old Bybee verb) and *ring – rung* (new Bybee verb, grey background) respectively.

Figure 5.12 shows very clearly that the new (non-standard) Bybee verbs, indicated by a light grey background in the figure, integrate into the existing verb class perfectly, one (*spring – sprung*) even occupying the most central ('the most prototypical') space together with *string – strung*. All others have at least one highly prototypical feature (ending in /ɪŋ/ or /ɪŋk/). The only member that is clearly more marginal to this verb class is *begin – begun*, and indeed we have seen that this verb is found far less often with a past tense in <u>, and also syntactically behaves quite differently.

Becoming class 2 verbs is also a strategy that avoids unnecessary redundancy in the system. The fact that a pattern with identical forms for past tense and past participle is defining the properties of the English verbal system indicates that a two-part-paradigm that preserves the morphological contrast between the two simple tenses, present and past, is fully sufficient to avoid morphological ambiguities. Three-part-paradigms like standard English *drink – drank – drunk* could therefore be regarded as 'gratuitous luxury' (or 'dumb' redundancy; see Dahl 2004: 10–11) in functional terms.

Perhaps, therefore, the question should be put the other way around: why do we find distinct forms for past tense and past participle in the standard? Relatively late in the standardization process, the standard seems to have chosen from the competing <a>–<u> forms the forms in <a> for the past tense in order to distinguish it formally from the past participle. Data from nineteenth-century grammars (Anderwald forthcoming) confirms that this process was still going on as late as the second half of the nineteenth century. It is clear from other investigations that during the process of standardization, variability as such is often eradicated (cf. Stein's principle

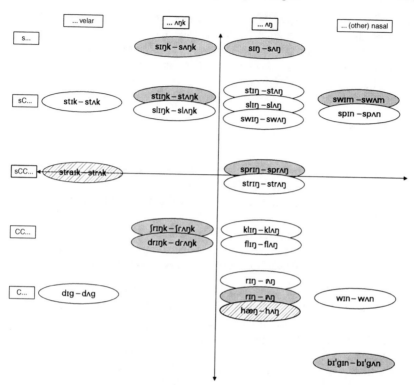

Figure 5.12 Prototypical structure of verb class (Bybee verbs)

of 'no variation'; Stein 1998: 36). On the other hand, it is quite clear that this distinction is in fact simply redundant also in the standard (as the system-defining structural properties of English would suggest), thus completely superfluous and uneconomical. It cannot very plausibly count as an instance of 'smart' redundancy in the sense of Dahl (2004: 10 et passim), defined as a situation in which 'redundancy is exploited gainfully in a system' (Dahl 2004: 291), because a confusion between a simple past context and a present or past perfect one (if the auxiliary is misunderstood, deleted, or dropped) is not very likely to lead to serious misunderstandings, as indeed the majority pattern of all other verbs shows.[19] Three-part paradigms of the standard can thus not be functionally motivated. Instead, the choice seems to have been motivated perhaps by a parallel with Latin (which after all does as a rule possess distinct past tense and past participle forms), more in line with Stein's principle 2a. This principle suggests that 'external principles determin[ing] the banning of types of forms NOT accepted into W[ritten] S[tandard] ...

[19] Very different from possible misunderstandings between present tense and past tense, of course.

may be of two basic types: (a) an ideology of language based on presumed Latin models and its "logic" … (b) factors derived from the ideology of essayist literacy' (Stein 1998: 38). The (standard English) choice of *drink – drank – drunk* over *drink – drunk – drunk* is thus very probably ideologically rather than functionally motivated.

5.3   Past tense *seen*

5.3.1   Introduction

(12) They all came down to the house and when they *seen* me, were shaking their heads like this. (FRED HEB 018) (Hebrides, Scotland)

(13) And that was the first time I *seen* the sea. (FRED LEI 002) (Leicestershire, Midlands)

(14) [I] went down in the cabin. When I went down first thing I *seen* was a thing a little bit bigger than, you know, square; was a brass plate with printing on it. (FRED SOM 028) (Somerset, South West)

As mentioned above in section 4.4.3.1, the past tense of *see* is regularized to *seed* occasionally in the Midlands and the South West, at a fairly stable rate of around 10 per cent, and it is levelled to *see* in the South East only, where *seed* and *see* are in almost perfect complementary distribution. *Seed* does, however, have another direct non-standard contender, the past tense form *seen*, which is much more frequent than *seed* or *see*. As this is the dominant non-standard form for this verb paradigm in FRED, it will be investigated in more detail in this section.

5.3.2   History

Although, today, a non-standard past tense form *seen* is usually described as being the past participle, extended to past tense functions, historically it can also be legitimately derived from the past plural form (preterite II). As mentioned above in section 4.4.3, attested forms of *see* have always been strong. The Old English paradigm was *séon – seah, sáwon/sǽʒon – ʒesewen*, but for the past tense forms a wide range of variants are attested. In all cases, however, the plural past tense ended in <n>, and the OED traces forms sufficiently similar to the past plural *sáwon/sǽʒon/séʒun, sǽʒun* across the centuries until *seen* appears as a past tense form in the fifteenth century (OED: s.v. *see* v.), so that we can indeed assume historical continuity for this feature. On the other hand, there are no attestations of past tense *seen* in the Helsinki corpus or in ARCHER (in any of the attested spelling variants), so that it must have been relegated to non-standard status quite early on. An interesting metalinguistic resource is the overview article by Poplack et al. (2002), introducing the authors' OGREVE (the Ottawa Grammar Resource on Early Variability in English) which collects (explicit or implicit) mentions of grammatical variation from grammars and other (contemporary) reference works and gives timelines for individual verb forms (Poplack et al. 2002: 97). Unfortunately, the information in OGREVE on *seen* is inconclusive, as Poplack et al. do not distinguish between past tense *seed* and *seen*, so that the non-standard history of this form remains to be investigated.

5.3.3   Historical dialects

In the historical dialect data that we have, past tense *seen* is only mentioned unsystematically, while the *English Dialect Grammar* (Wright 1905) does not mention this non-standard form at all. The *English Dialect Dictionary*, however, lists the following past tense forms in –*n*: *seen*, *sen*, *sin*, *zeen* and *zin* (Wright 1898–1905: s.v. *see*). Their geographical distribution by counties is shown in Map 5.1.

In traditional English dialects at the end of the nineteenth century, past tense *seen* seems to have been a predominantly 'central' phenomenon, with most counties clustering along a central axis from the central South through the central Midlands to the central North.

If we compare this to data from the SED, depicted in Map 4.3 (repeated here for convenience as Map 5.2), we can see that the over-general depiction in terms of counties is relativized somewhat in the more fine-grained Basic Material from the SED. Past tense *seen* is indicated by black dots.

In particular, Map 5.2 makes it clear that past tense *seen* is only a sporadic feature of the English North; although it does occur, past tense *seed* is much more frequent there. The only areas where *seen* is really frequent are the southwest Midlands (Herefordshire [15], Worcestershire [16] and Warwickshire [17]) as well as Monmouthshire [23] and Oxfordshire [25]. In East Anglia and the South East, *seen* is more in competition with the third non-standard form *see* (indicated by light grey in Map 5.2). The only area where *seen* competes with *seed* is along the coast (in Sussex [40] and Kent [35]), i.e. areas that historically belonged to the southern dialect area.

5.3.4   Data from FRED

In FRED, the southern/southwestern and Midlands distribution of *seen* that we found in the EDD and SED can still be confirmed. In general, data from FRED show that past tense *seen* is a very frequent phenomenon; in almost all cases, it is much more frequent than the other non-standard past tense forms, the weak form *seed* and unmarked *see*: *seen* is ten times as frequent as *seed* in the South West, the stronghold of non-standard past tense forms of *see*, and roughly four times as frequent in the Midlands, as Table 5.8 shows. Only the South East is exceptional here, as the regionally restricted form *see* is dominant in this dialect area. (Past tense *see* will be discussed in more detail in section 5.5.4.) As in the historical data, *seen* and *seed* are

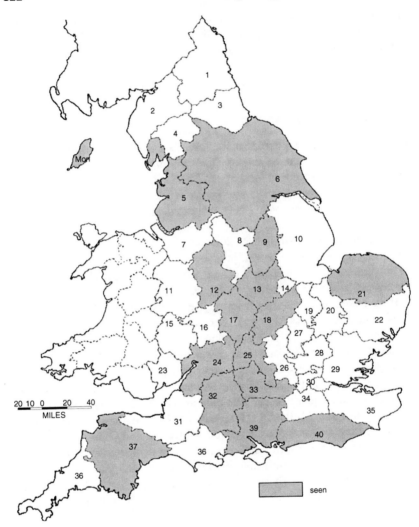

Map 5.1 Past tense *seen* in the EDD

generally not in complementary distribution. Instead, those areas that have
very high occurrences of past tense *seen* (the South West and the Midlands)
also have the highest occurrences of the non-standard weak form *seed*, as
Table 5.8 and Figure 5.13 show.

Like non-standard past tense *seed*, which is included in Figure 5.13, non-
standard past tense *seen* is clearly a western phenomenon. It is one of the rare
phenomena where the South East does not dominate, but displays a clearly
regional form instead (unmarked *see*). Nevertheless, past tense *seen* is a gen-

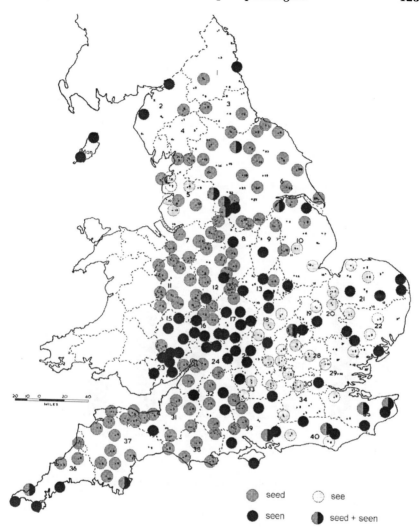

Map 5.2 Past tense *seed*, *seen* and *see* in the SED (Basic Material)

eral feature in that it occurs in all dialect areas.[20] Ratios for the South East
and the North are still around 10 per cent, the magic threshold for a stable

[20] The statistical analysis supports this picture. Overall, differences in Table 5.8 are significant (at df=5, p<0.001). If we break this down into pairwise comparisons, we get a group of
four dialects where differences are gradient: the South West is significantly different from
all other dialect areas (at df=1, p<0.001) except Wales, but Wales is neither different from
Scotland, nor from the Midlands (both at df=1, p<1). Wales is, however, significantly different from the South East and the North (at df=1, p<0.025). The same is true for Scotland
(each at df=1, p<0.001) and the Midlands (each also at df=1, p<0.001). Finally, the South

Table 5.8 *Relative frequencies of* seen *in FRED*

	seen	seed	see	saw	Sum	% seen	% seed	% see	% nStE forms
South West	91	9	9	85	194	49.2	4.9	4.6	56.2
Wales	9	0	0	18	27	33.3	0	0.0	33.3
Scotland	68	0	3	143	214	32.2	0	1.4	33.2
Midlands	37	9	6	81	133	29.1	7.1	4.5	39.1
South East	16	1	66	101	184	13.6	0.8	35.9	45.1
North	16	1	0	107	124	12.9	0.8	0.0	13.7
Total	237	20	84	535	876	Ø 9.92	Ø 5.2	Ø 9.6	Ø 38.9

Note: **bold** type indicates favoured forms in a dialect area.

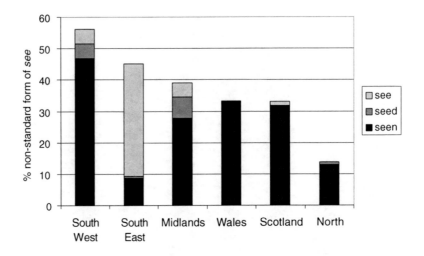

Figure 5.13 Past tense *seen*, *seed* and *see* per dialect area in FRED

feature (Halliday 1992). Non-standard past tense *seen*, therefore, does not look like a recessive feature, despite the fact that it is relegated to the conservative South West, or the Midlands. For one thing, frequencies are too high (almost 50 per cent in the South West, 30 per cent in the Midlands, Wales and Scotland); for another, frequencies even in the South East and the North seem to be stable.

Data from COLT also indicate the stability of this feature. If the recruits are divided according to their social classes, the picture is as shown in Table 5.9.

East and the North are not significantly different from each other. They therefore seem to form a coherent group.

Table 5.9 *Past tense* seen *in COLT*

	seen	see	saw	Sum	% seen	% see	% non-standard form
Social group 1 (high)	1	1	62	64	1.6	1.6	3.1
Social group 2 (middle)	1	1	57	59	1.7	1.7	3.4
Social group 3 (low)	6	3	40	49	12.2	6.1	18.4
Total	8	5	159	172	Ø 4.7	Ø 2.9	Ø 7.6

Although on average, past tense *seen* is only used in around 5 per cent of all cases, this average masks the (well-known) social differentiation. While in the higher and the middle social groups of London teenagers, past tense *seen* is hardly used at all, in the lower social group it is used at a comparable rate to the older FRED material (indeed, there is no statistically significant difference between these two groups of speakers[21]). Even today, then, past tense *seen* is a stable non-standard feature in the South East, if at a comparatively low frequency.

5.3.5 *Conclusion*

This section has shown that past tense *seen* is clearly a retention of a historically attested form that can be traced back – in dialectal forms – to the end of the nineteenth century, historically to the preterite II form in *–n*. Despite its considerable frequency in the west of the country, past tense *seen* does not seem to be increasing in frequency at the moment: data from the recent COLT corpus of London teenagers indicate very similar (low) relative frequencies for past tense *seen* as for the older FRED material for the South East. No increase since the times of FRED hints at the fact that past tense *seen* does not look like a candidate for a new supraregional feature of non-standard British English varieties. Instead, it is a stable low frequency feature of non-standard British English today.

5.4 Past tense *done*

5.4.1 *Introduction*

The verb *do* has two clearly distinct functions in standard English: it is used as an auxiliary and as a main verb (Quirk et al. 1985: 132–5). In examples (15) to (17), the main verb use is marked by *italics*, the auxiliary use by underlining.

---

[21] Calculated for a 2×2 table with df=1.

(15) I regularly *do* my homework.
(16) He <u>didn't</u> *do* any house cleaning.
(17) <u>Did</u> he *do* his work yesterday?

Although these uses are not distinguished morphologically in the stand-ard, the syntactic behaviour of the two verb functions is clearly distinct: the main verb *do* patterns with all other main verbs, e.g. it takes *do*-support for negation (see Anderwald 2002a: 24–5) and inverts with the auxiliary for interrogatives, as examples (16) and (17) illustrate, whereas the auxiliary has its own domain (it is used chiefly for negating main verbs, for inversion in interrogatives or other constructions, in elliptical constructions and for emphasis; see Quirk et al. 1985: 133–4). In standard English, *do* is a strong verb with the three-part paradigm *do – did – done*. This situation is quite different in the dialects, however. In at least some dialects this three-fold distinction is levelled, and at the same time this levelling is combined with a functional differentiation. Both possible paradigms *do – did – did* (levelled participle to the StE past tense form) and *do – done – done* (levelled past tense form to the StE past participle) are attested and, at least for some dia-lects, exist side by side. These forms are not freely variable, though: *do – did* is restricted to the auxiliary,[22] *do – done – done* is restricted to the main verb uses of *do*, as examples (18) and (19) illustrate.

(18) *Didn't* get paid for that [raising pigeons]. I *done* it for the love of ani-mals, really. (FRED LND 001) (London, South East)
(19) I think I *done* the right thing. (FRED DEV 001) (Devon, South West)

This development seems to be a true innovation. Although it has been spec-ulated that this re-functionalization continues an older distinction, there seems to be no historical evidence in support of such a distinction.

5.4.2 *History*

In a (related) discussion about present tense *do*, Cheshire (1982: 34–9) finds that her adolescent informants from the town of Reading preserve an older (non-standard) morphological contrast between auxiliary and main verb *do*: they tend to use *dos* [duːz] for all persons for the main verb, but *do* for all persons for the auxiliary in the present tense. According to Cheshire, only in standard English were the two forms redistributed (distinguishing the third person singular from all other forms), disregarding the functional differentiation.

The OED, however, does not mention the auxiliary–main verb distinc-tion as being relevant for the morphological paradigm. Instead, we can see

---

[22] As the paradigm *do – did* is restricted to the auxiliary, it is not quite correct to posit a past participle form, as the auxiliary only possesses simple present and simple past forms; see Quirk et al. (1985: 132–3).

that the past tense had *did* unanimously from a very early time onwards (for the first and third person singular, as well as the plural), *didst* in the second person singular. Past tense *done* is only mentioned as a colloquial or dialectal form from the middle of the nineteenth century onwards. The first example of past tense *done* is from 1847 from an American source, but is so closely followed by quotations from the *English Dialect Dictionary* from 1848 that it would be difficult to maintain that it was an Americanism (OED: s.v. *do* v.). Any purported historical split in the verb *do* between auxiliary and main verb can thus not be substantiated on the basis of the OED – which is otherwise a reliable source for spotting and tracking fine-grained morphological and semantic differences.

5.4.3   *Previous studies*

Past tense *done* seems to be an inconspicuous form that has not attracted much notice by dialectologists. Only overview articles sometimes note past tense *done*, e.g. Poplack et al. (2002). In OGREVE, past tense *done* is not commented on before 1830, much in contrast to many other non-standard past tense forms like past tense *come* or *eat* (cf. the table in Poplack et al. 2002: 97). *Done* thus seems to be a genuinely newer form. On the other hand, this dating conforms well to the first attestation of past tense *done* in print some twenty years later, so that we can date the establishment of this new non-standard form with reasonable certainty to the first half of the nineteenth century.

5.4.4   *Historical dialects*

Wright briefly notes on the past tense of *do* that 'in many dialects the *pp.* [past participle] is used for this tense' (Wright 1898–1905: s.v. *do* v. I.2), but does not comment on a possible functional split. All the collected examples with *done* in the past tense, however, are examples of the full verb rather than the auxiliary. Wright has examples of past tense *done* for the following counties or dialects: Irish, Wexford, Derby [8], south Nottinghamshire [9], Leicestershire [13], Northampton, Warwickshire [17], Herefordshire [15], Gloucestershire [24], Suffolk [22], Berkshire [33], west Midlands, Surrey [34], Sussex [40], Hampshire [39], and Cornwall [36] (Wright 1898–1905: s.v. *do* v. I.2).

As a look at Map 5.3 makes clear, past tense *done* is a Midlands and southern phenomenon in the nineteenth century. Unfortunately, Wright again does not have data from all counties. For this reason, I have indicated by a lighter grey where the EDD gives *did* (or a variant thereof) for a county. White areas indicate that no data are available from Wright. (Somerset [31] has a doubly marked past tense form *doned* or *don'd* which is indicated by a dark grey.)

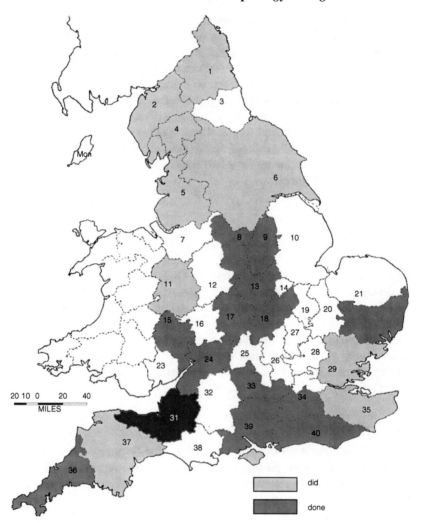

Map 5.3 Past tense *done* in the EDD

Map 5.3 shows that past tense *done* is certainly not a northern phenomenon. The distribution in the South is not so easily described, partly due to
the high number of white areas in the Midlands, partly due to the fact that
Essex [29], Kent [35] and Devon [37], as well as the Isle of Wight, seem to
pattern differently from the rest. This might indicate that in the nineteenth
century, past tense *done* is used variably with *did* in the South.

Moving on some fifty or more years, the SED records some forms of past
tense *done*, but unfortunately only in negative environments (responses to
question IX.5.5 *Your wife suddenly says to you: This vase is broken, and you at*

once say: Well, I can truthfully say I … it.). As alternatives of the most wide-spread answer *I didn't do it* they record *I never done it* in Monmouthshire [23], Gloucestershire [24], Oxfordshire [25], Leicestershire [13], Norfolk [21], Suffolk [22], Buckinghamshire [26], Essex [29], Somerset [31], Wiltshire [32], Kent [35], Dorset [38] and Hampshire [39], as well as in Yorkshire [6] (however, the response here has a different negator: *I noan done't* with the negator *noan* and the clitic pronoun*'t*). Very probably, this response is not directly comparable to the 'ordinary' phenomenon of past tense *done* as listed in the EDD above, as the use of *never* as a past tense negator plays a role in the choice of this answer as well. (For those dialects where *never* is not available in this function obviously *done* cannot appear in this particular response, either.) Nevertheless, if we collect the *done* responses to SED question IX.5.5 in a map (following Upton et al. 1994: 498), the result is as displayed in Map 5.4.

We can see more clearly than in the data from the EDD that *done* here is a southern phenomenon in the widest sense, where some of the Midlands (especially Leicestershire [13]) may have to be included. The exact distribution cannot be asserted without recourse to the individual responses in the Basic Material, and this distribution is displayed in Map 5.5.

It has to be stressed again, however, that the availability of *never* as a past tense negator plays into the choice of *done* over *did* as the past tense form in this environment. In this combination, at least, *never done* is clearly the minority option and is restricted mainly to the South West and East Anglia.

5.4.5 Data from FRED

Only with the help of data from FRED can the geographical spread of the functional differentiation be investigated in more detail. Data from FRED present some fascinating insights. In FRED, past tense *done* is found in all dialect areas, but with widely different frequencies. It is far more frequent both in the South East and the South West than in all other dialect areas, which might suggest a southern origin for this phenomenon. However, even in those dialect areas that make only limited use of past tense *done*, this *done* is always restricted to the main verb use. Although the auxiliary use of past tense *do* is far more frequent than the main verb (only about one in four occurrences of past tense *do* are the main verb[23]), *done* never encroaches on the auxiliary territory. A functional differentiation then seems to be spreading hand in hand with this morphological form. When considering the raw figures, it has to be stressed that figures for *done* might even be slightly higher in reality as some instances of *'d done* could well have been transcribers' 'hypercorrections' (I doubt the difference between *'d done* and *done* is really audible for non-phoneticians).

---

[23] In FRED, we find 1,366 main verb occurrences vs. 4,225 auxiliary ones for past tense *do*.

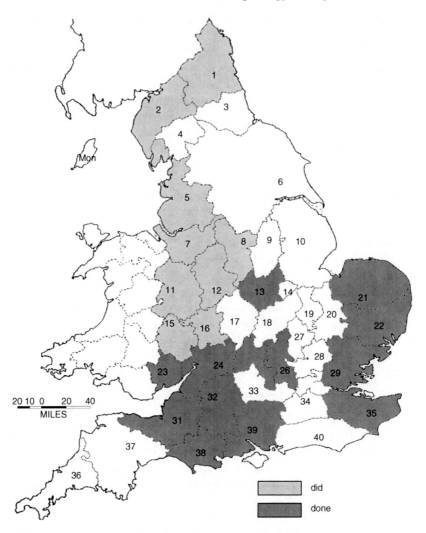

Map 5.4 Past tense *done* in the SED (by counties)

In particular, I searched all instances of *done* and *did* per dialect area. All occurrences of *did* were manually disambiguated between auxiliary and main verb uses. Only *did* used as a main verb is included in Table 5.10.

Past tense *done* is clearly a southern phenomenon, as Figure 5.14 indicates. Frequencies in the South East with almost 80 per cent are nearing categoricity; frequencies in the South West are still extremely high at 62 per cent or nearly two-thirds of all cases. These figures are in striking contrast to the rest of the country, with the Midlands employing past tense *done* in around one in four cases (26 per cent), Wales, Scotland and the North even less

Map 5.5 Past tense *done* in the SED (Basic Material)

frequently.[24] Past tense *done* is therefore a candidate for a newer phenomenon that may be spreading from the South, extending its regional restriction gradually.

[24] Again, this is confirmed by a statistical analysis. The overall figures are significantly different at df=5, p<0.001. Pairwise comparisons single out the South East and the South West, which are significantly different from all other dialect areas (at df=1, p<0.001 in all cases), but are also significantly different from each other (at df=1, again at p<0.001). For the other areas, individual comparisons show a rather gradient picture, with the Midlands patterning not significantly differently from Wales (but significantly differently from Scotland and the North), Wales patterning not significantly differently from Scotland (but significantly differently from the North), and Scotland and the North also not differing significantly.

Table 5.10 *Past tense* done *(main verb) in FRED*

	done	did	Sum	% done
South East	279	70	349	79.9
South West	250	153	403	62.0
Midlands	46	126	172	26.7
Wales	10	37	47	21.3
Scotland	17	108	125	13.6
North	22	261	283	7.8
Total	624	755	1379	Ø 45.3

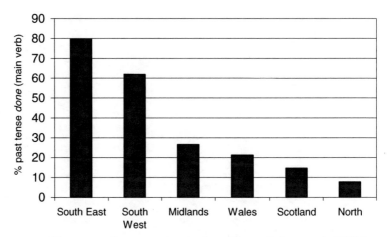

Figure 5.14 Past tense *done* (main verb) per dialect area in FRED

5.4.6 Data from COLT

Indeed, data from COLT confirm that past tense *done* is a highly frequent phenomenon in the language of London teenagers at the end of the twentieth century, as Table 5.11 shows.

Table 5.11 shows the distribution of a typical dialect marker, with the lower social group leading the middle as well as the higher social groups.[25] In addition, however, the (high) relative frequencies indicate that past tense *done* is a feature that may be spreading not only geographically, but also socially. Percentages for both the higher and the middle social groups are anything but negligible, but by far exceed, e.g., frequencies of a stable traditional dialect feature like *seen* as discussed in section 5.3.4 (which occurs at a frequency of 13 per cent in the lower social group).

[25] This difference is statistically significant at df=2, p<0.001.

Table 5.11 *Past tense* done *(main verb) in COLT*

	done	*did*	Sum	*% done*
Social group 1 (higher)	12	46	58	20.7
Social group 2 (middle)	12	19	31	38.7
Social group 3 (lower)	31	16	47	66.0
Total	55	81	136	Ø 40.4

5.4.7   Done *in American English*

There are (at least impressionistic) indications that past tense *done* is also widely used in American English, but as for British English, the literature is very scarce. In the middle of the nineteenth century, Bartlett in his *Dictionary of Americanisms* notes that 'DONE, instead of *did*; as, "They *done* the business." [is] A common vulgarism in the State of New York' (Bartlett 1848: 118). Similarly based on anecdotal evidence and his own intuition, Mencken very generally notes that the preterite of *do* is *done* in American 'common speech' (Mencken 1921: 271, 273), indicating that by the beginning of the twentieth century, this feature must have spread considerably geographically. The *Dictionary of American Regionalisms* DARE (Cassidy and Houston 1991), collecting data from over 1,000 informants in the 1960s, also indicates that *done* is used quite generally. In particular, the additional examples collected on tape seem to cluster in the American South (examples come from Florida, Arkansas, Louisiana and Oklahoma), but there are also attestations from Massachusetts, Michigan, Ohio and even Washington state on the West coast. Strikingly, in all quotations *done* is only ever used as a full verb. In the absence of an accessible dialect corpus for American English, this feature can unfortunately not be investigated further, but seems to be extremely well established in informal speech today.

    The lexicalized incidence of past tense *done*, the noun *whodunit*, is first attested in an American source around 1930 (OED: s.v. *whodunit*), i.e. a whole century after *done* is reported as non-standard British English speech, but as there are quotations from British sources around the same time, it would be difficult to pin down the word *whodunit* as an Americanism. As the typical 'whodunit'-literature reached its height in the 1920s to 1940s in Britain (consider the 'classical' authors of detective stories such as Agatha Christie, Dorothy L. Sayers, etc.) and was copied by American authors of the same time, it is not implausible to speculate that the term *whodunit* might also be more British in origin.[26] The derivational form *whodunitry* on the other

---

[26] In addition, (British English) native speaker intuitions do not mark out *whodunit* as being peculiarly 'American' (Georgie Robins, personal communication, 23 September 2005).

hand, attested another 30 years after *whodunit*, definitely sounds like tongue-in-cheek British English.

Finally, it has to be noted and stressed that past tense *done* does not seem to be related to the pervasive use of *done* as an aspect marker in Southern American English or African American Vernacular English (AAVE), which is well described and indeed frequently analysed (Labov 1998; Green 1998; 2002 and references therein). Two examples typical of AAVE are given in (20) and (21) below.[27]

(20) They *done* washed the dishes.
    'They have already washed the dishes.'
(21) The children *be done* ate by the time I get there.
    'The children have usually already eaten by the time I get there.'

It is clear that these uses of *done* have nothing in common with the British dialect use of *done* as a full verb, neither formally nor semantically. In AAVE *done* is used as an auxiliary, i.e. always together with a lexical verb, whereas in non-standard British English, *done* is always a main verb, i.e. can never occur with another lexical verb. Semantically, in AAVE this auxiliary *done* is used as an aspect marker, indicating perfectivity (the action denoted is completed), whereas non-standard British *done* denotes the simple past of the main verb use of *do*, i.e. is semantically not more finely differentiated than StE *did*.

5.4.8 Cognitive explanation

For those dialects that have it, past tense *done* is motivated in a two-fold manner, quite similar to the Bybee verbs discussed at the beginning of this chapter: there is abstract analogy, resulting in conformity with the system-defining property PRES ≠ PAST = PPL.; in addition, past tense *done* also contains the verb class marker $/\Lambda/$ for past tense forms, followed by a nasal. In other words, the verb paradigm of *do – done – done* is also a Bybee verb: it conforms to the product-oriented schema of (i) or (ii) and can in fact easily be expanded to the full schema as depicted in Figure 5.15.

The integration of *done* into the prototype figure in Figure 5.16 shows that *done*, although situated near the margin, is still a 'better' Bybee verb than, e.g. *begun*, and is as well integrated as *win – won* or indeed *dig – dug*.

The motivation for past tense *done* is more complex, however. As we have seen, only main verb *do* is levelled to *done* in the past tense. For the auxiliary uses, *did* is employed invariably. In other words, main verb *do* patterns with other main verbs (namely the large group of main verbs clustering around *string*), while auxiliary verb *do* has a purely idiosyncratic pattern. Analogy as the motivating factor for the use of non-standard *done* can thus only account

---

[27] Examples are taken from Green (1998: 43).

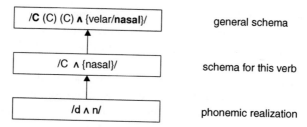

Figure 5.15 Schema for past tense *done*

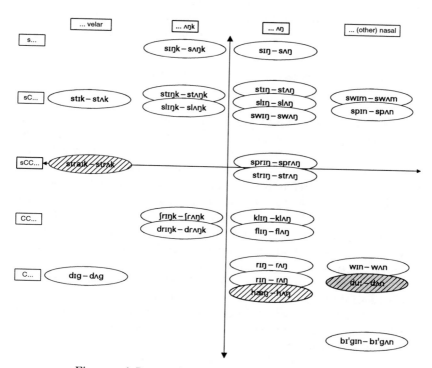

Figure 5.16 Prototypicality grid of Bybee verbs, including *done*

for its main verb uses. It is important to realize the concomitant functional differentiation which – in the past tense – establishes a new (morphological) distinction that appears to be cognitively salient for its users. The (syntactically redundant) morphological contrast between past tense form and the past participle of the standard (in the three-part paradigm *do – did – done*) is re-morphologized into the two syntactic functions (auxiliary use vs. main verb use) in non-standard systems which are clearly perceived as cognitively more salient and/or communicatively more important. This is a striking example of *exaptation* in the sense of Lass (1990): language users employ linguistic 'junk', i.e. morphological distinctions that do not code a grammatical distinction any longer, to express new functions. This process also adds 'smart redundancy' to the system (in the sense of Dahl 2004): the distinction main verb vs. auxiliary is strengthened, as it is now morphologically expressed; on the other hand, the morphological distinction past tense vs. past participle is weakened, as this is always expressed periphrastically anyway. This morphological split in the verb paradigm thus makes the verb system more complex. In this case, then, we can see quite clearly that 'simplification', whichever way conceived, is not the main motivating factor for selecting non-standard variants that are then spread to other (social and geographical) dialects. Rather, two-fold analogy, coupled with exaptation used to code a cognitively salient category can account for this verb form.

5.5 Counterexamples: past tense *eat*, *give* and *see*

5.5.1 Introduction

This section deals with three verb paradigms, those of *eat*, *give* and *see*, that seem to constitute counterexamples to the main direction of change for the verbs in this chapter. We have seen that both for the group of new 'Bybee' verbs (*drunk*, etc.) as well as for *done*, a change from a three-part paradigm to a two-part paradigm proceeds by making past tense and past participle identical, bringing these verbs (among other things) in line with the dominant characteristic of the English verb system overall, namely the pattern PRES ≠ PAST = PPL. *Eat* and *give* (and in its third non-standard form, *see*) on the other hand have non-standard paradigms where the present tense form and the past tense are identical: the paradigms are *eat – eat – eaten*, *give – give – given* or *see – see – seen*, resulting in the marginal pattern PRES = PAST ≠ PPL that is only found once in the standard English verb system, namely for the verb *beat – beat – beaten*. Whether the history of these verbs can explain their diverging behaviour, and whether we are dealing with a frequent or a rather infrequent phenomenon here shall be the subject of this section.

5.5.2 Past tense eat

Surprisingly, the OED gives as the standard English past tense forms of *eat* both *ate* and *eat*, with three pronunciations: /eɪt//ɛt//iːt/.[28] This indicates that up to the end of the nineteenth century, past tense *eat* (/iːt/) must have been quite acceptable in standard English.[29] More recent dictionaries like

---

[28] This heading has not changed in the internet edition (seen 24 February 2005).

[29] Ekwall also notes the pronunciation /iːt/, but as 'less common'; interestingly the 1980 editor Ward comments that it is 'not now [iːt] … probably … it was a mistaken pronunciation used by persons who did not recognize *eat* as a written form of the pret. [et]' (Ekwall 1980: 109, n. 170).

the MED on the other hand only mention *ate* as the past tense, though the pronunciation remains variable between /eɪt/ and the more conservative /ɛt/. (Quite possibly, the first of these is another example of a spelling pronunciation undoing phonological changes.) Quirk et al. also do not include *eat* as a past tense form of *eat* in their overview of irregular verbs (Quirk et al. 1985: 116). Quite possibly, then, past tense *eat* is a recessive feature that until quite recently was an acceptable past tense form of *eat*.

5.5.2.1 History

Eat derives from the Old English paradigm *etan – æt, æton – eten*. *Etan* was the only paradigm in verb class V that did not have a short vowel in the preterite I stem. In all other verbs, the past tense stems in Old English differed in vowel quantity (but, as opposed to the verb class III verbs ('Bybee verbs') discussed above, not in vowel quality). According to Ekwall, both *eat* and *give* went over to verb class IV in Middle English (Ekwall 1980: 108). The OED cites a range of forms for past tense *ate*. As the OED also points out, *eat* differed 'from other verbs of the same conjugation in having a long vowel in the pa[st] tense sing[ular] *æt*, whence the mod. *eat* (iːt); but a form *æt*, with short vowel, must also have existed, as is proved by the ME. form *at*, mod. *ate*' (OED: s.v. *eat* v.).

In other words, the non-standard past tense form *eat* can be plausibly derived from the attested past tense form of *etan*, as both the past tense singular and plural stems had a long *æ*. The present-day standard form *ate* is in more need of explanation. If we assume that the only long singular past tense stem *æt* in verb class V was shortened, simplifying the verb class considerably, we have a plausible precursor of present-day *ate*, as the OED points out. Wyld quotes analogy with other past tense forms as a possible motivation for the short past tense *ate*: 'the short type of Pret[erite] is found already in the fourteenth century, and is probably due to the analogy of the weak Pret[erite]s *led*, M.E. *ledde* from *lead* E.Mod. and M.E. *bet* from *beat* etc.' (Wyld 1927: 276).[30]

It is important to note, however, that we need not assume that past tense *eat* is an extension of the present-day present tense form. Instead, it is the natural heir to both Old English past tense stems, whereas the present-day standard form seems slightly younger and presupposes either a variable Old English form (between long and short *æ*) or a Middle English innovation.

5.5.2.2 Historical dialects

In the *English Dialect Grammar*, Wright cites the forms /at, ēt, īt/ (roughly corresponding to /æt/, /eːt/ and /iːt/ in IPA) for Scotland, Wexford, Westmoreland [4], Yorkshire [6], Lancashire [5], Cheshire [7], Shropshire

---

[30] Although we do not have a paradigm *beat – bet* any more, Wright still lists the past tense forms *bet* and *bæt* for some northern counties (Wright 1905: 281).

[11] and west Somerset [31], without, however, regionally distinguishing the three forms further (Wright 1905: 282). In keeping with our historical conjectures above, Poplack et al. mention *eat* as one of the oldest non-standard past tense forms; their overview shows that this form is continually commented on since about 1640 (Poplack et al. 2002: 97). Characteristically, as the OED already mentions, no stigma seems attached to this form until relatively recently. Although Poplack et al. mention one disparaging comment on the use of *eat* as a past tense form in 1803, major criticism does not really set in before 1855, much later than for most other non-standard past tense forms.

In data from the SED luckily the complete paradigm of *eat* was collected. Question IV.5.11 *When I have an apple, I ___ it* was also converted for the past tense and the past participle, and responses are available from practically all informants. Most notable is the fact that, despite the huge amount of phonetic variation for this verb, overall identity of present tense and past tense is a frequent feature and occurs across the country almost uniformly. Interestingly, and again in keeping with our historical observations, some informants noted that past tense *eat* is the 'older form' (see the Basic Material, responses to IV.5.11). All relevant responses in the Basic Material have been collected in Map 5.6.

Although identical past and present tense forms for *eat* do occur all across the country, there are two clusters observable where these non-standard forms seem to be more frequent: the very North, and an area from the Midlands to the South West. Past tense *eat* is notably infrequent in the South East, as well as the West Midlands. Whether this regional distribution also holds for data from FRED is investigated next.

5.5.2.3   Data from FRED

(22) They all had a good do, and drank plenty and *eat* plenty and then you ended up with a row. (FRED YKS 007) (Yorkshire, North)

(23) I says, my goodness, many a dandelion I've eaten, I says, just pulled at the roadside and *eat* it, as if I thought it was clean. (FRED PEE 002) (Peeblesshire, Scottish Lowlands)

Eat is not a very frequent verb – past tense forms occur only thirty-seven times in the whole of FRED (this is not due to the fact that the subject of eating is not mentioned, but probably to the fact that more idiomatic expressions are available, like *have breakfast, have lunch*, etc.). It is perhaps all the more surprising that well over a third of the attested instances are in fact non-standard *eat*. This can hardly be attributed to 'ignorance', as Ekwall's editor Ward would have it. Rather, a legitimate descendant of the Old and Middle English past tense forms with a long vowel is apparently still alive and well in traditional dialects in twentieth-century Britain. The regional distribution is given in Table 5.12.

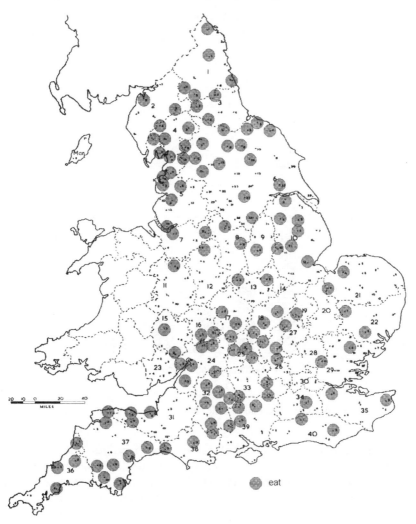

Map 5.6 Past tense *eat* in the SED (Basic Material)

A regional distribution very similar to the older SED data is apparent from Table 5.12 and Figure 5.17. Clearly, past tense *eat* is still strongest in the South West, a region not generally known for being particularly innovative. In fact, we know from many phenomena that the South West in particular is highly conservative, and this fits well with the impression that past tense *eat* might be a recessive feature that may have been much more frequent in the past. Past tense *eat* is also comparatively frequent in the Midlands and in the North, but occurs in the South East with frequencies that are far below the overall average, again mirroring the distribution in the SED quite closely.

Table 5.12 *Past tense* eat *in FRED*

	eat	*ate*	Sum	% *eat*
South West	11	3	14	78.6
Midlands	3	3	6	50.0
North	3	7	10	30.0
Scotland	2	5	7	28.6
South East	4	19	23	17.4
Wales	0	1	1	0.0
Total	23	38	61	Ø 37.7

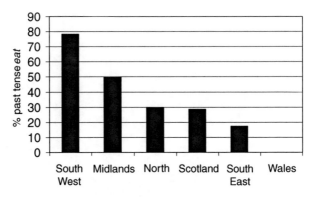

Figure 5.17 Past tense *eat* per dialect area in FRED

Past tense *eat* is thus a candidate for a conservative feature that has survived in the more marginal areas of Britain, especially the South West, but also in the Midlands. Nevertheless, it should be borne in mind that absolute figures are comparatively low, and that statistical tests are therefore not reliable.

5.5.2.4   *Conclusion past tense* eat

In sum, we can say that past tense *eat* is today a regional phenomenon that occurs especially in the South West, but also in the Midlands, less frequently in the North and Scotland, and is comparatively rare in the South East. Although it is a feature with a long-standing history, today it seems to be recessive, as speakers in the influential South East do not seem to have taken it up. While this may be a historical and geographical coincidence, it must also be noted that past tense *eat* results in a paradigm that is functionally less than optimal in several ways: changing verb class from verb class 1 to verb class 4 is strongly disfavoured in the system (only one verbal paradigm makes up verb class 4, namely *beat – beat – beaten*, although this verb admittedly has a very similar phonemic shape), and it results in the overall pattern PRES = PAST ≠ PPL which is not system-congruent. It is therefore perhaps not surprising that this non-standard verb paradigm is disfavoured, and does not seem to be spreading to other regions presently.

In COLT, the verb *eat* in general is again very rare (there are seven past tense instances altogether), so that not much can be said on its present-day distribution in London adolescent speech.

5.5.3   *Past tense* give

(24) She *give* me the basin I took it and *give* her half a loaf of bread. (FRED NTT 013) (Nottinghamshire, Midlands)
(25) He took out his wallet and he *give* me a ten shilling note. (FRED WIL 001) (Wiltshire, South West)

When we look at past tense *give*, a pattern rather similar to past tense *eat* emerges, as this section will show. Although, in contrast to *eat*, *give* is a highly frequent verb (the standard past tense *gave* occurs over 500 times in FRED alone), the non-standard past tense form *give* is comparatively rare and, like *eat*, does not seem to be a candidate favoured for spreading into a supralocal non-standard today.

5.5.3.1   *History*
Like *eat*, the past tense of *give* must have been variable over the last centuries. The Old English paradigm *ȝiefan – ȝeaf, ȝéafon – ȝiefen* shows vowel quantity alternation between the preterite I and the preterite II stems. This quantity distinction between singular and plural stem in the past tense is interesting, as the long vowel in the plural seems to have been the source for Middle English *gave*. If we take the singular vowel, this may have led to a short past tense vowel, e.g. *give*, and can thus be regarded as the source for the modern non-standard form *give*. Both long (*gave*) and short (*give*) past tense forms of present-day English can in this way be regularly derived. As noted in section 4.4.2.2, the initial /g/ we find today probably goes back to Scandinavian influence, cf. Old Norse *gefa*, as Old English <g> regularly became /j/.

5.5.3.2   *Historical dialects*
In the EDD, past tense *give* is only one of forty-seven (!) past tense forms noted for *give*. (One of them, past tense *gived*, has already been discussed in section 4.4.2.2.) Occurrences of past tense *give* are noted in Lincolnshire [10], Leicestershire [13], Kent [35], Surrey [34] and Dorset [38], confirming that – if anything – this is an 'eastern' phenomenon, perhaps with the exception of Dorset [38], as Map 5.7 illustrates.

In the OGREVE (Poplack et al. 2002), past tense *give* is mentioned later than the early forms *eat, run* or *come*, not before 1685. In fact, past tense *give* is commented on only twice, in 1685 and 1688. This is astonishing, since past tense *give* must have continued to exist. As data from FRED indicate, it is a highly frequent phenomenon in traditional British dialects today.

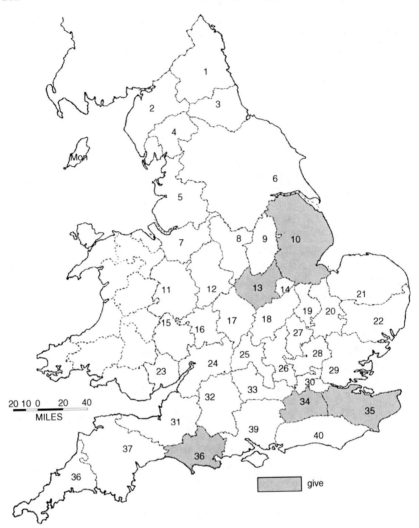

Map 5.7 Past tense *give* in the EDD

5.5.3.3 *Data from FRED*

In FRED, all instances of *give* were manually disambiguated for tense, and then counted per dialect area. In particular, the extended context was employed to determine past time reference (or not) for all cases of *give*, especially where this was not preceded by a third person singular. All unclear examples were excluded. The results are displayed in Table 5.13 and in Figure 5.18.

Past tense *give* in traditional British dialects is clearly a South East phenomenon, where over three-quarters of all instances of the past tense of this lexeme are *give* rather than *gave*. The South West, the Midlands and the

Table 5.13 *Past tense* give *in FRED*

	give	*gave*	Sum	*% give*
South East	154	51	205	75.1
South West	64	92	156	41.0
Midlands	37	76	113	32.7
North	42	95	137	30.7
Wales	4	34	38	10.5
Scotland	8	93	101	7.9
Total	309	441	750	Ø 41.2

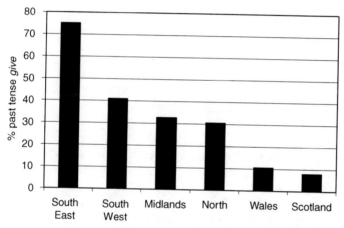

Figure 5.18 Past tense *give* per dialect area in FRED

North form the second group of dialect areas with similar ratios of between 30 and 40 per cent – past tense *give* clearly is still a frequent phenomenon here, but patterns at only half the rate of the highly frequent South East. Finally, the 'Celtic fringes' Wales and Scotland have minimal occurrences of past tense *give* at around or under 10 per cent.[31] While past tense *give* in general can therefore be said to be very well established in the traditional dialects of England, the South East stands out by a large margin. For a fre-

---

[31] These divisions are supported by statistical analyses. Again, the overall comparison suggests that there are significant differences between dialect areas (at df=5, p<0.001). The South East patterns significantly differently from all other dialect areas (at df=1, p<0.001 in all pairwise comparisons). The South West, Midlands and the North are not significantly different from each other, but are different from Wales and Scotland, respectively (at df=1, p between 0.025 and 0.001). Wales and Scotland with df=1 and p<1 are not significantly different from each other.

quent verb like *give*, a non-standard past tense in around 75 per cent of all cases is a highly frequent phenomenon indeed.

In data from COLT, however, past tense *give* has become very rare. Despite the strong standing in traditional dialects, in London teenagers' language at the end of the twentieth century, past tense *give* is almost non-existent. It occurs exactly three times, while the standard form *gave* occurs 111 times, giving past tense *give* a text frequency of under 3 per cent in COLT. Past tense *give* thus seems to be a phenomenon that is recessive. As discussed above for *eat*, there may be functional reasons for this.

5.5.4   *Past tense* see

(26) Then he looked down and he *see* this pair o' cod britches. (FRED SFK 038) (Suffolk, South East)
(27) Yeah. Yes, that was the last time I *see* him. (pause) (FRED KEN 006) (Kent, South East)

As noted above (in section 4.4.3.1 on past tense *seed* and in section 5.3 on past tense *seen*), there is a third – regionally very restricted – non-standard past tense form for *see*, namely the unmarked past tense *see*.[32]

5.5.4.1   *Historical dialects*
In the data from the SED, the distribution of past tense *see* seems to centre in the South East, but its regional distribution is spread beyond the Home Counties, as Map 5.8 shows.

Especially noteworthy is the little enclave of past tense *see* forms in Lancashire [5] – an area otherwise dominated by *seed*. Incidentally, the regional distribution of past tense *see* complements the distribution of both *seen* and *seed* almost perfectly. There are no more than a handful of informants who use *see* as well as another past tense form. This also makes it strikingly clear that past tense *saw* – the standard English form – is in the minority by far in the SED. It is almost always outnumbered by one of the non-standard strategies.

5.5.4.2   *Data from FRED*
Data from FRED have been cited before (in the sections on past tense *seed* 4.4.3.1 and on past tense *seen* 5.3); here we shall concentrate on past tense *see* only. As Table 5.14 indicates, past tense *see* is noticeably frequent in the South East only, closely mirroring the older distribution of this dialectal form in the SED. Past tense *see* is in fact the dominant non-standard form for this paradigm in the South East, although the relative frequency is 'only' just over a third of all instances, while past tense *seen* is rather marginal in the South East.

---

[32] I am very grateful to Peter Trudgill for drawing my attention to this phenomenon.

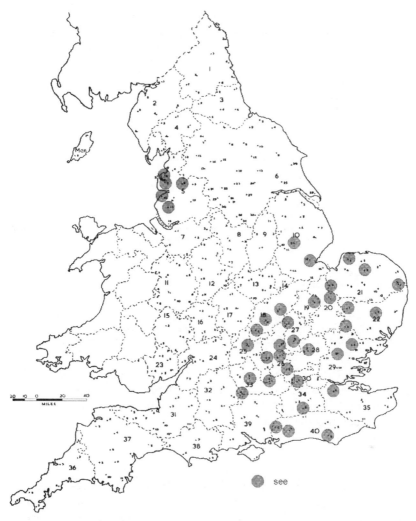

Map 5.8 Past tense *see* in the SED (Basic Material)

5.5.4.3   *Data from COLT*

As we have also seen above, past tense *see* still occurs in data from COLT in a handful of instances, as Table 5.9 (repeated here as Table 5.15) has shown. However, even for speakers of social group 3, past tense *see* is noticeably less frequent than the more widespread non-standard past tense form *seen*. This is a clear change in trend for younger speakers in London, then. The form *see*, traditionally dominant in the South East, is receding at the expense of the more widespread non-standard form *seen*. However, both are much rarer for teenage speakers in London than they were for the older speakers in FRED,

Table 5.14 *Past tense* see *in FRED*

	seen	seed	see	saw	Sum	% see
South West	91	9	9	85	194	4.6
Wales	9	0	0	18	27	0.0
Scotland	68	0	3	143	214	1.4
Midlands	37	9	6	81	133	4.5
South East	16	1	66	101	184	35.9
North	16	1	0	107	124	0.0
Total	237	20	84	535	876	Ø 9.6

Table 5.15 *Past tense* see *in COLT*

	seen	see	saw	Sum	% seen	% see	% non-standard form
Social group 1 (high)	1	1	62	64	1.6	1.6	3.1
Social group 2 (middle)	1	1	57	59	1.7	1.7	3.4
Social group 3 (low)	6	3	40	49	12.2	6.1	18.4
Total	8	5	159	172	Ø 4.7	Ø 2.9	Ø 7.6

or indeed the SED. Both *seen* and *see* have become marginalized non-standard forms at the expense of standard English *saw*. While *saw* was still clearly in the minority in the data from the SED, it has become more frequent in FRED (often constituting the majority option) and even more so in COLT.

5.5.5   Conclusions

The comparison of data from FRED with the (regionally very restricted) data from COLT suggests that *eat, give* as well as *see* have all become comparatively rare, although in the traditional dialects they were relatively strong even in the South East, or even exclusive to it. The (admittedly restricted) comparison with COLT may suggest tentatively that these forms therefore obviously do not constitute good candidates for new supraregional non-standard forms. This indicates that a possible new supraregional non-standard form has to fulfil several criteria. First of all, it should have a geographical base in the (rich, influential, trendsetting) South East. Dialect features like *give* that are comparatively rare in the traditional South Eastern dialects do not seem very likely to spread into a national non-standard, although they might be extremely frequent in other dialect areas.

Secondly, there also seem to be functional considerations. Probably the most widespread pattern in the verb system is that of Bybee verbs. Verbs which go against this popular pattern, like *eat*, *give* or *see*, apparently do not spread easily, even if they have a strong regional base in the South East, as the example of *see* has shown.

A combination of these two criteria (geographical origin, linked to the status of its speakers and thus clearly a sociolinguistic criterion, and the functional system-internal criteria discussed here and in Chapter 7) together seem to be a good predictor of future language change, especially where the establishment of a supralocal non-standard for British English is concerned. This discussion will be taken up again in section 7.2.

5.6   Chapter conclusion

As Robert Lowth has already noted (unfavourably) at the end of the eight-eenth century, three-part paradigms in English tend to be levelled to just two (see the quotation at the beginning of this chapter). As this chapter has shown, non-standard strong verbs can be grouped into several classes in this respect. Logically, several possibilities obtain: the standard English three-part paradigm as depicted in Figure 5.19 could be simplified so that (a) the simple past form is used for the past participle; (b) the infinitive could be used as the past participle; (c) the past participle could be used as the simple past; or (d) the infinitive could be used as the simple past, as illustrated in Figure 5.20.[33] Strikingly, only the last two options seem to constitute majority patterns.[34]

As a result, the StE simple past tense forms are much rarer in non-stand-ard discourse, as they do not appear in either of the majority patterns. Put the other way around, we could say that while infinitive and past participle tend to remain the same as in standard English, only the simple past tense form is subject to change: either becoming identical with the infinitive, or with the past participle. These two major non-standard patterns are also not equivalent to each other. As this chapter has shown, many verb types follow the first pattern (pattern (c) in Figure 5.20): all Bybee verbs, including *do – done – done*, but also *see – seen – seen*, and as this pattern conforms to the abstract structural property of the English verb system, PRES ≠ PAST = PPL, it also becomes very stable.

The second pattern is only followed by the three verb types *eat – eat – eaten*, *give – give – given* as well as *see – see – seen*. In all three cases, these non-iconic forms (with identical present tense and simple past tense forms)

---

[33] There are other, intuitively more nonsensical possibilities, such that StE forms would 'jump' to another function (e.g. StE past tense used for only the nStE past participle, or StE past tense and past participle reversing functions in nStE), but this does not seem to depict a possible paradigm. Historical continuity is an obvious reason why these scenarios do not take place. Synchronically, it looks as if StE forms tend to 'extend' only to a neigh-bouring function, at least in the majority patterns.

[34] The first option is attested historically (*I have wrote*); it is not clear, however, whether this pattern was ever anything but marginal.

Same shading implies identity of forms

Figure 5.19 Standard English three-part paradigm

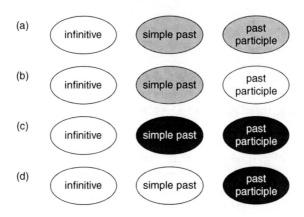

Same shading implies identity of forms

Figure 5.20 Non-standard English two-part paradigms

are mainly historically motivated. These three paradigms are characterized by the abstract pattern PRES = PAST ≠ PPL., which is not system-congruous in the English verb system and can thus be expected to evince considerable instability. And indeed in the case of *eat*, we have seen that this might be a recessive feature where the (new) standard English forms of the twentieth century are encroaching on the older standard and dialectal forms. In the case of *give*, we have seen the interesting development that in those areas where levelled *give* is strongest, non-standard systems have reacted to this levelling by introducing new weak forms, resulting in a paradigm *give – gived – gived*, which re-establishes the abstract structural property of the English verb system, PRES ≠ PAST = PPL. Neither past tense *give* nor the regionally restricted *see* seem to be spreading to a newer supralocal non-standard.

The pattern PRES ≠ PAST = PPL then does indeed play a most important role in English non-standard verb paradigm systems. It is much more prominent than in the standard, where most three-part paradigms are still intact, especially the medium frequency ones under discussion in this chapter. With regard to this system-defining structural property of English, then, we can indeed claim that the non-standard systems are more natural than the standard counterpart.

6   *Come* and *run*: non-standard strong verbs with a one-part paradigm

Run (rʌn), *v.* [...] A verb of complicated history in Eng[lish] ...
(OED: s.v. *run* v.)

6.1   Past tense *come*

6.1.1   Introduction

(1) He was at sea f' Christmas and she *come* in – there was just the wheel there. (FRED SFK 033) (Suffolk, South East)
(2) We had to stop it when he *come* from the war. (FRED NTT 006) (Nottinghamshire, Midlands)
(3) She wouldn't cut the bread when it *come* out the bakehouse, it was too hot. (FRED LAN 002) (Lancashire, North)

The non-standard use of *come* in the past tense is generally well known and seems to be a feature of enormous geographical spread – indeed Chambers includes it under his vernacular universals as one of 'the most ubiquitous' 'markers of W[orking] C[lass] speech in widely scattered areas of the English-speaking world' (Chambers 1995: 240). Chambers' inclusion of past tense *come* as a general indicator of 'mainstream non-standard' English (Chambers 1995: 241) equally means that this feature is so frequent it would qualify not as a dialect feature in the strict sense, but as a general non-standard feature. Past tense *come* is also mentioned by Wolfram and Schilling-Estes (1998: 332) for the majority of vernaculars in the US North and South, and is one of the most frequent non-standard past tense forms in Poplack and Tagliamonte's study of diaspora varieties of African American English (Poplack and Tagliamonte 2001). Poplack and Tagliamonte give an interesting overview of a number of African American English varieties (Samaná English, the Ex-Slave Recordings, African Nova Scotian English from North Preston and Guysborough Enclave) and one White English Vernacular, their control variety (Nova Scotian Vernacular English from Guysborough Village). Despite the often widely diverging methodologies and informant backgrounds, they document relatively consistent usage of past tense *come* of between 10 and 17 per cent (of all strong verbs used in past-reference contexts). Comparing standard vs. non-standard past tense of *come*, figures are more divergent (indeed they range from just under 40 per cent in Samaná English to almost 100 per cent in the Ex-Slave Recordings). What unites all speech communities, however, is that non-standard *come* is far more frequent than any other non-standard strong verb form. Tagliamonte (2001) has studied past tense *come* further, partly drawing on the same materials, but in addition concentrating on a British non-standard variety, namely material from York. (This study seems, however, rather exploratory in nature, and comes to contradictory conclusions.)

In the case of *come*, a levelling of the past tense/past participle contrast to *come* results in an (almost completely) undifferentiated paradigm for all tenses – the only remaining contrast being third person singular *–s*, which differentiates present from past tense for this person. Poplack and Tagliamonte strongly argue for idiosyncrasy for this verb form (Poplack and Tagliamonte 2000: 136 et passim). In this chapter I will show that past tense *come* is by no means an idiosyncrasy, although its historical development is of course specific to this verb paradigm (recalling Grimm's dictum that every word has its own history; see Chapter 4). However, past tense *come* can be linked to other non-standard past tense forms in a regular way, and can indeed be functionally motivated.

6.1.2   History

6.1.2.1   Regular development

Come is a verb form of considerable historical complexity. It belonged to the Old English verb class IV with the paradigm *cuman – c(w)ōm, c(w)ōmon – cumen* (Krygier 1994: 49–50). Quoting the OED, the following forms are attested for the present tense stem: *cuman* in Old English, *cumen, cume, cum* as well as the spelling variant *comen* in Middle English, and *come* since the fourteenth century, the form that eventually became the standard (OED: s.v. *come* v.). What we have here is the regular development of present tense form *cuman*. It developed into /kum/ (losing its ending), laxed to /kʊm/[1] and then in the seventeenth century centralized, unrounded and lowered to /kʌm/ in those dialects that underwent the /ʊ/ – /ʌ/ split, i.e. basically in the South of England and in Scotland. This regular development is slightly obscured by the convention of Middle English scribes to spell <u> as <o> before <m, n, v>, etc. in Middle English in the so-called *minim*-environments, which gives us the current spelling for the present tense *come*.

---

[1] I am assuming laxing according to the majority position, although Lass (1999: 90) claims that short tense /u/ must have started to move towards /ʌ/ before centralization and lowering to /ʊ/ occurred. This does not affect my argument, however.

The development of the current past tense form of standard English is more complicated to trace, as the Middle English dialects here underwent different developments. The OED documents the following forms for the past tense singular and plural: *cwóm*, *cuóm*, *cóm* and *cōm*, for the singular, which regularly developed into Middle English *coom* and *come*; and the parallel plural forms *cwómon*, *quómon*, *cómon* for Old English, *cōmen* for Middle English, which also regularly developed into Middle English *come* (OED: s.v. *come* v.). (For details on the Old English forms in individual manuscripts, see also Campbell 1959.)

What is central to note here is that the Old and Middle English past tense forms unanimously indicate a long vowel, long /o:/. The natural development for the class of words containing the ME long /o:/ vowel was a little varied. Three main scenarios can be distinguished:

Scenario A (regular development of long vowels)
Undergoing the Great Vowel Shift, Middle English long close /o:/ typically became long /u:/ in present-day English (cf. *boot*, *shoot*, *broom*, *pool*). If the past tense of *come* had developed regularly, this should have given us a present-day English form *coom* /ku:m/. Clearly, however, this is not the case. Also dialectally, past tense /ku:m/ is hardly attested today. Map 6.6 (on page 163) collects the few attestations there are in the SED Basic Material. *Coom* in the traditional dialects recorded after the Second World War was obviously a sporadic northern phenomenon. In the standard, past tense *coom* disappears from the written records around 1500. This phonological development of the past tense therefore remains as good as unattested.

The regular development is indicated by a bold arrow in Figure 6.1 (adapted from the general overview in Lass 1999: 90).[2]

There is another possibility, though.

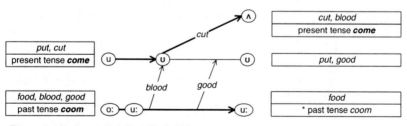

The regular development is indicated by **bold** arrows

Figure 6.1   Postulated regular development of present and past tense *come*

---

[2] The development Lass proposes in addition (lowering of tense /u/ to schwa, without first laxing to /ʊ/) can be safely disregarded for our purposes, for the sake of simplifying the diagram considerably.

Scenario B (raising, shortening)
If we assume that *coom* underwent the Great Vowel Shift as in scenario A, changing /oː/ to /uː/, and that the resultant /uː/ was then shortened, as in many other – highly frequent – words, this would result in a past tense form /kʊm/ for the time before the seventeenth century, which accords well with the documented evidence. (Remembering that short *u* was regularly spelled <o> before <m>.) If this shortening took place before the /ʊ/ – /ʌ/ development stopped being productive in the seventeenth century, this would give us a past tense /kʌm/ today in the South, /kʊm/ in the North. This is exactly the non-standard past tense form that is widely attested throughout Great Britain (and indeed in the rest of the English speaking world).[3]

It is not implausible that the regular Old and Middle English past tense form of *come* underwent this development (especially shortening). *Come* is one of the most frequent verbs of English, and it is the frequent words in particular that were prone to the shortening of Middle English long /oː/ which is necessary for this explanation. This regular (if marked) development also explains why (non-standard) past tense *come* is homophonous with the present tense *come* both in the South (/kʌm//kʌm/) as well as in the Midlands and the North, where the /ʊ/ – /ʌ/ split is well known not to have occurred (here the forms are /kʊm/ and /kʊm/): the infinitive and thus the present tense stem developed regularly from short /u/, whereas the past tense took a slightly more roundabout way from long /uː/, which was shortened at some stage. This marked regular development is illustrated in Figure 6.2.

Scenario C (raising, later shortening)
In an exception to the regular development depicted above in scenarios A and B, some words split from the ME long /oː/ class after having undergone the Great Vowel Shift, and /uː/ was shortened to /ʊ/ comparatively later than in scenario B. Again, this seems to have affected high frequency words in particular (cf. *good, foot, wool*). As this /ʊ/ is still present in /gʊd fʊt wʊl/ and has not changed further into /ʌ/, the /uː/ to /ʊ/ shortening must have been relatively recent – at any rate, it must have happened after the /ʊ/ – /ʌ/ split, in which it would otherwise have taken part: 'later shortenings apparently go directly to /ʊ/ (since there is no short [u], and the changes leading to [ʌ] are no longer active)' (Lass 1999: 90). From the evidence available, *coom* does not seem to have taken part in this late shortening, as it has not changed to short /kʊm/ in the South of England today, unlike *good, foot, wool*, and scenario C can in all probability be discarded.

As a summary of the regular development of all forms of *come*, the preceding diagrams can be combined as in Figure 6.3.

---

[3] See also Ekwall (1980: 107).

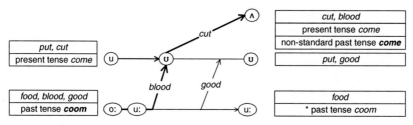

Figure 6.2 Marked regular development of past tense *coom*

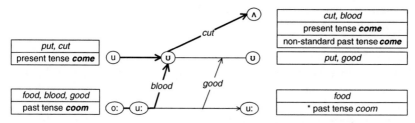

Figure 6.3 Phonological development of *come*

In other words, past tense *come* can be traced directly from the attested Old and Middle English forms, undergoing the same development as the word *blood* (Figure 6.3). Although this development has resulted in a levelled paradigm, levelling was in all probability not a motivating factor. Instead, we have seen that a past tense form *come* can be explained as being a by-product of converging historical phonological changes that also made words like *cut* and *blood* sound alike today in many accents of English.

6.1.2.2 *Standard English past tense* came

Clearly, however, this does not explain how the current standard English past tense form *came* evolved. The OED suggests the following path of development:

just as, in late W[est] S[axon], *nóm, nómon,* became *nam, námon,* so in late Northumbrian *cóm, cómon* appear to have become *cam, cāmen,* which are found in the earliest specimens of northern ME. These forms were used by Wyclif, and soon afterwards drove out *com, come,* which hardly appear after 1500 in the literary language, though still widely prevalent in midland and southern dialects. In northern dialect, the pronunciation is still (kam), but in standard Eng[lish] it has duly passed into (keɪm), cf. *Cambridge.* (OED: s.v. *come* v.)

Jespersen also proposes the development in analogy with *niman*: 'the Mod[ern] E[nglish] prt[preterite] *came* goes back to ME *cām,* earlier *cam,* which is a new formation, probably on the analogy of *niman, nam* (now extinct). The old prt[preterite] *come* died out in the literary language about 1600; Sh[akespeare] has it once' (Jespersen 1942: 56).

However, for various reasons, an analogy with *niman – nam* is not very convincing. Although both *niman* and *cuman* belong to the same Old English verb class (verb class IV), the infinitives and attested Old English past tense forms *niman – nam* and *cuman – cwom* are sufficiently unlike each other to permit an easy analogy. (They become more alike after *cwom* changes to *cam*, but that is hardly the correct basis of deduction.) Wyld similarly writes that 'it is clear that no other verbs of this class [i.e. class IV] could have influenced the forms of *come*, as they are quite differentiated from it by various combinative changes' (Wyld 1927: 275). Secondly, variation between *nom* and *nam* is attested since earliest times, and the past tense *nam* is well established even in Old English. *Cam*, very differently, is first attested around 1250, and then only for the North (OED: s.v. *come* v.) – a time-lag of several hundred years, which does not make an explanation purely along the lines of analogy very convincing. In addition, *niman* was slowly being ousted by *take* (*tacan*) during Middle English times, a verb of Old Norse origin which is attested since the eleventh century, until *niman* gradually disappeared out of the verb system altogether (OED: s.v. *nim*, *take* v.). Clearly a verb that is in the process of becoming obsolete is not a convincing basis for positing analogical extensions to high frequency members of the same class.

An interesting alternative suggestion comes from the *Oxford Dictionary of English Etymology* (ODEE). Although it basically supports the OED in its dating, it is indeed a little more specific, dating the beginnings of *came* to the fourteenth century, and in addition suggesting Old Norse influence: 'pt. [past tense] *came*, originally ME. *cam*, *cāme*, pl. *cāmen* (XIII, first in north and east, prob[ably] after O[ld] N[orse] *kvam*)' (ODEE: s.v. *come*).

Data from LALME, however, do not support the impression of a northern preponderance of *came*. Two dot maps compare past tense forms in <a> and <o> (LALME dot maps 381 and 382, Vol. 1: 400), reproduced here as Map 6.1 and Map 6.2.

A comparison of these two maps shows clearly that in the fourteenth century, the regionally unmarked past tense form was *come*, supporting also Jespersen's impression above that *come* was the 'old preterite' (Jespersen 1942: 56). Forms of the type *came* were restricted to the Midlands and the South – the opposite of what one would expect if this form had its origin in language contact with Old Norse. (Cf. the clearly Old Norse-influenced distribution of *rin* below in Map 6.8.)

If we actually look at the developments in Old Norse, especially the East Scandinavian forms (in Icelandic, Faroese and Norwegian Nynorsk) can be directly derived from Old Norse *kvam* (the putative source form of present-day English *came*). However, language-internal developments in the Scandinavian languages seem not to have resulted in forms in <a>. In Icelandic, arguably the most conservative of the Nordic languages, the

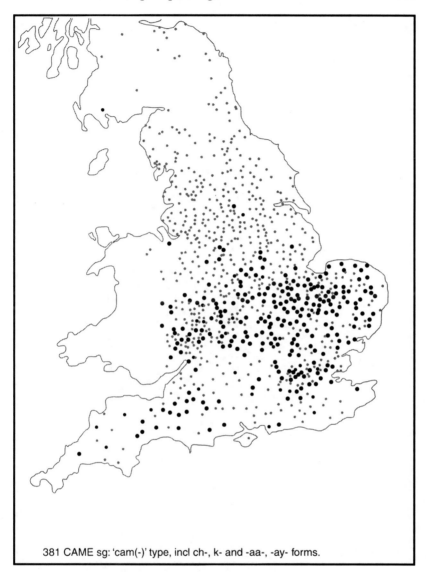

381 CAME sg: 'cam(-)' type, incl ch-, k- and -aa-, -ay- forms.

Map 6.1 Past tense *came* in LALME

present tense stem has developed to <e> in the singular, while it is <o> in the plural, leading to syncretism between present and past plural forms – strikingly similar to non-standard English (the full paradigm in the present tense is: *ég kem, þú kemur, hann kemur, við komum, þið komuð, þeir koma*; in the past tense: *ég kom, þú komst, hann kom, við komum, þið komuð, þeir koma*). The West Scandinavian forms (Swedish, Danish and Norwegian

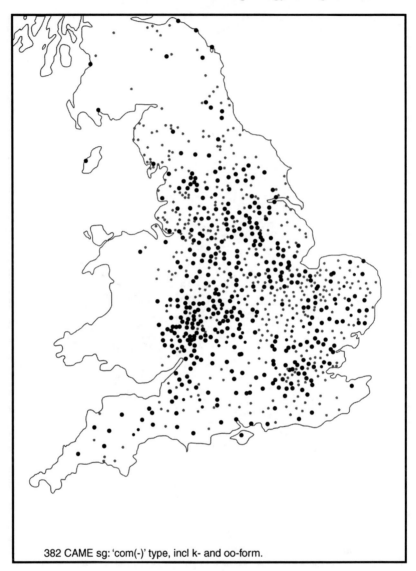

382 CAME sg: 'com(-)' type, incl k- and oo-form.

Map 6.2 Past tense *come* in LALME

Bokmål), on the other hand, probably go back to alternative Old Norse forms, e.g. *kom*. The morphological contrast in these three languages (Bokmål in this respect is identical to Danish) is carried by the ending and consonant length (present tense *kommer* vs. past tense *kom* in all persons for Danish, Bokmål and Swedish), but not by vowel quality. Clearly, then, the Old Norse antecedent of all four languages has developed to <o> in the past tense in all Scandinavian languages, and from this short overview as well as the medieval distribution of forms detailed in Map 6.1 it seems unlikely that Old Norse was indeed the decisive influence on the development of past tense *came*.[4]

As the OED notes, the precursors of *came* are practically standard in literary language by 1500. Although the first attestation in the OED is from around 1250 and indeed comes from northern sources, these early instances must have been sporadic. A detailed study of the diachronic part of the Helsinki corpus shows only three instances of *came* in the period from 1350 to 1420, roughly corroborating the ODEE claims. In the late Middle English period from 1420 to 1500, *came* becomes increasingly frequent, and in the first Early Modern texts (from 1500 to 1570) *came* is practically without competition from past tense *come*. If we only concentrate on the rise of *came*,[5] figures from the Helsinki corpus suggest, however, that the complete ousting must have been later than 1500. Absolute figures as well as normalized ones (related to subcorpus word number) bear a striking resemblance to the S-curves well known from language change, where a change typically starts off slowly, gathers momentum and finally slows down again. (This has sometimes been called the fox-trot of language change: Slow-Slow-Quick-Quick-Slow.) The steepest slope in Figure 6.4 is clearly situated *after* 1500 (namely from 1570 to 1640), which indicates that the complete change from *come* to *came* is an Early Modern English phenomenon rather than a Middle English one. This time-lag further corroborates the argument against analogy with *niman – nam* as the original motivation for this change – all the more so as by 1500 the verb *niman/ nim* had fallen almost completely out of use, being superseded by the Scandinavian loan word *take*.

This late change looks like it might have been propelled by emerging standardization, and it is not implausible that a regional phenomenon of the general South was chosen for this function. As we have seen in section 5.2.5, forms where present and past tense stems were different must have been favoured during the process of standardization – together with its (southern) regional provenance as detailed in Map 6.1, this is a second argument in favour of *came*. Even though the origin of this past tense form is still unclear, its subsequent path of development can be plausibly traced.

---

[4] However, it is also true that all West Germanic languages today have past tense forms of *come* with <a> (cf. Modern Frisian, Modern German and Modern Dutch forms), so that the standard English past tense *came* curiously looks like an areal typological phenomenon.
[5] A study of just the frequency of the incoming form *came* (and, marginally, *camen*), rather than a comparison of old *come* vs. new *came*, e.g. in percentages, is justified by the general phenomenon that 'in many morphosyntactic phenomena frequency follows the pattern of variable percentages' (Nevalainen and Raumolin-Brunberg 2003: 216).

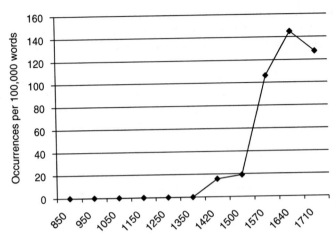

Figure 6.4 The rise of past tense *came* (Helsinki corpus, normalized figures)

6.1.3 Historical dialects

The *English Dialect Dictionary* (Wright 1898–1905) records a baffling diversity of forms for both present and past tenses of *come*. In volume I (A–C) the entries are still grouped according to similarity of form, a practice apparently given up in subsequent volumes, and the past tense forms recorded for the past tense are: *cam, co', coh, com, come, comed, comm'd, coom, coom'd, coome, cum, cum'd, kam, keame, kem, kim, kom, kom'd.* As these reflect the dialect spellings of many different authors, several forms can legitimately be grouped together. The easiest to pick out is the regular dental suffix *–ed* that characterizes *comed, comm'd, coom'd, cum'd* and *kom'd*, forms which are documented for Nottinghamshire [9], Lincolnshire [10], Shropshire [11], Gloucestershire [24], Norfolk [21], Suffolk [22], Northamptonshire [18], west Somerset [31], Huntingdonshire [19], northeast Yorkshire [6], east Yorkshire, west Yorkshire [6] and Devon [37]. As in many cases, this is just one form among others; regularization to *–ed* for *come* seems to be a sporadic feature, situated mainly in the Midlands, but also covering East Anglia and some of the South West, as Map 6.3 makes clear.

The remaining forms differ in vowel quality and/or presumably in quantity.

Very interesting from a historical point of view are the forms with <oo>, indicating a long /uː/. This is the 'missing link', the regular development of ME ō without shortening. Already in late Middle English, forms with <oo> spelling are very rare (LALME Vol. 4: 142–3). In the EDD, remnants of

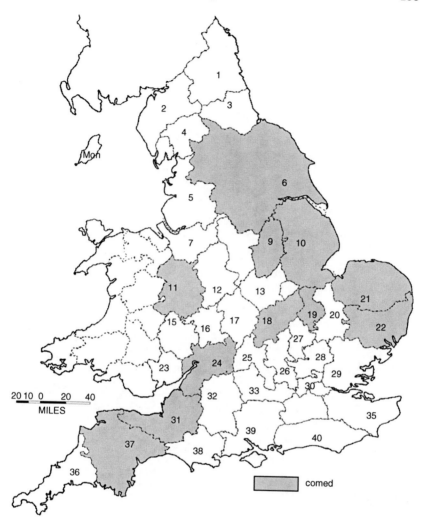

Map 6.3 Past tense *comed* in the EDD

<oo> are present in *coom, coom'd, coome* in west Yorkshire [6], Lancashire [5], south Cheshire [7], Lincolnshire [10] (also additionally with *−ed*) and Surrey [34] (Wright 1898–1905: s.v. *come* v. I.2), and thus this seems to be mainly a central northern phenomenon (with the striking exception of Surrey [34]), as Map 6.4 shows.

The present ubiquitousness of *come* in the past tense can already be traced back to the EDD, where it is widely attested, as Map 6.5 illustrates. *Come* – together with *com, cum* as a quasi-phonetic spelling as well as

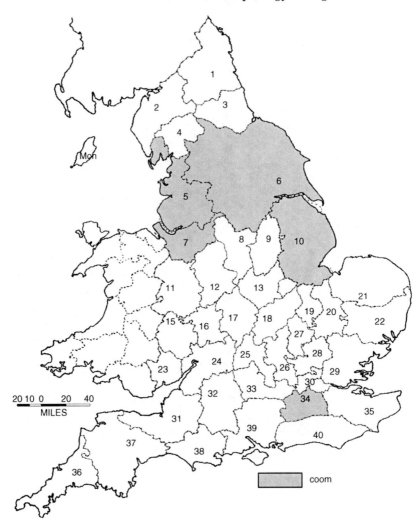

Map 6.4 Past tense *coom* in the EDD

kum – is documented for Northumberland [1], Durham [3], Cumberland [2], Westmoreland [4], Yorkshire [6], Lancashire [5], Warwickshire [17], Cheshire [7], Nottinghamshire [9], Northamptonshire [18], Shropshire [11], Gloucestershire [24], Oxfordshire [25], East Anglia, Sussex [40], Dorset [38], west Somerset [31] (where it is explicitly noted that '*came* is unknown'), Devon [37], Lincolnshire [10], Isle of Wight, i.e. across the country. White areas are mainly due to the fact that not all counties are featured in Wright's list.

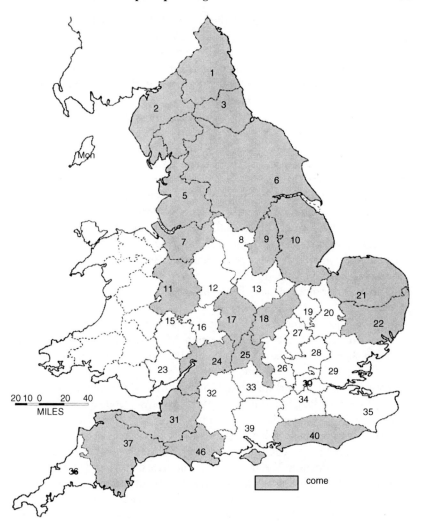

Map 6.5 Past tense *come* in the EDD

The majority option even in the time of the EDD then seems to have been past tense *come*, across the country. The striking *coom* is a minority phenomenon with a very restricted regional distribution, only encountered in the central North, whereas regularization to *comed* (with vowel variation in the stem) occurs sporadically across the country. Unfortunately, of course, even where we can conclude that individual dialects must have been variable, no quantification of these early observations is possible, and we cannot therefore say with certainty how dominant the majority option really was.

Past tense *come* is also one of the few verb forms elicited by the SED questionnaire. Question IX.3.4. reads: *Afterwards Father went out, but then he remembered that he had forgotten something else, so back he ___.* The recorded responses (cf. also the map form, Orton et al. 1978: M14) show that past tense *come* occurs all over England, particularly in the east. However, the map is oversimplifying and in fact the legend is incorrect (*come* and *came* are the wrong way round), so that it makes more sense to investigate the Basic Material directly. Surprisingly, Orton et al. write that 'the St[andard] *came* is the norm in most of England but several sizeable enclaves of *come* and *comed* are to be found in the eastern half of the country and in small sections of the West Midlands' (Orton et al. 1978: introduction, no pagination). The apparent uniformity is, however, belied by the Basic Material, which suggests a similar diversity of forms as Wright's EDD (cf. responses to IX.3.4. in Orton and Halliday 1962–64; Orton and Barry 1969–71; Orton and Tilling 1969–71; Orton and Wakelin 1967–68). The apparently clear division of the map into StE *came*, dialectal *come* and marginal *comed* does not take account of the marginal *coom* which still occurs sporadically in the SED. All occurrences of *coom* from the Basic Material have been collected in Map 6.6.

Map 6.6 shows a very similar regional distribution of *coom* to the earlier material collected in the EDD (cf. again Map 6.4); if anything, the distribution has moved slightly to the north (the northernmost counties Northumberland [1] and Durham [3] were not mentioned in Wright's list; the counties south of Yorkshire like Lincolnshire [10] and Cheshire [7] which still had *coom* in Wright's time no longer have any instances of *coom* in the SED). Forms of *coom* indeed seem to have survived in the North only, and only very marginally so. Their marginality is also expressed by the individual occurrences in the counties where they do occur – something the more sweeping assignment in Wright to whole counties could not depict.

Although the marginality of *coom* has begun to become clearer, proper quantification is of course not possible on the basis of material from the SED. FRED unfortunately records no instances of *coom*. Although this may be partly due to transcription errors (*coom* is not a dialect form generally known even to students of dialectology, and may therefore have gone unnoticed in the process of transcription), it is equally possible that this form has become increasingly marginal and was out of use by the time of the FRED recordings.

Where the most frequent past tense form of *come* is concerned, what was indicated by the widespread distribution already in Wright seems also confirmed in the SED. Contrary to Orton et al., who perhaps relied on their (mistakenly transposed) legend to the map for their introductory comment, past tense *come* in the SED is in fact the majority option and covers the whole country. For this reason a map would not be very helpful. Instead, it would be interesting to compare these older data with data from FRED, to

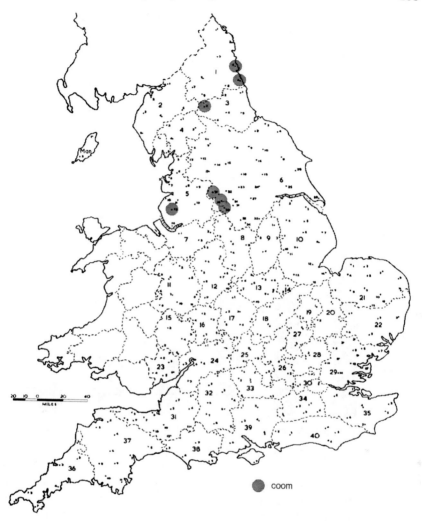

Map 6.6 Past tense *coom* in the SED (Basic Material)

investigate relative frequencies and to see whether increasing access to the standard may have changed the dominance of *come* over *came*.

6.1.4 Data from FRED

Because *come* is a highly frequent verb, and because disambiguating the past tense meaning of *come* for any but third person singular subjects involves an incredible amount of time while still remaining questionable, I restricted searches in FRED to *he/she/it come* vs. *he/she/it came*. For these forms,

Table 6.1 *Past tense* (he/she/it) come *in FRED*

Dialect area	*come*	*came*	Sum	% *come*
South East	137	63	200	68.5
Midlands	91	77	168	54.2
South West	139	131	270	51.5
North	77	206	283	27.2
Scotland	44	143	187	23.5
Wales	6	42	48	12.5
Isle of Man	3	2	5	60.0
Total	497	664	1,161	Ø 42.8

Ø = average.

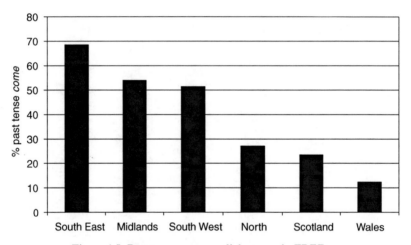

Figure 6.5 Past tense *come* per dialect area in FRED

presence and absence of *–s* unambiguously signals present vs. past tense. (Except of course in those dialects where third person *–s* is frequently deleted, i.e. especially East Anglia. Here, all instances of *come* were checked manually, and all dubious cases were excluded.) Oblique forms of the pronouns were also included in the search, as in some dialects, especially the South West, we can observe pronoun exchange – this applied in particular to *her come* (for *she come*). There are no occurrences of oblique pronouns in subject position with the standard *came*, so these two non-standard features (pronoun exchange and non-standard past tense *come*) seem to go together obligatorily.

All instances where *it* was the object preceding a verb were of course excluded (e.g. *let it come*). Figures of *he/she/it come* are simple percentages of all possible occurrences and thus indicate the extent to which this non-standard strategy is employed.

Table 6.1 and Figure 6.5 indicate strikingly that past tense *come* is indeed still a highly frequent phenomenon. Averages are above 50 per cent in three

Table 6.2 *Past tense* (he/she/it) come *in COLT*

	come	*came*	Sum	*% come*
Social group 1 (higher)	2	33	35	5.7
Social group 2 (middle)	0	12	12	0.0
Social group 3 (lower)	10	8	18	55.6
Total	12	53	65	18.5

dialect regions (the South East, the Midlands and the South West), and indeed the overall average is well above 40 per cent as well. Nevertheless, Table 6.1 also indicates a clear regional distribution, most clearly visible inside England. While the South West and the Midlands pattern very similarly (just over 50 per cent), the South East uses past tense *come* slightly more frequently (in almost 70 per cent of all cases), while the North uses *come* far less than the average (just under 30 per cent), or than its direct neighbour, the Midlands.[6]

Inside Scotland, only the Lowlands use past tense *come* to a significant degree (at around 27 per cent not really so differently from the English North). The Highlands and the Hebrides as the only areas that cannot look back onto a medieval English past seem to have taken over the standard English system after their switch from Gaelic to (Scottish) English.

The older, marginal form *coom* has been completely lost, and the non-regional *come* seems to have taken over as the general non-standard form, levelling more specifically regional dialectal differences.

6.1.5   Data from COLT

To compare the traditional dialect data from the South East with more present-day material, COLT was also searched for forms of *he/she/it come* vs. *came*. Again, all occurrences were manually disambiguated. The results are displayed in Table 6.2.

Table 6.2 shows that past tense *come* is clearly a socially stratified feature; it only really occurs in social group 3. Here, however, it is very frequent; in fact it is the majority option over standard *came*. A comparison with figures from FRED, where *come* occurred at a frequency of 68.5 per cent for the South East, shows that there is no statistically significant difference between

---

[6] Again, this distribution is supported by the statistical analysis. Overall, the dialect areas are significantly different at df=6, p<0.001. More specifically, the South East behaves significantly differently from all other dialect areas (at df=1, p<0.001 for every pairwise comparison). The Midlands and the Scottish Lowlands show no significant difference, but are different from all other dialect areas (at df=1, p between 0.025 and 0.001 for all other dialect areas). Finally, Scotland and the North seem to be quite similar to each other (at df=1, p<1).

them.[7] Past tense *come* is thus still a frequent feature of non-standard dialects, albeit a sharply stratified one.

6.1.6   Summary and explanation

The use of non-standard past tense *come* leads to a paradigm that is almost maximally levelled and that features little redundancy. Levelling of *come* results in a paradigm with no morphological distinctions, i.e. a class 3 verb with the pattern PRES = PPL ≠ PAST is instead found in class 5, where all three forms are identical (PRES = PAST = PPL). Indeed, such a levelled paradigm is highly speaker economical, but not very hearer economical. (Nor is it very researcher friendly.) It may impede communication, because the context has to provide all the information on tense; disambiguation is therefore always difficult (for the listener and much more so for the linguist). This of course only holds for the past tense, as the participle is marked for the perfect (or the passive) analytically, which might be a reason why *come* is acceptable in the standard as the past participle. Furthermore, in the past tense, non-distinction holds only for non-third person subjects, as Figure 6.6 shows.

The third person past tense can as a rule unambiguously be recognized by the fact that the present tense –*s* is missing (at least in those dialects – most – that do preserve the third person singular –*s*). Nevertheless, levelling of *come* leads to an extremely odd typological situation, as it results in a construction that contradicts all markedness relations: in the system that contains past tense *come*, only the present is marked by 'something' (namely –*s*), but the past is not marked morphologically at all, or is marked by zero, resulting in a counter-iconic paradigm in Mayerthaler's terms (see section 2.9.1). This seems to be a

Present tense		Past tense		Present perfect	
he		he		he	
she	comes	she		she	has come
it		it		it	
I		I	come	I	
we	come	we		we	have come
you		you		you	
they		they		they	

Figure 6.6 Paradigm of non-standard *come*

[7] Calculated for a 2×2 table with df=1.

very strange coincidence of history and stresses the fact that typology does not seem to be a main motivating factor in morphological change.

This raises the question why past tense *come* seems to be so remarkably stable. Of course it is the historically attested form that simply persists, but its counter-iconic pattern should make it unstable and subject to change. Yet the opposite seems to be the case. In my view, this is due to the phonological shape of the past tense form. The pattern /kʌm/ looks suspiciously like Bybee's prototypical template for a 'good' past tense form (see section 5.2), as Figure 6.7 explicates.

In other words, I would argue that *come* has become a Bybee verb (Figure 6.8). It fits the general past tense schema without adaptations (although its present tense form is of course quite different). The past tense form *come* is stabilized by the phonologically similar Bybee verbs, which it has come to resemble due to historical coincidences. (For the integration of *come* into the prototypicality grid, see Figure 6.13.)

Note that I am not claiming that the existence of the large class of past tense verb forms conforming to the Bybee pattern was the motivation for the establishment of the non-standard form *come*. We have seen quite clearly above that *come* is motivated through historical continuity; it is simply the 'regular' past tense form derived from the Old English and Middle English

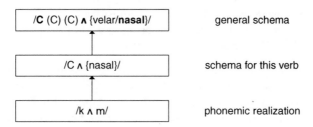

Figure 6.7 Schema for past tense *come*

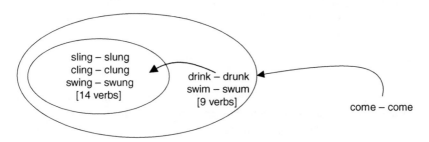

Figure 6.8 *Come* as a Bybee verb

forms. However, when we ask about the present-day stability of this form, I would argue that non-standard past tense *come* is stable through sufficient similarity with a stable class. In fact, one could call the phonotactic pattern [C (C) (C) Λ{velar/nasal}] a stable marker of the past tense in (non-standard) English. Having the same stable marker in its tense paradigm also makes the otherwise system-incongruent past tense *come* more natural in the sense of Wurzel, and through this higher system-dependent naturalness it becomes more stable itself.

6.2 Past tense *run*

6.2.1 Introduction

(4) Myself and another girl – we went and *run* and jumped on this tramway car. (HEB 033) (Hebrides, Scotland)

(5) He *run* away from home when he were a young lad. (FRED LAN 005) (Lancashire, North)

(6) I stood there like a mug, I got the one, oh he hit me alright, so I *run* after that, and when I got home I thought I'll tell my parents and that all what happened like. (FRED NTT 013) (Nottinghamshire, Midlands)

(7) It was a spanking place, and, but it was girls what *run* it. Three or four-hundred girls what *run* the, made the cordite then. There wasn't no men on the factory. (FRED KEN 003) (Kent, South East)

(8) We sailed from there to Huelva, in Spain with a cargo of iron ore. On the way back we *run* into rough weather, and I'd had just about a bellyful of it. (FRED GLA 006) (Glamorgan, Wales)

The analysis for *run* is similar to *come*, although the history as well as the regional patterns are quite different. *Come* and *run* do have in common, however, that they on their own constitute the standard English verb class 5 (with the pattern PRES = PPL ≠ PAST). Both *come* and *run* are noticeably more frequent than the other verbs under discussion in this book: as detailed on page 13 (footnote) in Francis and Kučera (1982) *come* is the eleventh most frequent verb; counting only lexical verbs, it is even the fifth most frequent verb overall (after *say*, *make*, *go* and *take*). *Run* is not quite as frequent, but still ranks among the top thirty irregular verbs, i.e. is highly frequent.

6.2.2 History

6.2.2.1 Present tense
In contrast to the verb *come*, the fact that the one form *run* is used for all tenses in at least some non-standard systems seems to be due not to a levelling (or a historical coincidence) of the past tense form, but to divergent developments in the present tense stem, which became identical to past tense and past participle.

The OED points out that present-day English *run* has precursors in several lexemes, which eventually fell together. In particular, they note that the causative verb was *ærnan* or *earnan* (a weak verb), which later extended to the transitive meaning and then fell together with the strong intransitive verb (OED: s.v. *run* v.).[8] The Old English precursor of the strong intransitive verb *run* belonged to verb class IIIa with the paradigm *rinnan* – *ran*, *runnon* – *runnen* (Krygier 1994: 44–5), i.e. together with what later became Bybee verbs (*clingan* – *clang*, *clungon – *clungen*) and non-standard Bybee verbs (*drincan* – *dranc*, *druncon* – *druncen*). However, at least part of the reason why *run* subsequently developed quite differently from *cling* or *drink* may lie in the fact that already in Old English, *run* underwent different developments. Krygier notes that '*brinnan* ["to burn"] and *rinnan* … were metathesized in prehistoric times and moved to the subclass IIIb' (Krygier 1994: 45); the metathesized paradigm being *irnan* – *arn*, *urnon* – *urnen* with vowel variants (Krygier 1994: 46–8). Jespersen also notes that next to the Old English infinitive *rinnan*, the metathesized form *irnan* was more frequent (Jespersen 1942: 55), pointing out that Middle English *rinne(n)* may be (partly) of Scandinavian origin. The OED equally stresses that the usual present tense stem had metathesis: 'The prevailing form in all [Old English] dialects appears to have been that with metathesis, *irnan, iernan, yrnan*' (OED: s.v. *run* v.), with the past tense *arn* or *orn*, plural *urnon*, and the participle *urnen* (OED: s.v. *run* v.). The Scandinavian influence can, however, only explain the choice of the unmetathesized over the metathesized form, i.e. the position of the *r* in the present tense stem, not the shape of the present-day vowel. As Jespersen admits, 'the ModE present stem *run* is hard to explain' (Jespersen 1942: 55).

Like Jespersen, the ODEE also cites Old Norse as the most likely influence on the forms without *r*-metathesis: 'The common ME. present tense forms *rinne, renne*, were prob[ably] due to ON[Old Norse] *rinna, renna*, with pt. *ran*, pp. *run*, reinforced from the same source' (ODEE: s.v. *run*1). This explains why the more traditional metathesized forms could persist especially in the South West, perhaps until today.

Data in the *County Dictionary* in LALME document that in the fourteenth century, metathesized forms are still present regionally in the upper South West, as well as sporadically in the South East, as Map 6.7 indicates (data from LALME Vol. 4: 238–9; see also LALME Vol. 1: map 1060).

Data from the EDD some four centuries later still confirm this medieval regional distribution. The only 'dialectal' grammatical forms noted for the present tense are *arn, hirn, hurn* and *urn*, mirroring the variety of metathesized forms in LALME above. With the exception of one attestation from

---

[8] As the OED points out, cf. the etymologically related German *rinnen* vs. *rennen* vs. *gerinnen* for some differences in meaning.

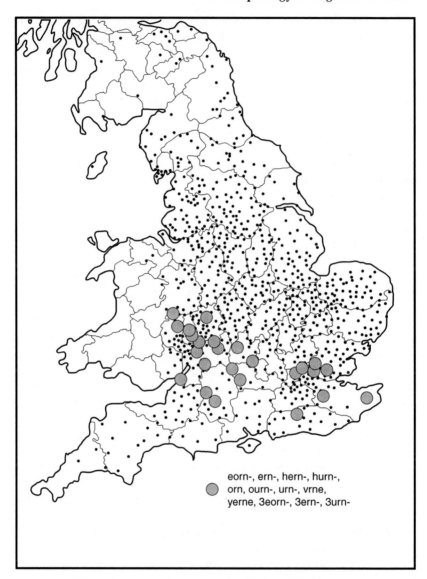

eorn-, ern-, hern-, hurn-,
orn, ourn-, urn-, vrne,
yerne, 3eorn-, 3ern-, 3urn-

Map 6.7 Present tense *run* metathesis in LALME

mid-Yorkshire [6] (*arn*), all come from the South West (Somerset [31] and Devon [37]).

While language contact with Old Norse is thus a plausible explanation for the emergence of verbal forms without metathesis, it does not account for the present-day English present tense vowel <u> in *run*. From the attested

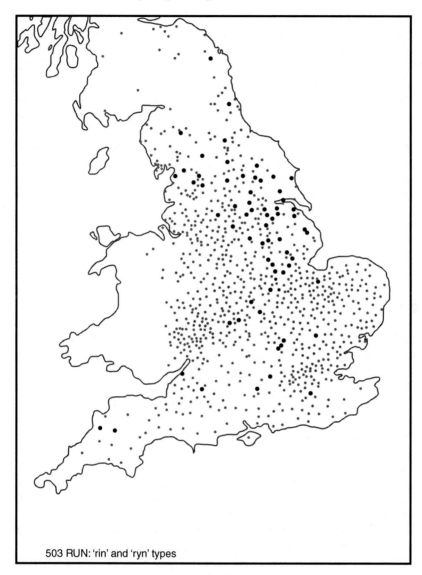

503 RUN: 'rin' and 'ryn' types

Map 6.8 Present tense *rin* in LALME

sources, we would expect a regular paradigm **rin – ran – run*, instead of
present-day English *run – ran – run*. *Rin* is indeed attested for late Middle
English in LALME in an area that looks suspiciously like the Danelaw (see
dot map 503 in LALME Vol. 1: 430, reproduced as Map 6.8).

Present tense *rin* today is still found dialectally, especially in Scots, as in
the well-known 'bairnsang' (Scottish nursery rhyme) by William Miller,
'Wee Willie Winkie rins through the toun' (Stedman 1895) (although this

is probably better known in the English version, 'Wee Willie Winkie *runs* through the town'). The OED confirms that forms like *rin* were and indeed still are 'chiefly northern and Scottish' (OED: s.v. *run* v.).

Forms in <u> in the present tense are not quoted in the OED before the fifteenth century, e.g. *run, runnande, runnyng*; in fact, inflected forms appear much later (e.g. the first person singular *runne* not before the seventeenth century, the imperative likewise, as the ODEE also notes, cf. the quote immediately below). While Jespersen is basically silent on the history of present tense *run*, the ODEE adduces early levelling with past tense/past participle forms: 'in finite parts of this vb.[verb] the present form with −*u*- is not current before XVI [the seventeenth century] (*runne*), but the var.[iant] *ronne* is earlier. The vowel resulted from levelling through forms in which it was original, viz. pt. [past tense] pl. *runnen* (OE *runnon*), and pp. [past participle] *runne(n), ronnen* (pp. [past participle] *gerunnen* coagulated, curdled)' (ODEE: run1). Wyld on the other hand speculates that 'the old Sthn.[Southern] *yrnan* would become M.E. *ürnen*, which with metathesis would give *rünnen* and Mod[ern] *run*. On the other hand, this might be derived from Merc[ian] *eornan*, which would also become *ürnen* in W[est] Midl[ands] (*y* from *æ*)' (Wyld 1927: 274).

When we look at actual data on Middle English verb forms, in over 500 entries for present tense *run*, the *County Dictionary* in LALME cites only one form with a clear <u> (*runn-* from Cheshire), and only three forms with <o> before the <n>, which as a *minim*-spelling might indicate /u/ (LALME Vol. 4: 238–9).[9] All three attestations with <o> are from Norfolk. Even taken together, these four forms amount to well under 1 per cent of all attested present tense forms of *run*. The majority form of present tense *run* in LALME is *renne* (and spelling variants), with *rynne* a poor second. Therefore, the spread of present tense *run* clearly has to be dated after late Middle English.

If we trace the spelling of unmetathesized present tense (and infinitive) *run* in the Helsinki corpus over the periods of interest here, i.e. Middle English and Early Modern English, the shift from *renne* to *run* becomes a little easier to date. Table 6.3 indicates the number of all spelling variants of the present tense stem of *run* over the Middle and Early Modern English periods, subdivided by the Helsinki corpus subdivisions (four for Middle English, three for Early Modern English, of roughly seventy years each – with the exception of the first period, which spans a century). Only unmetathesized forms were included.

The Middle English dominance of *renne* (and spelling variants) is apparent already from the raw figures (between 1250 and 1500 it is the only, or else the dominant option), supporting the data from LALME for the end of

---

[9] It should be borne in mind that LALME indicates types per manuscript, not tokens. Even so, the figures are very small.

Table 6.3 *Diachronic development of present tense* run *(Helsinki corpus)*

		<i> or <y>	<e>	<o>	<u>	Sum
Middle English	−1250	5	0	0	**4**	9
	−1350	0	**8**	0	0	8
	−1420	0	**27**	0	0	27
	−1500	4	**19**	1	0	24
Early Modern	−1570	0	13	8	**17**	38
English	−1640	0	0	3	**38**	41
	−1710	0	0	0	**69**	69

Note: dominant forms in bold type.

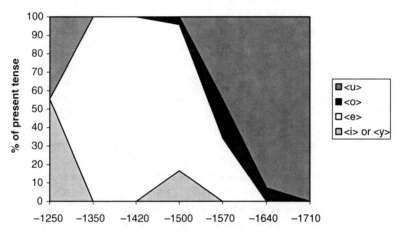

Figure 6.9   Present tense *run* (Helsinki corpus)

the fourteenth century above. The dominance of *run* is clear for the last two periods, where *ron* – in all probability – serves as a mere spelling variant. The two intermediate periods, roughly between 1500 and 1640, seem to be a period of rapid change, at least in writing, where *run* came to be determined as the standard English form. Graphically, this change can best be displayed in an area chart, as in Figure 6.9.

The lightest area indicates spellings in <e> in percentages for the individual points in time. The mere surface area of this variant already indicates its dominance from 1350 onwards. <i> or <y> at least in Middle English seems to have been no more than a minority option (we have seen the regional restriction of this form in Map 6.8). From 1500, we see that first forms in <o>, then forms in <u> rapidly take over, in fact displaying an impressive

S-curve of change. By 1710, the change to a present tense form *run*, at least in writing, is complete.

Unfortunately, this result still does not answer the question 'why'.[10] Why was a minority variant chosen: was it in fact the Norfolk variant, as the data from LALME tentatively suggest, and if so, what influence did Norfolk speech have in sixteenth-century London? Was *run* chosen in the new emerging standard because it was clearly different from a perceived regional, northern form *rin?*[11] And why did it spread so rapidly? Unfortunately, these questions cannot be answered with the materials at hand, but they might prove to be an interesting starting point for an in-depth study of this neglected verbal paradigm.

6.2.2.2 Past tense

After this complicated history of the present tense form of *run*, the past tense is a little more straightforward. At least in the Helsinki corpus, the past tense in written texts was *ran* from Middle English onwards, with very little or even no variation. This is slightly different in LALME. The *County Dictionary* gives forms for the past tense of *run*, but restricts itself to the south of the country (LALME Vol. 4: 239). (Unfortunately, the north was not sampled for the past tense, only for the present tense, cf. LALME Vol. 1: 553, Vol. 4: xvii, 238–9.) Of the 129 forms and texts attested, 40 still display metathesis (i.e. *arnde, ornen, urnen* or *gorn*), i.e. roughly one-third.[12] A tiny minority of three attestations have forms in <e>, but *ran* or *ranne* is the majority option in almost half of all instances (63 out of 129). However, there is the sizeable number of 23 texts which display an unmetathesized past tense form in <u>. Their regional distribution is indicated in Map 6.9.

Map 6.9 shows that in the late Middle English period, past tense *run* is restricted to a narrow belt in the South to Midlands. Although here metathesized forms still play a role, it is interesting to note that in general, 'mixed' paradigms (of metathesized and unmetathesized forms) do not seem to occur. Based on a careful comparison per text of present and past tense forms, data from LALME clearly indicate that metathesized present and past tense forms tend to co-occur in a text, as do past tense <ron> and present tense <renne> (LALME Vol. 4: 238–9).[13] Unfortunately, we cannot say anything

---

[10] As a curious aside, Halle and Mohanan in their much criticized version of Lexical Phonology and Morphology – and probably completely unintentionally – do in fact propose /rin/ as the underlying form of the present tense form /rʌn/, which is derived through a battery of phonological rules (Halle and Mohanan 1985).

[11] On the difficulty (and danger) of projecting backwards our present-day notions of 'northern' vs. 'southern' and their antagonism, see Wales (2000, 2006).

[12] LALME does not distinguish the transitive or causative weak verb. *Arnde* at least looks as if it belonged to this category.

[13] Although it has to be noted that for many texts, one of the forms is not attested. In particular, of twenty-six present tense metathesis forms, ten also have metathesis in the past, twelve have no attested past tense forms. Of twenty-two past tense forms <ron>, seven have present tense <renne>. Nine have no attested present tense.

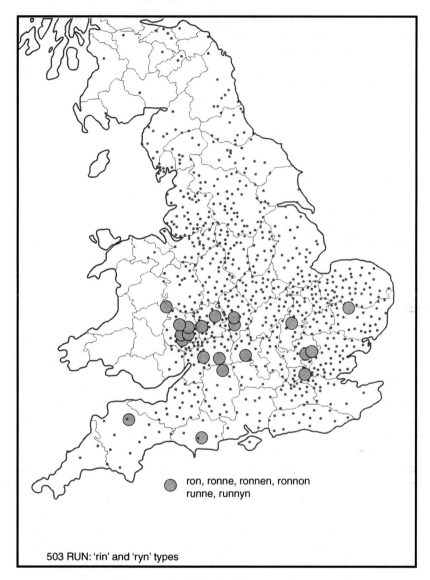

ron, ronne, ronnen, ronnon
runne, runnyn

503 RUN: 'rin' and 'ryn' types

Map 6.9 Past tense *run* in LALME

on the more northern distribution of past tense *run* in late medieval English, although from later evidence it is highly likely that Middle English past tense *run* was not a purely southern phenomenon.

As we have seen, like *cling* or *drink*, the paradigm of *run* used to rely on two stems in the past tense, one in <a>, one in <u>. It is therefore hardly surprising that after the breakdown of number inflection in Middle English, forms in <a> and <u> should have been variable (see the discussion in section 5.2.1.). It is perhaps more remarkable that instead of free variation, LALME displays a very orderly regional distribution of variants. Past tense *run* can thus be shown to have been a truly regional phenomenon at least since the fourteenth century.

Perhaps because of the regional distribution that is already apparent in Middle English, past tense *run* must early have acquired the connotation of being a dialectal form, as Jespersen writes: 'A [preterite] *run* is found, by the side of the more common *ran*, in a great many writers from the 16th to the 19th century ... The form is used to characterize dialectal speech ...' (Jespersen 1942: 55–6).

Past tense *run* is also noted in contemporary reference grammars from the very beginning (i.e. from the second half of the sixteenth century onwards, e.g. in OGREVE; see Poplack et al. 2002: 97). Unlike some of the other past tense forms, notably *eat*, past tense *run* was commented on unfavourably relatively early on, since 1771. This also supports the observations from Jespersen above, as past tense *run* must have served as a characteristic of dialectal speech.

6.2.3   Historical dialects

Apart from the continuation of metathesized forms as documented in the EDD, Wright also notes cases where *run* is used as a past tense form. In particular, he notes this for northern Ireland, west Yorkshire [6], south Cheshire [7], Lincolnshire [10] on the one hand, Surrey [34] and Kent [35] on the other, thus basically establishing a northern and a distinct southern regional distribution, as Map 6.10 shows. As LALME is unfortunately silent on the northern distribution of past tense forms of *run*, it cannot be established whether *run* might also have historical antecedents in that part of the country. Note, however, that the philosopher David Hume in 1752 marked out past tense *run* as one of the Scotticisms (probably of his) to be avoided (and to be substituted by standard English past tense *ran*) (quoted in Dossena 2005: 67).

Strangely, despite considerable dialectal variation and interesting regional distributions historically (in both the present and the past tenses), not to mention its high frequency, the verb *run* is not part of the established SED questionnaire, and we cannot therefore draw on the fine grid of informants for this phenomenon. We will turn to data from FRED instead.

6.2.4   Data from FRED

6.2.4.1   Procedure
For past tense *run*, searches in the FRED texts were not restricted to third person singular contexts. Although *run* is a frequent verb, it is not nearly as frequent as *come*, and where a dialect area might have five or six occurrences of third person *run*, it might have around twenty or so with other subjects. Since a concentration on the third person singular may have distorted results,

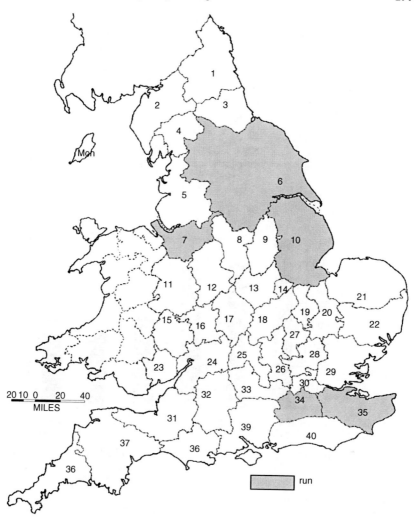

Map 6.10 Past tense *run* in the EDD

all instances of *run* were manually checked and analysed. One instance of a metathesized form seems to have survived; this one is, as expected, from the South West, and runs like this:

(9) Well now there's about sixty, I think they've got on the register and actu-
     ally I don' know if it's gonna work, been trying to get *urn* a Thursday
     afternoon meeting for people that don' like coming out n' out t' is dark
     nights n' that. (FRED SOM 034) (Somerset, South West)

Table 6.4 *Past tense* run *in FRED*

Dialect area	*run*	*ran*	Sum	*% run*
North	19	5	24	79.2
Midlands	40	17	57	70.2
South East	76	38	114	66.7
Wales	4	5	9	44.4
Scotland	13	25	38	34.2
South West	30	59	89	33.7
Total	182	149	331	55.0

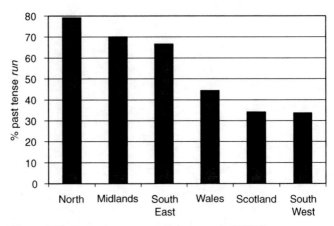

Figure 6.10   Past tense *run* per dialect area in FRED

6.2.4.2   *Quantification*

All unambiguous instances of past tense *run* (examples in (4) to (8) above) were calculated per county and then per dialect area, and the same was done for the standard English equivalent *ran*. Instances of *did run*, especially in the South West, were excluded.[14]

Counted by dialect region, occurrences of past tense *run* vs. *ran* are detailed in Table 6.4. As Table 6.4 and Figure 6.10 show, figures for past tense *run* are exceptionally high; past tense *run* is used in the majority, in fact in two-thirds to three-quarters, of all cases in the North, the Midlands and the South East. On the one hand, this confirms Wright's (and Hume's)

---

[14] There are only a handful of examples, but from the context it is not feasible to determine which examples are unemphatic. Because of the small number, figures are not seriously skewed by this exclusion.

documentation of past tense *run* in the North as well as the South East; on the other hand, the high frequency in the Midlands links these two strongholds of past tense *run*. Past tense *run* is still common in the South West, in Wales and in Scotland, but at around 33 per cent only about half as frequent as in the first group.[15] The high frequency group forms a coherent area that can be described as basically 'eastern' and is striking in comparison with the medieval distribution in LALME in Map 6.9, where past tense *run* was clearly a minority variant in the South.[16]

6.2.5 Data from COLT

Unfortunately, the verb *run* is comparatively less frequent than *come* in COLT, and quantification is therefore not a very sensible strategy. Although all occurrences of *run* were checked manually, only four cases of a clear past tense form could be identified. Interestingly, however, two come from social class 1, and two from social class 3. In both cases, past tense *ran* is the majority option (with twelve occurrences in both cases, resulting in a percentage for non-standard past tense *run* of just over 14 per cent). However, absolute figures are so low that no sensible analysis follows from these numbers. It could perhaps be argued that past tense *run* today in the South East is not a frequent phenomenon, but in the absence of more data little can be said at the moment about its present-day status.

6.2.6 Cognitive explanation

Although the use of past tense *run*, rather than the StE *ran*, results in a maximally levelled paradigm as for *come – come – come* above, the use of *run* as a past tense form is well motivated historically, as we have seen, and we can also motivate it functionally. Past tense *run* again conforms to Bybee's template of a prototypical past tense form, as Figures 6.11 and 6.12 indicate.

Again, we have seen that the choice of this form is due to historical coincidences (although these are not entirely clear yet for this verb form, as this discussion has shown, especially in their sociolinguistic impact). The form

[15] The statistical analysis confirms the strong differences, but also hints at gradience for this phenomenon. Overall, Table 6.4 shows significant statistical differences (at df=5, p<0.001). There are no differences between the North, Midlands, South East and Wales in pairwise comparisons, but the first three areas are significantly different from Scotland and the South West (at df=1, p<0.001). Wales seems to have an in-between status, as it is not significantly different either from the high frequency areas (North, Midlands and South East) (at df=1, p between 0.20 and 1), or from the lower frequency ones (Scotland and the South West) (at df=1, p<1 in both cases). Finally, Scotland and the South West are also not significantly different (at df=1, p<1).

[16] As noted above, however, we cannot say anything about past tense forms of *run* in the North in LALME.

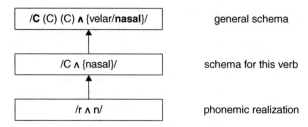

Figure 6.11 Schema for past tense *run*

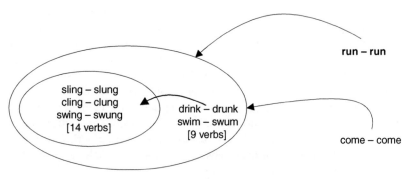

Figure 6.12 *Run* as a Bybee verb

as such seems to be able to persist at such astonishing frequencies of up to 80 per cent in FRED, however, despite the fact that it results in a counter-iconic paradigm that also runs counter to the system-defining structural properties of the English verbal inflectional system. Again, I would argue that this is due to the fact that it conforms to Bybee's template and is thus a 'good' past tense form – despite having identical forms in present and past tense. Bybee's template represents a stable marker of past tense inflection and confers stability on the whole paradigm as well. As such, past tense *run* is indeed a more natural past tense form than the standard English past tense *ran*.

6.3   Chapter conclusion

We have seen that in the cases of *come* and *run*, the maximally levelled paradigms that we can observe and that seem to be remarkably stable in non-standard speech today are due to various historical coincidences. In the case of *come*, past tense *come* can be explained as the historically continuous form that, through regular phonological changes, happened to converge on the same vowel (as do *cut* and *blood* today), although they can be traced

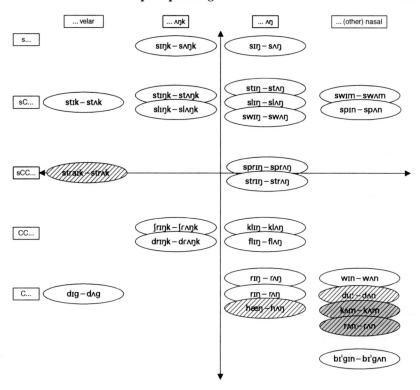

Figure 6.13 Prototypicality grid of Bybee verbs, including *come* and *run*

back to quite different vowel sounds in Middle English. In the paradigm of *come*, we have seen that it is only the standard English form *came* that is in need of explanation (although its rise in the context of emerging standardization can be documented and traced convincingly). We have seen that non-standard past tense *come* is not only the historically continuous form, it is also well motivated functionally, as it conforms to the schema for Bybee verbs – a template that, as we have argued, confers considerable stability on its paradigms.

In the case of *run*, on the other hand, it is the present tense *run* that is in need of explanation. The alternation between *run* and *ran* in the past tense can, as in the case of non-standard Bybee verbs, be traced to the variability between the preterite I and preterite II stems in Middle English after the breakdown of number inflection during this time, and is thus ultimately parallel to the non-standard Bybee verbs discussed in Chapter 5. Again, non-standard past tense *run* conforms to the schema for Bybee verbs, which in turn confers considerable stability on this past tense form. As a summary, we can integrate both past tense *come* and past tense *run* into the overall prototypicality grid for Bybee verbs in Figure 6.13. *Come* and *run* can be found near the bottom right corner (marked for easier identification by a grey background), indicating that they are rather marginal members of this verb class. (However, they are slightly better exemplars than *begun*.) The diagonal lines indicate that like *strike*, *hang* and *do*, *come* and *run* have present tense forms that do not include the vowel /ɪ/ – recall that this was Bybee's original motivation in postulating product-oriented schemas, as input-oriented rules cannot account for this phenomenon. Although *come* and *run* have a slightly marginal position, then, one can see that they are well integrated into this verb class overall. It is therefore highly likely that they will continue to profit from this association by remaining stable past tense forms in non-standard systems.

7 Conclusion: supralocalization and morphological theories

Much regional variation is being lost as the large number of traditional dialects covering small geographical areas gradually disappear from most, though by no means all, parts of the country. These, however, are being replaced by a much smaller number of new modern dialect areas covering much larger areas. The dialects and accents associated with these areas are much less different from one another, and much less different from RP and Standard English, than the traditional dialects were.
(Trudgill 2001: 179)

7.1 Summary of findings

The most striking result of this investigation is the fact that processes predicted by universal morphological naturalness (Mayerthaler) play only a minor role. If anything, universal natural morphology predicts in the realm of the verb a continuous shift of strong verbs into the weak verb class ('weakification'). However, the investigation in Chapter 4 has shown that while weakification does take place, it is by no means frequent and, in the majority of cases, can be explained by the retention of historically attested forms. Weakification, contrary to Mayerthaler's predictions, thus constitutes only a minor strategy. In the comparison with more modern data especially (e.g. from COLT, representing London teenage speech in the 1990s), we can see that strong verbs are remarkably resilient and resist the trend towards weakification on a grand scale.

Interestingly, non-standard verb systems do not employ the standard English verb forms to a great extent either (although in place of non-standard weak forms, they do in fact employ the respective (standard English) strong verbs in the majority of cases). On the contrary, the verb systems investigated in this book are in fact characterized by a high degree of non-standardness. This is mainly due to the fact that highly frequent strong verb paradigms have different strong forms. Non-standard strong verbs differ from standard English in particular in one respect: the dominant marker of standard English strong verbs – past tense <u> as in *string – strung – strung* or *cling – clung – clung* – has expanded at the cost of distinctive past tense vs. past participle forms in three-part (and even two-part) paradigms: it is found in the group of verbs clustering around *drink – drunk – drunk* and even in *come – come – come* and *run – run – run*. While in standard English this past tense marker <u> characterizes the historically continuous group of Bybee verbs, it has extended in non-standard British English into the whole class of new Bybee verbs (*sing – sang – sung*). Recalling section 3.3.1, we have seen that the present-day English verb class 1 is characterized by two intersecting features: vowel mutation and a participle <-en>. The reader will recall that the group of verbs around *sing – sang – sung* is the only subclass in this verbal class in standard English that employs vowel mutation only to indicate paradigmatic contrasts. Merging this subclass with verb class 2, which only has two distinctive forms, in effect eliminates in these dialects all verb paradigms that have three distinct forms by way of vowel mutation only. In these dialects, the verbal system is simplified considerably, as verb class 1 can now be characterized by the fact that all verb paradigms have a participle in <-en>.

The past tense marker <u> has spread further, however. Apart from Bybee verbs and new Bybee verbs, as summarized above, it has also expanded its territory to *done* (another class 1 verb), effecting a functional split between main and auxiliary verb uses – a process that is perhaps best characterized as exaptation in the sense of Lass (1990), which utilizes linguistic 'junk' to express a new morphological distinction where the standard has none.

Finally, the past tense marker <u> has spread also to the two very frequent verbs *come* and *run*, in this case effectively attracting a complete verb class (verb class 3) – albeit a very small one. Although the actual forms have come about through a number of historical coincidences and completely idiosyncratic developments, as Chapter 6 has shown in detail, today the past tense forms of these two verbs (past tense *come* and past tense *run*) conform to the Bybee schema $[C\,(C)\,(C) \wedge \{velar/nasal\}]_{past}$ and thus constitute typical, or 'good', past tense forms phonologically. We have seen that these forms are remarkably stable, probably because of the phonological similarity with Bybee verbs proper. Again, in those dialects that employ past tense *come* and *run*, the verbal system is simplified considerably: with the switch of verb class 3 to verb class 2 only four verb classes remain instead of five.

By all these extensions, the past tense marker <u> (more exactly: the Bybee schema $[C\,(C)\,(C) \wedge \{velar/nasal\}]_{past}$) has become a very stable marker in the non-standard tense system, in return conferring stability upon verbal paradigms that contain it. The theoretical implications of this mechanism will be discussed below.

7.2   Supralocalization?

We can now turn to the question whether we can actually observe the emergence of some kind of new supraregional dialect when we look at non-standard verb systems in British dialects. As Trudgill observes, supralocalization is not really an appropriate concept for phonology, as here even the more general modern dialect areas mentioned above in the quotation 'are for the most part currently diverging, not converging' (Trudgill 2001: 179). On the other hand, there seem to be at least some features of phonology that currently seem to be spreading extremely rapidly, e.g. T-glottalization (cf. e.g. contributions in Foulkes and Docherty 1999; or Milroy et al. 1994), with concomitant de-stigmatization, while other, equally stereotypical features of South East England phonology have remained much more regionally restricted (e.g. L-vocalization, referred to by Trudgill as a 'specific regional feature'; see Trudgill 2001: 179).[1] A rapid spread, including 'city-hopping', has on the other hand been observed for discourse features such as the 'new' quotatives among teenagers (Andersen 2001; Macaulay 2001). These features, phonological or pragmatic, seem to have in common that they are spreading from the South East of England outwards, rather than in the opposite direction.

The interesting question in the context of this book certainly is: can we say anything about the spread of *morphological* non-standard features? If a new supraregional non-standard is emerging in Great Britain in these decades, is it also characterized by a more uniform morphology than the traditional dialects? If so, where do new supraregional forms originate, and what do they look like?

It is very noticeable in the individual analyses in this book that wherever we can discern some kind of diachronic development in the realm of verb paradigms, the South East of England is always in the vanguard. We do not find, say, features typical of traditional northern English, e.g. *tellt* or *sellt*, being imported into the speech of London teenagers today. (Although it has to be noted again that, in the absence of a nation-wide corpus of reliably transcribed speech, conclusions on real-time differences have to be mostly conjectures.) Secondly, in agreement with Trudgill's observation above, the wide array of attested dialectal variants seems to be giving way to few, but comparatively highly frequent variants which appear to be extremely resilient

---

[1] Cf. also the ongoing discussion of Estuary English, where modified features of Cockney can now be heard by a much larger part of the population. Whether this really constitutes a spread of non-standard features from London outwards to the Home Counties and possibly beyond, or whether this is an epiphenomenon of a change in social structure, a wider access (in)to the media, or a matter of prestige reversal ('not wanting to sound like a snob') is still being discussed; see Mugglestone (2003: 273–88) and Trudgill (2001: 176–80) and references therein.

in the face of 'opposition' from standard English and, more than that, which even seem to expand at the expense of the standard.

It is also noticeable that these fewer variants can be functionally motivated, and as a rule are more 'natural' than their standard counterpart (in the sense of Wurzel 1984). From the limited material available, I would like to postulate two hypotheses on criteria that a morphological feature has to fulfil in order to have a chance of spreading regionally (and, perhaps concomitantly, socially).

In order to become part of a supralocalized non-standard in Britain, a morphological feature has to be:

- More natural than the standard English, or indeed any other non-standard, alternative. This is an intralinguistic principle, but is ultimately related to cognitive motivation: in order to diffuse, a morphological feature has to be functionally motivated, either originally, or new learners have to be able to reconstruct a functional motivation. We will call this the PRINCIPLE OF HIGHER NATURALNESS.
- Strong in the South East, preferably endorsed by the (linguistically) powerful (because prestigious) trendsetting group of London teenagers. This is an extralinguistic principle, relating to – covert – prestige ('coolness'): in order to diffuse, a morphological feature has to be promoted by a prestigious, preferably trendsetting group. We will call this the PRINCIPLE OF HIGHER PRESTIGE.

Since we possess no dialect corpus of present-day young speakers that would be comparable to FRED (i.e. that would be regionally representative like the BNC, but reliably transcribed also for possibly stigmatized morphological features), these hypotheses, as mentioned above, at present remain at best working hypotheses. My preliminary tests against COLT really serve nothing else but the establishment of some first proposals. Very generally, however, results from COLT can also be supported by data from the internet. Results from weblogs, discussion forums and similarly informal meeting grounds tentatively suggest that in unmonitored informal written English (comparable to results from COLT) non-standard weak verbs hardly ever occur, whereas non-standard Bybee verbs are extremely frequent and seem quite well established in informal English today (Anderwald 2007).

My distinction of functional vs. social criteria may be reminiscent of Croft (2000). However, Croft claims that only language innovation is functionally motivated.[2] We have seen, however, that in all cases, those morphological forms that are good candidates for spreading are time-honoured: they can be traced back at least several centuries for the most part. In other words, only relatively recently has long-standing variation been resolved in favour of a small number of non-standard forms that are being distributed more widely

---

[2] For a critique, see Seiler (2006).

Table 7.1 *Supralocalization features*

	More natural	COLT	Less natural	COLT
South Eastern	Bybee verbs	+	past tense *give*	−
	past tense *done*	++	past tense *see*	−
	past tense *come*	++		
	past tense *run*	+		
Not South Eastern	past tense *seen*	−−	past tense *eat*	−

+ = attested, ++ = frequent, − = marginal, −− = not attested in COLT.

geographically. In the process of social as well as geographical diffusion, those dialectal variants seem to get selected that new speakers can motivate functionally. In particular, this applies to the group of new Bybee verbs and in general to the spread of the past tense marker <u>, but also to the functional split of *done*. I would therefore argue, *pace* Croft, that successful variants do not necessarily *come into existence* for functional reasons – instead, their origin is mostly idiosyncratic and unmotivated. Later on, however, in the process of widespread diffusion, variants may be re-interpreted in functional terms, and only those forms that can be given a functional interpretation have a good chance of being chosen for diffusion.

The second feature seems more straightforward. Only those (functionally motivated) variants are selected that are dominant in the influential group of South Eastern dialects.[3] In sum, a combination of the two criteria results in a two-by-two matrix, into which we can now add the verb forms under investigation in this book. I exclude non-standard weak verbs because they show no particular regional distribution and they are demonstrably infrequent in the traditional material as well as today, as pointed out above.

As Table 7.1 shows, all four fields can be filled by actual examples discussed over the course of this investigation. Starting with the least likely candidate for a supralocal morphological feature, past tense *eat* in the bottom right field (indicated by the white) fails both the intra and the extra-linguistic criterion. It is non-functional (in so far as present and past tense are identical) and not natural (it does not conform to the system-defining structural property PRES ≠ PAST = PPL, and also does not conform to the Bybee schema). On the regional criterion, we have seen that past tense *eat* is mostly a southwestern phenomenon (as section 5.5.2 has shown, it is not very frequent in the traditional dialects of the South East). We have also seen that past tense *eat* is not particularly frequent in data from COLT and thus it seems extremely unlikely that it will become part of a more general non-standard.

[3] In the absence of at least a nation-wide corpus of informal present-day speech, not to mention longitudinal studies, this remains conjectural, of course.

Moving to candidates that score a little better at least on one of the two criteria (indicated by a light grey), past tense *seen* in the bottom left field is more natural than *eat* (it conforms to the system-defining pattern PRES ≠ PAST = PPL, although it is not a Bybee verb), but it is not the dominant southeastern dialect form historically. Nevertheless, there are some indications that it is accepted on a moderate scale into the language of London teenagers. However, a geographical spread is not documented in the dialect literature (and can, unfortunately, not be detected on the basis of the current database); and COLT does not indicate any social spreading of this feature either. For this reason, it does not seem likely that past tense *seen* will become part of a supralocal non-standard in the foreseeable future, although it has slightly better chances than past tense *eat* above.

Past tense *give* and *see* on the other hand (in the top right field, also light grey) are as little natural as past tense *eat* (both share the system-incongruous pattern PRES = PAST ≠ PPL and neither are Bybee verbs), but both are traditional features of dialects of the South East, where they are indeed very frequent, as we have seen in the data from FRED. Strikingly, neither form really survives in COLT. Again, it therefore seems extremely unlikely that either verb form will become part of a supralocal non-standard in Britain.

We are left with the result that the Bybee verbs especially, extended by *done* as well as *come* and *run* in the top left field in Table 7.1, are 'alive and kicking', i.e. present to a high degree in the speech of London teenagers in the 1990s, and spreading into the higher social classes. They are extremely well motivated historically, functionally as well as sociolinguistically, and it is therefore not surprising that they are the first candidates for the possible supralocalization of non-standard morphological forms.

7.3   Morphological theories revisited

7.3.1   *Rules vs. representations*

As Bybee has pointed out, at least logically, rules and representations should be isomorphic, in that any representation can be expressed as a rule, and vice versa (Bybee 1988: 121–2). For example, an idiosyncratic past tense form (like *be – was*) that is found in a single individual lexeme is typically specified in the lexicon entry of that lexeme. This is the 'standard' solution in dual-route approaches and is clearly a solution that is based on representation. On the other hand, a lexeme-specific rule that changes the lexeme *be* (and only the lexeme *be*) to *was* in the past tense can be shown to work equally well, so that the outcome (the 'correct' past tense form *was* for *be*, and only for *be*) could in fact be modelled by either procedure. This (purely rule-based approach) is the approach hinted at by Chomsky and Halle (1968) for the English past tense forms, and implemented by Halle and Mohanan (1985) for practically all English strong verbs, where phonological rules apply to groups of fewer or more lexemes. In fact, Halle and Mohanan explicitly state that their 'rules of verb inflection constitute a continuum of productivity and generality that extends from affixation of the *–ed* suffix … to total suppletion' (Halle and Mohanan 1985: 104).[4]

The same claim of isomorphism between rules and representations may be intuitively less convincing if applied to the other end of the scale, namely typical 'rules'. It is, however, possible to show that the stronghold of rules, e.g. the 'wug' test, can also be modelled in a purely representational model. A very productive and general process like assigning the weak past tense form <-ed> to all regular, novel or loan verbs can be modelled not just by explicit rules, but can be shown to emerge from representations: it is clear that the recurring phonological forms /t/, /d/ and /ɪd/ are always systematically linked with the semantics 'past tense', and can thus be shown to emerge as an apparent 'morphemic rule' from the mere representations of the lexemes (in the sense of Bybee 1995), without being present in the system as an explicitly formulated rule.

If these two extremes (lexeme-specific forms – the prototypical domain of a representation; and very general forms – the prototypical domain of a rule) can be modelled by either method (rule or representation), it is clear that this will also hold for anything in between these two poles.

Although rules and representations may therefore in fact be logically equivalent to each other, Bybee points out that there are nevertheless points that a theory based only on rules misses, such as differences in paradigmatic relations, productivity or allomorphy (Bybee 1988: 121–2). In fact, all theories based on rules (i.e. Chomsky and Halle 1968, Lexical Phonology and Morphology, but also words-and-rules theories) fail to account for Bybee verbs, as Bybee herself has pointed out repeatedly. The investigation in the preceding chapters supports this point, as neither Bybee verbs proper, nor especially the attraction of the new Bybee verbs, as well as *done, come* and *run*, can be captured by input–output rules, since verbs become progressively unlike the prototype *string – strung*.

The most important point for our purposes here is the internal prototypical structure of the group of Bybee verbs (depicted, e.g., in Figure 6.13). The fact that this verb group has attracted verbs that do not have a present tense stem in <i> cannot be explained by an input–output rule, just as the internal structure of this verb class is only badly characterized by sufficient and

---

[4] It is clear that a host of lexeme-specific 'rules' may not be a particularly efficient or elegant way of building a system, but that is a meta-theoretical aspect that need not concern us here at the moment. A compromise solution is offered by McMahon, whose constrained model of Lexical Phonology and Morphology 'makes a distinction between a small subclass of strong verbs whose surface alternations are derivable from a single underlier without recourse to special rules, and the great majority where a productive phonological account is ruled out for the present day language' (McMahon 2000: 130).

necessary criteria. It is clearly similarity to the prototypical past tense forms *strung* or *sprung* that holds this verb class together. In Bybee's model, on the other hand, the similarity in output form can be captured by a product-oriented schema which emerges from the lexical association of these lexemes; in Wurzel's model, we would speak of a stable past tense marker across paradigms (two analyses that do not contradict each other). Bybee's associative network can in fact account for Wurzel's observation that stable (= frequent) markers can become hyperstable ('überstabil' in Wurzel's terms), 'detach' from their verb class and spread further through an inflectional system, conferring stability on the paradigms that adopt them and thus resist morphological change (Wurzel 1984: 136–42). We could picture this association in the style of Bybee's well-known diagram, expanded by the new Bybee verbs, as in Figure 7.1.[5]

As we have seen, Pinker (1998: 223–6) has modified his words-and-rules theory accordingly and added an associative component in the memory part of his theory, as he acknowledges explicitly, in order to 'show the kinds of associative effects that are well-modelled by pattern associators: families of similar irregular verbs are easier to store and recall … and people are prone to generalize irregular patterns to new verbs similar to known ones displaying that pattern' (Pinker 1998: 225), resulting in a compromise solution that can be shown to work well for English.

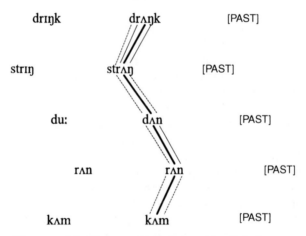

Figure 7.1 New Bybee verbs (as before, identical phonemes are marked by uninterrupted lines, similar ones by dotted lines)[6]

---

[5] Again, it has to be stressed that these diagrams are severely reduced; anything approaching a more realistic description would have to be multi-dimensional, taking into account many more properties of words and a multitude of cross-lexical links that are virtually impossible to depict in a two-dimensional diagram.

[6] Continued from Bybee (1985: 130; 1988: 135; 1995: 430, 1996: 250).

7.3.2   The role of frequency

From psycholinguistic data, in particular, it is clear that frequency has an important role to play in any theory that tries to model verb paradigms in a psychologically realistic way.[7] It is by now commonplace to claim that only highly frequent verbs can retain their irregular forms, while rare verbs tend to be regularized – a process that seems to accord well with cross-linguistic data, and of course also with the historical observation that strong verbs have tended to become weak in English over the course of the last millennium or so.[8] While the role of token frequency has thus long been acknowledged, only a few theories can incorporate the importance of type frequency. Especially in Bybee's network theory we have seen (graphically, in Figure 7.1) how the fact that a part of the past tense stem recurs over different types of verbs leads to the emergence of a past tense marker that may become detached from the present tense form altogether. Wurzel has formalized this to a greater degree and in fact built his theory on the fact that type frequency determines the size (and thus the power of attraction) of inflectional classes (e.g. Wurzel 1984: 86).

Rule-based accounts on the other hand would have to incorporate different types of rules to account for different ranges of productivity, at worst listing the group of verbs that can act as input to a particular rule. As long as rules typically are input–output rules, they will fail to account for this frequent phenomenon. As we have seen, Bybee's network model and Pinker's associative memory component can be shown to fare much better, as Bybee verbs as a group can clearly be structured on the basis of a product-oriented schema, also explaining the continuing attraction of this pattern.

7.3.3   Accounting for diachronic developments

The strict division of synchrony and diachrony – perhaps one of the major lasting impacts of de Saussure's dichotomy[9] (Saussure 1959) – is exemplified par excellence in expressly synchronic theories like Chomsky and Halle (1968) or Lexical Phonology and Morphology. As we have seen in sections 2.2 and 2.3, a diachronic dimension is completely (and of course

---

[7] This probably excludes generative accounts by definition. As Sankoff puts it, 'highly frequent phenomena ... are ... of no interest to the generativist, who does not encounter frequencies in the course of his or her analyses' (Sankoff 1988: 147).

[8] Against this commonplace statement it should perhaps be pointed out that the majority of strong verbs of Old English (if they haven't survived as strong verbs) have in fact simply died out. Although it is true that towards Middle English many verbs became weak, today only a handful of former strong verbs have survived with a weak paradigm, among them *help* (formerly *healp, hulpon – holpen*), *bake* (*boc, bocon – bacen*), *melt* (*mealt, multon – molten*) and *climban* (*clamb, clumbon – clumben*). See the overview in Krygier until Early Modern English (Krygier 1994).

[9] 'The opposition between the two viewpoints, the synchronic and the diachronic, is absolute and allows no compromise' (Saussure 1959: 83).

intentionally) missing from these synchronic models of English phonology and morphology; diachrony is built into native speakers' competence in the form of various rules instead, in order to account for the obvious residue of these long-standing phonological processes. Some examples may suffice: we find rules for x-deletion (to account for the absence of surface /x/ in *night* or *fought*, historically a late Middle English process), g-deletion (to account for *long/-ŋ/* vs. *longest /-ŋg-/*, an Early Modern English process), trisyllabic shortening (to account for the difference between *serene – serenity*, an Old English to early Middle English process), velar softening (to account for the alternation *critic – criticize* or *matrix – matrices*, this was no native English process at all, but has been inherited from Romance in loan words) or, of course, the famous Vowel Shift Rule (which includes reflexes of the Great Vowel Shift, but goes beyond it in many ways).[10]

Despite the obvious historical parallels, it should be borne in mind, as McMahon points out, that 'synchronic phonological rules and the diachronic sound changes which are their source need not be identical, or indeed bear much resemblance to one another' (McMahon 2000: 138) – as a consequence of which theorists are quite at liberty to stipulate any number of rules that can be made to account for the synchronically observable variation between lexemes, and indeed to stipulate almost any (often widely divergent) underlying form.[11] Apart from the fact that many other rules are stipulated ad hoc and are not motivated historically,[12] it may in fact be theoretically undesirable to separate synchronic and diachronic descriptions as rigorously as is still common in much linguistic theory. As the examples of rules above make clear, this division unnecessarily forces the theory to duplicate historical processes in synchronic description. As Blevins points out,

> simpler grammatical models are usually preferred to more complex ones ... if we can demonstrate that principled diachronic explanations exist for particular sound patterns, considerations of simplicity would seem to dictate that explanations for the same phenomena should not be imported into, or otherwise duplicated within, synchronic accounts. In all cases where clear diachronic explanations exist for a particular synchronic pattern, this diachronic explanation makes a synchronic account redundant, since the optimal description should not account for the same pattern twice.
> (Blevins 2004: 5)

---

[10] All rules are quoted according to Halle and Mohanan (1985). The historical assignment is mine.

[11] This is in fact one of the points of the theory criticized most frequently, and most vociferously, and the development after Halle and Mohanan (1985) seems to have gone in the opposite direction. Cf. McMahon (2000: 129–39) for a more restrained model with only modestly divergent underlying forms.

[12] For example the reverse of x-deletion: x-insertion, or yod-insertion ('y-insertion'); see the overview in Halle and Mohanan (1985: 100–1).

As a further consequence, purely synchronic theories run into trouble once they try to account for diachronic variation. As Kroch puts it: 'the [synchronic] grammatical perspective provides no vocabulary for the discussion of process' (Kroch 1989: 201). As is typical of generative approaches, language change in this school necessarily has to be abrupt and discontinuous;[13] the difference between two dialects (a term which would also include historical stages of the language) is modelled either as a different ordering of rules (e.g. in dialect A, rule 1 may apply before rule 2, but in dialect B the reverse order is stipulated), as differences in the rule inventory (e.g. dialect A may have three rules, dialect B just two, and dialect C four, etc.), or as differences in the application of rules (e.g. dialect A may not apply rule 1 to feature x, whereas dialect B does, etc. Cf. again Halle and Mohanan 1985; and also the application to dialect material by Harris 1989). As a generative model of language acquisition does not provide for the part acquisition of rules, language learners can only change the language by not acquiring a rule, reordering rules or inventing a new rule – processes that in any case cannot account for gradual change.[14]

Including as much diachrony as possible in a synchronic description, in addition, robs a theory of explanatory (and perhaps predictive) powers for processes of language change, not to mention intralinguistic variation. If we cannot model in this theory why a certain verb class has acted historically as an attractor, while others have in fact lost members, not only will it be explanatorily unsatisfactory, it will also be difficult to project this process into the future.

Natural morphology, especially language-specific naturalness in the sense of Wurzel (1984), on the other hand is notable for including diachronic developments in its theory and is in fact drawing much explana-

---

[13] 'When a language changes, it simply acquires a different grammar. The change from one grammar to another is necessarily instantaneous and its causes are necessarily external' (Kroch 1989: 201).

[14] This is a long-standing debate that I will not go into in more detail here; suffice it to say that the usual generative argument against gradual language change (as evinced in S-curves; for many historical examples, see Nevalainen and Raumolin-Brunberg 2003) is that gradualness is an epiphenomenon of sampling populations, rather than a characteristic of single speakers. As late as 1991, Lightfoot for example speaks of 'the *apparent* gradualness of change' by which linguists have been 'overimpressed' (Lightfoot 1991: 158 - my emphasis) – generativists generally hold instead that individual speakers show categorical behaviour, either displaying a certain feature (if they have rule x) or not. Lightfoot for example says that 'syntactic structures ... are not generally amenable to incremental modification' (1991: 160), and claims that 'the spread of a new parameter setting through a speech community is typically manifested by categorically different usage on the part of different authors rather than by variation within the usage of individuals, although the data are sometimes not as clean as that idealization would suggest, because a writer often commands more than one form of a language' (Lightfoot 1991: 162). Where speakers are variable in their behaviour, they operate with two (or more) different rule systems, i.e. are bi- or multi-dialectal (for one of the rare generative accounts in sociolinguistics, see Henry 1995).

tory power from diachronic shifts, e.g. between inflectional classes.[15] In the description of English verb classes we have seen that the diachronic development is responsible for idiosyncrasies like the behaviour of *have – had* and *make – made* (virtually the only lexical verbs that Halle and Mohanan have to exclude from treatment completely – probably because their rules cannot account for the deletion of the stem consonants; see Halle and Mohanan 1985: 105); diachronic processes are also responsible for coherent groups of verbs that used to be regular, but have come (through phonologically regular processes) to be morphologically highly irregular, like *keep – kept, bite – bit* or even *bring – brought*. We have also seen that many present-day inflectional classes are characterized by a high degree of diachronic continuity (e.g. verb class 5, *hit – hit – hit*, etc., is almost exclusively derived historically from apocopated verbs; what is left of Old English verb class IV, *bear – bore – borne*, is only found in verb class 1; survivors of Old English verb class V, *give – gave – given*, have also only entered verb class 1, whereas verbs based on quantitative changes, e.g. *feed – fed – fed*, are found almost exclusively in verb class 2). Finally, analogical pressure seems to affect historically continuous classes in particular (consider the behaviour of *knowed, blowed, growed*, etc. in the non-standard dialects in sections 4.4.2.3 and 4.4.4.1, but of course also the Bybee verbs, both old and new, in sections 5.2 and 5.4 and Chapter 6, which first seem to have extended to the historically related sister verb class, and then later to other verbs like *come* and *run*). It is therefore clearly desirable to work in a theory that can at least accommodate historical data.

7.3.4 *Non-standard data*

Finally, non-standard data present a problem for almost all linguistic theories. This is not a problem of principle: as any enlightened linguist knows, non-standard varieties are as systematic as standard languages, and can just as well be described with the help of sophisticated linguistic theories as the standard. As pointed out above in section 7.3.3, postulating separate sets of rules, differential rule ordering or differences in the extension of rules are some of the mechanisms that rule-based systems employ to describe (and 'explain') differences between dialects. Thus, in the framework of Lexical Phonology and Morphology, Harris (1989) investigates *æ*-tensing in different groups of dialects (northern US cities, mid-Atlantic, Belfast, Norwich, received pronunciation) and assigns the same rule to the postlexical stratum for some of these dialects, to the lexical strata for others (Harris 1989: 50).

---

[15] It has to be noted, though, that the synchronic description of the individual stages of a language in fact takes precedence also in this model. A main point of Wurzel's work on nominal classes is, however, the subsequent comparison of synchronic stages of the language, and the explanation in terms of verb class attractiveness. Many of his basic concepts are inherently diachronic, e.g. the distinction between stable and instable inflectional classes can only be observed in diachronic developments.

The problem therefore is not accounting for non-standard data as such, but accounting for inherent variability. Harris, for example, treats his dialects as monolithic, because the linguistic model forces him to do so.

The standard answer in modern sociolinguistic studies used to be the concept of the 'variable rule', which speakers apply with stochastic probabilities, and sophisticated statistical models have evolved to model speaker variation and the factors that constrain this variation (e.g. Labov 1969; see also the Varbrul algorithm developed by Cedergren and Sankoff 1974 and subsequent publications). While variable rules originated as a reaction to categorical rules e.g. in Chomsky and Halle (1968), they have subsequently not followed theoretical developments in the generative frameworks. Today, they are a very powerful descriptive tool (for some of the most prominent exponents, see Poplack and Tagliamonte 2001; and especially Tagliamonte 2006), whose theoretical status is, however, not clear any longer:[16] a body of variable rules does not constitute a linguistic theory per se and should in fact not be misunderstood as such, but amounts to a sophisticated descriptive apparatus; usually, these variable rules are not integrated further into current syntactic theories.

A study by Guy (1991; 1996) is a notable exception; working like Harris above in the framework of Lexical Phonology and Morphology, Guy tries to account for the inherent variability of sociolinguistic phenomena (rather than differences between dialects), in his case *t/d*-deletion. Guy introduces the concept of variable rules into Lexical Phonology and Morphology, claiming that, e.g., deletion rules may apply variably, and at all strata. In a multi-stratum structure, monomorphemic words will therefore be affected by the same deletion rule several times, as they proceed through the strata, resulting in a comparatively high ratio of deletion. Derived forms on the other hand will undergo the rule only once at a higher stratum. In this way, not only does the model predict the variability of this deletion process for an individual speaker, but it even predicts different ratios of deletion for different kinds of lexemes, depending on their morphological structure.

While this seems to work well for the phonological phenomenon under discussion, it is not clear how level ordering could account for variably strong verb forms. A fixed set of rules can probably never account for the fact that [*know*]+[PAST] sometimes surfaces as *knowed*, but sometimes as *knew*. As we have seen above for explanations of historical variability, the classical answer in generative accounts is the postulation of multiple grammars (e.g. a formal and an informal one), between which speakers would switch, perhaps according to the extralinguistic parameters of the situation.

---

[16] The application of variable rules presupposes, of course, that speakers are in fact variable in their behaviour, and that variability is not just an epiphenomenon of speaker aggregates – from sociolinguistic studies of the speech of individuals it is probably not contentious by now to claim that indeed, an individual's speech varies with intra and extralinguistic factors, *pace* Lightfoot (1991). For some recent arguments in this debate, see Preston (2004).

The answer in classical Optimality Theory is similar (if variation is discussed at all); Anttila for example postulates discrete constraint hierarchies for variable data (Anttila 2002), making Optimality Theory in this respect more similar to classical generativist accounts. The equivalent of variable rules in generative frameworks would perhaps be the status of constraints in stochastic Optimality Theory, where probabilities are built into the grammar, as detailed in section 2.5. The assumption is that all constraints are variable, and speakers modify the range and possibly the distance between constraints in the process of acquisition. Provided a language learner is exposed to variable input, stochastic Optimality Theory is one of the few frameworks that can be shown to model variability well.

Finally, it has to be said that Bybee's network model as well as Wurzel's natural morphology, employed in this book, can be shown to model non-standard data equally well as standard data, but also run into some difficulties in the representation of speaker variability. (As with most other theories, both models are not explicit on this point.) In Bybee's network model, variable input would presumably lead to branching representations, with *know* becoming part of two networks for its past tense forms. Apart from semantic labels (like [PRESENT] or [PAST]), forms could presumably also carry situational (formality) data ('this form is used in relaxed situations/with friends/in my village' vs. 'this form is used on the television/at school/with strangers'). (In the absence of explicit statements to this effect by Bybee herself, these ideas remain conjecture.) Different situations would then activate different networks, or parts of the network. Other effects, like the immediately preceding linguistic context (linguistic 'persistence', or priming, Szmrecsanyi 2006), could also be accommodated. (See also again Baayen's spreading activation network, e.g. Baayen 2003.) An example of such a branching network is provided in Figure 7.2.

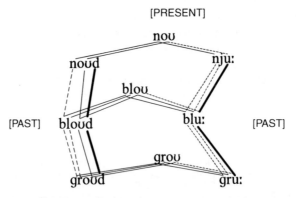

Figure 7.2 Extension of network model to variable data

The advantage that Wurzel's model of language-specific (but not universal) natural morphology has is that it can account for the direction of paradigm simplification and the stabilization of the inflectional system, which seems to be a prerequisite for a verb paradigm spreading further in the course of supralocalization. In so far as the modelling of non-standard data is linked to diachronic developments, Wurzel's and Bybee's models can be shown to fare reasonably well.

7.4   Summary

We have seen that virtually all theories have particular weaknesses modelling individual variability – this has not been the main concern of this book. Many theories can be seen to fare much better for diachronic variability, although also here much remains to be discussed. It is certainly the case that non-standard data can throw an interesting light on these theoretical debates, in many cases complicating matters considerably. Finally, psychological realism is probably still difficult to obtain as long as we cannot observe small-scale neuron and glia activities as they pertain to language use. In sum, this is a discussion where we obviously still seem to be very much at the beginning, but it is clear that non-standard data should be taken into account much more than has previously been the case, as this has the potential to enrich the discussion enormously. For this aim we need a thorough descriptive basis, one small part of which this book has tried to provide.

Appendix 1: Verb classification

List of Quirk et al.'s irregular verbs in alphabetical order (Quirk et al. 1985: 115–120); my classification in the right-hand column (Verb class in roman, Vowel pattern in *italics*, other features).

(Note: morphologically complex forms that were excluded from all counts are shown in italic.)

Base	Past tense	Past participle	LA classification		
			Class	*Vowel*	Other features*
abide	abode (abided)	abode (abided)	2	*V2a*	stem in /d/
arise	*arose*	*arisen*			
awake	*awoke (awaked)*	*awoken (awaked)*			
be	was/were	been	1	*V3*	ppl <-en>
bear	bore	borne	1	*V2a*	ppl <-en>
beat	beat	beaten (beat)	4	*V1*	ppl <-en>
become	*became*	*become*			
befall	*befell*	*befallen*			
beget	*begot*	*begotten*			
begin	began	begun	1	*V3*	
behold	*beheld*	*beheld*			
bend	bent	bent	2	*V1*	/d/ > /t/
bereave	bereft (bereaved)	bereft (bereaved)	2	*V2a*	+ /t/
beseech	besought (beseeched)	besought (beseeched)	2	*V2a*	C > /t/
beset	*beset*	*beset*			
bestride	*bestrode*	*bestridden (bestrid, bestrode)*			
bet	bet (betted)	bet (betted)	5	*V1*	
betake	*betook*	*betaken*			
bid	bad(e) (bid)	bade (bid, bidden)	5	*V1*	
bind	bound	bound	2	*V2a*	stem in /d/
bite	bit	bitten (bit)	1	*V2a*	ppl <-en>

(*cont.*)

			LA classification		
Base	Past tense	Past participle	Class	*Vowel*	Other features*
bleed	bled	bled	2	V_{2a}	stem in /d/
blow	blew	blown	1	V_{2c}	ppl <-en>
break	broke	broken	1	V_{2a}	ppl <-en>
breed	bred	bred	2	V_{2a}	stem in /d/
bring	brought	brought	2	V_{2a}	C > /t/
broadcast	broadcast	broadcast			
build	built	built	2	V_1	/d/ > /t/
burn	burnt (burned)	burnt (burned)	2	V_1	+ /t/
burst	burst	burst	5	V_1	
buy	bought	bought	2	V_{2a}	C > /t/
cast	cast	cast	5	V_1	
catch	caught	caught	2	V_{2a}	C > /t/
chide	chid (chided)	chidden (chid, chided)	1	V_2	ppl <-en>
choose	chose	chosen	1	V_{2a}	ppl <-en>
cleave	cleft (clove, cleaved)	cleft (cloven, cleaved)	2	V_{2a}	+ <t>
cling	clung	clung	2	V_{2a}	Bybee
come	came	come	3	V_{2c}	
cost	cost	cost	5	V_1	
creep	crept	crept	2	V_{2a}	+ <t>
cut	cut	cut	5	V_1	
deal	dealt	dealt	2	V_{2a}	+ <t>
deepfreeze	*deepfroze,- freezed*	*deepfrozen,- freezed*			
dig	dug	dug	2	V_{2a}	Bybee
do	did	done	1	V_3	ppl <-en>
draw	drew	drawn	1	V_{2c}	ppl <-en>
dream	dreamt (dreamed)	dreamt (dreamed)	2	V_{2a}	+ <t>
drink	drank	drunk	1	V_3	
drive	drove	driven	1	V_3	ppl <-en>
dwell	dwelt (dwelled)	dwelt (dwelled)	2	V_1	+ <t>
eat	ate	eaten	1	V_{2c}	ppl <-en>
fall	fell	fallen	1	V_{2c}	ppl <-en>
feed	fed	fed	2	V_{2a}	stem in /d/
feel	felt	felt	2	V_{2a}	+ <t>
fight	fought	fought	2	V_{2a}	+ <t>
find	found	found	2	V_{2a}	stem in /d/
flee	fled	fled	2	V_{2a}	+ <d>
fling	flung	flung	2	V_{2a}	Bybee
fly	flew	flown	1	V_3	ppl <-en>
forbear	*forbore*	*forborne*			
forbid	*forbade (forbad)*	*forbidden (forbid)*			
forecast	*forecast*	*forecast*			
foresee	*foresaw*	*foreseen*			

(*cont.*)

			LA classification		
Base	Past tense	Past participle	Class	*Vowel*	Other features*
foretell	*foretold*	*foretold*			
forget	*forgot*	*forgotten (forgot)*			
forgive	*forgave*	*forgiven*			
forgo	*forwent*	*forgone*			
forsake	forsook	forsaken	I	$V_{2}c$	ppl <-en>
forswear	*forswore*	*forsworn*			
freeze	froze	frozen	I	$V_{2}a$	ppl <-en>
get	got	got (gotten <Am E>)	2	$V_{2}a$	
give	gave	given	I	$V_{2}c$	ppl <-en>
go	went	gone	I	V_{3}	ppl <-en>
grind	ground	ground	2	$V_{2}a$	stem in <d>
grow	grew	grown	I	$V_{2}c$	ppl <-en>
hamstring	*hamstrung*	*hamstrung*			
hang	hung	hung	2	$V_{2}a$	Bybee
have	had	had	2	V_{1}	C > /d/
hear	heard	heard	2	$V_{2}a$	+ /d/
heave	hove (heaved)	hove (heaved)	2	$V_{2}a$	
hew	hewed	hewn (hewed)	I	V_{1}	past <-ed> ppl <-en>
hide	hid	hidden (hid)	I	$V_{2}a$	ppl <-en>
hit	hit	hit	5	V_{1}	
hold	held	held	2	$V_{2}a$	stem in /d/
hurt	hurt	hurt	5	V_{1}	
inset	inset	inset	5	V_{1}	
keep	kept	kept	2	$V_{2}a$	+ /t/
kneel	knelt (kneeled)	knelt (kneeled)	2	$V_{2}a$	+ /t/
knit	knit (knitted)	knit (knitted)	5	V_{1}	
know	knew	known	I	$V_{2}c$	ppl <-en>
lead	led	led	2	$V_{2}a$	stem in /d/
lean	leant (leaned)	leant (leaned)	2	$V_{2}a$	+ /t/
leap	leapt (leaped)	leapt (leaped)	2	$V_{2}a$	+ /t/
learn	learnt (learned)	learnt (learned)	2	V_{1}	+ /t/
leave	left	left	2	$V_{2}a$	+ /t/
lend	lent	lent	2	V_{1}	/d/ > /t/
let	let	let	5	V_{1}	
lie	lay	lain	I	$V_{2}a$	ppl <-en>
light	lit (lighted)	lit (lighted)	2	$V_{2}a$	stem in /t/
lose	lost	lost	2	$V_{2}a$	+ /t/
make	made	made	2	V_{1}	C > /d/
mean	meant	meant	2	$V_{2}a$	+ /t/
meet	met	met	2	$V_{2}a$	stem in /t/
miscast	*miscast*	*miscast*			
misdeal	*misdealt*	*misdealt*			
misgive	*misgave*	*misgiven*			
mishear	*misheard*	*misheard*			

(*cont.*)

			LA classification		
Base	Past tense	Past participle	Class	*Vowel*	Other features*
mislead	*misled*	*misled*			
misspell	*misspelt* (*misspelled*)	*misspelt* (*misspelled*)			
misspend	*misspent*	*misspent*			
mistake	*mistook*	*mistaken*			
misunderstand	*misunderstood*	*misunderstood*			
mow	mowed	mown (mowed)	1	V_1	past <-ed> ppl <-en>
offset	*offset*	*offset*			
outbid	*outbid*	*outbid* (*outbidden*)			
outdo	*outdid*	*outdone*			
outfight	*outfought*	*outfought*			
outgrow	*outgrew*	*outgrown*			
outrun	*outran*	*outrun*			
outshine	*outshone*	*outshone*			
overbear	*overbore*	*overborne*			
overcast	*overcast*	*overcast*			
overcome	*overcame*	*overcome*			
overdo	*overdid*	*overdone*			
overeat	*overate*	*overeaten*			
overfeed	*overfed*	*overfed*			
overhang	*overhung*	*overhung*			
override	*overrode*	*overridden*			
overrun	*overran*	*overrun*			
oversee	*oversaw*	*overseen*			
overshoot	*overshot*	*overshot*			
oversleep	*overslept*	*overslept*			
overtake	*overtook*	*overtaken*			
overthrow	*overthrew*	*overthrown*			
partake	*partook*	*partaken*			
put	put	put	5	V_1	
quit	quit (quitted)	quit (quitted)	5	V_1	
read	read	read	2	V_{2a}	stem in /d/
rebind	*rebound*	*rebound*			
rebuild	*rebuilt*	*rebuilt*			
recast	*recast*	*recast*			
redo	*redid*	*redone*			
remake	*remade*	*remade*			
rend	rent	rent	2	V_1	/d/ > /t/
reread	*reread*	*reread*			
rerun	*reran*	*rerun*			
reset	*reset*	*reset*			
restring	*restrung*	*restrung*			
retell	*retold*	*retold*			
rethink	*rethought*	*rethought*			
rewind	*rewound*	*rewound*			
rewrite	*rewrote*	*rewritten*			

(*cont.*)

			LA classification		
Base	Past tense	Past participle	Class	*Vowel*	Other features*
rid	rid (ridded)	rid (ridded)	5	V_1	
ride	rode	ridden	1	V_3	ppl <-en>
ring	rang (rung)	rung	1	V_3	
rise	rose	risen	1	V_3	ppl <-en>
run	ran	run	3	V_{2c}	
saw	sawed	sawn (sawed)	1	V_1	past <-ed> ppl <-en>
say	said	said	2	V_{2a}	+ /d/
see	saw	seen	1	V_{2c}	ppl <-en>
seek	sought	sought	2	V_{2a}	C > /t/
sell	sold	sold	2	V_{2a}	+ /d/
send	sent	sent	2	V_1	/d/ > /t/
set	set	set	5	V_1	
sew	sewed	sewn (sewed)	1	V_1	past <-ed> ppl <-en>
shake	shook	shaken	1	V_{2c}	ppl <-en>
shear	sheared	shorn (sheared)	1	V_{2b}	past <-ed> ppl <-en>
shed	shed	shed	5	V_1	
shine	shone (shined)	shone (shined)	2	V_{2a}	
shit	shit (shat)	shit	5	V_1	
shoe	shod (shoed)	shod (shoed)	2	V_{2a}	
shoot	shot	shot	2	V_{2a}	
show	showed	shown (showed)	1	V_1	past <-ed> ppl <-en>
shrink	shrank (shrunk)	shrunk	1	V_3	
shrive	shrove (shrived)	shriven (shrived)	1	V_3	ppl <-en>
shut	shut	shut	5	V_1	
sing	sang (sung)	sung	1	V_3	
sink	sank (sunk)	sunk	1	V_3	
sit	sat	sat	2	V_{2a}	stem in /t/
slay	slew	slain	1	V_{2c}	ppl <-en>
sleep	slept	slept	2	V_{2a}	+ /t/
slide	slid	slid	2	V_{2a}	stem in /d/
sling	slung	slung	2	V_{2a}	Bybee
slink	slunk	slunk	2	V_{2a}	Bybee
slit	slit	slit	5	V_1	
smell	smelt (smelled)	smelt (smelled)	2	V_1	+ /t/
smite	smote	smitten	1	V_3	ppl <-en>
sow	sowed	sown (sowed)	1	V_1	past <-ed> ppl <-en>
speak	spoke	spoken	1	V_{2a}	ppl <-en>
speed	sped (speeded)	sped (speeded)	2	V_{2a}	stem in /d/

(*cont.*)

Base	Past tense	Past participle	Class	*Vowel*	Other features*
			LA classification		
spell	spelt (spelled)	spelt (spelled)	2	V_1	+ /t/
spend	spent	spent	2	V_1	/d/ > /t/
spill	spilt (spilled)	spilt (spilled)	2	V_1	+ /t/
spin	spun (span)	spun	2	V_{2a}	Bybee
spit	spat (spit)	spat (spit)	2	V_{2a}	stem in /t/
split	split	split	5	V_1	
spoil	spoilt (spoiled)	spoilt (spoiled)	2	V_1	+ /t/
spread	spread	spread	5	V_1	
spring	sprang (sprung)	sprung	1	V_3	
stand	stood	stood	2	V_{2a}	stem in /d/
steal	stole	stolen	1	V_{2a}	ppl <-en>
stick	stuck	stuck	2	V_{2a}	Bybee
sting	stung	stung	2	V_{2a}	Bybee
stink	stank (stunk)	stunk	1	V_3	
strew	strewed	strewn (strewed)	1	V_1	past <-ed> ppl <-en>
stride	strode	stridden (strid, strode)	1	V_1	ppl <-en>
strike	struck	struck	2	V_{2a}	Bybee
string	strung	strung	2	V_{2a}	Bybee
strive	strove (strived)	striven (strived)	1	V_3	ppl <-en>
swear	swore	sworn	1	V_{2a}	ppl <-en>
sweat	sweat (sweated)	sweat (sweated)	5	V_1	
sweep	swept	swept	2	V_{2a}	+ /t/
swell	swelled	swollen (swelled)	1	V_{2b}	ppl <-en>
swim	swam (swum)	swum	1	V_3	
swing	swung	swung	2	V_{2a}	Bybee
take	took	taken	1	V_{2c}	ppl <-en>
teach	taught	taught	2	V_{2a}	C > /t/
tear	tore	torn	1	V_{2a}	ppl <-en>
telecast	*telecast*	*telecast*			
tell	told	told	2	V_{2a}	+ /d/
think	thought	thought	2	V_{2a}	C > /t/
throw	threw	thrown	1	V_{2c}	ppl <-en>
thrust	thrust	thrust	5	V_1	
tread	trod	trodden (trod)	1	V_{2a}	ppl <-en>
unbend	*unbent*	*unbent*			
unbind	*unbound*	*unbound*			
underbid	*underbid*	*underbid (underbidden)*			
undergo	*underwent*	*undergone*			
understand	*understood*	*understood*			
undertake	*undertook*	*undertaken*			
underwrite	*underwrote*	*underwritten*			
undo	*undid*	*undone*			
unfreeze	*unfroze*	*unfrozen*			
unmake	*unmade*	*unmade*			
unwind	*unwound*	*unwound*			

(*cont.*)

Base	Past tense	Past participle	LA classification		
			Class	*Vowel*	Other features*
uphold	*upheld*	*upheld*			
upset	*upset*	*upset*			
wake	woke (waked)	woken (waked)	1	V_{2a}	ppl <-en>
wear	wore	worn	1	V_{2a}	ppl <-en>
weave	wove	woven	1	V_{2a}	ppl <-en>
wed	wed (wedded)	wed (wedded)	5	V_1	
weep	wept	wept	2	V_{2a}	+ /t/
wet	wet (wetted)	wet (wetted)	5	V_1	
win	won	won	2	V_{2a}	Bybee
wind	wound	wound	2	V_{2a}	stem in /d/
withdraw	*withdrew*	*withdrawn*			
withhold	*withheld*	*withheld*			
withstand	*withstood*	*withstood*			
wring	wrung	wrung	2	V_{2a}	Bybee
write	wrote	written	1	V_3	ppl <-en>

* Explanation of feature abbreviations employed:

Feature	Long version	Example
stem in /d/	the verbal stem ends in /d/	*abide – abode – abode*
stem in /t/	the verbal stem ends in /t/	*light – lit – lit*
ppl <-en>	the past participle has added <-en>	*bear – bore – borne*
/d/ > /t/	/d/ of the verbal stem is devoiced to /t/	*bend – bent – bent*
+ /t/	/t/ is added	*bereave – bereft – bereft*
C > /t/	the final stem consonant is changed to /t/	*beseech – besought – besought*
C > /d/	the final stem consonant is changed to /d/	*have – had – had*
Bybee	past tense and past participle follow the template [C (C) (C) Λ {velar/nasal}]	*cling – clung – clung*
past <-ed>	the past tense has added <-ed> (=weak)	*hew – hewed – hewn*

Appendix 2: SED localities and list of counties

(from Orton and Halliday 1962–64: 30)

List of counties (by numbers)

1	Northumberland	21	Norfolk
2	Cumberland	22	Suffolk
3	Durham	23	Monmouthshire
4	Westmoreland	24	Gloucestershire
5	Lancashire	25	Oxfordshire
6	Yorkshire	26	Buckinghamshire
7	Cheshire	27	Bedfordshire
8	Derbyshire	28	Hertfordshire
9	Nottinghamshire	29	Essex
10	Lincolnshire	30	Middlesex and London
11	Shropshire	31	Somerset
12	Staffordshire	32	Wiltshire
13	Leicestershire	33	Berkshire
14	Rutland	34	Surrey
15	Herefordshire	35	Kent
16	Worcestershire	36	Cornwall
17	Warwickshire	37	Devonshire
18	Northamptonshire	38	Dorset
19	Huntingdonshire	39	Hampshire
20	Cambridgeshire	40	Sussex

List of counties (alphabetical)

Bedfordshire	27	Lincolnshire	10
Berkshire	33	Middlesex and London	30
Buckinghamshire	26	Monmouthshire	23
Cambridgeshire	20	Norfolk	21
Cheshire	7	Northamptonshire	18
Cornwall	36	Northumberland	1
Cumberland	2	Nottinghamshire	9
Derbyshire	8	Oxfordshire	25
Devonshire	37	Rutland	14
Dorset	38	Shropshire	11
Durham	3	Somerset	31
Essex	29	Staffordshire	12
Gloucestershire	24	Suffolk	22
Hampshire	39	Surrey	34
Herefordshire	15	Sussex	40
Hertfordshire	28	Warwickshire	17
Huntingdonshire	19	Westmoreland	4
Kent	35	Wiltshire	32
Lancashire	5	Worcestershire	16
Leicestershire	13	Yorkshire	6

Bibliography

Andersen, Gisle. 2001. *Pragmatic Markers and Sociolinguistic Variation*. Amsterdam & Philadelphia: John Benjamins.

Anderwald, Lieselotte. 2002a. *Negation in Non-Standard British English: Gaps, Regularizations and Asymmetries*. London & New York: Routledge.

2002b. "**I amn't sure*: Why is there no negative contracted form of first person singular *be?*" In Dieter Kastovsky, Gunther Kaltenböck and Susanne Reichl, eds. *Anglistentag 2001: Wien*. Trier: WVT, 7–17.

2004. "The morphology and syntax of the varieties of English spoken in the Southeast of England." In Bernd Kortmann, ed. *Handbook of Varieties of English*. Vol. 2: *Morphology and Syntax*. Berlin & New York: Mouton de Gruyter, 157–78.

2007. "'He rung the bell' and 'she drunk ale' – non-standard past tense forms in traditional British dialects and on the internet." In Marianne Hundt, Nadja Nesselhauf and Carolin Biewer, eds. *Corpus Linguistics and the Web*. Amsterdam & New York: Rodopi, 271–85.

Anderwald, Lieselotte. forthcoming. "Norm vs. variation in British English strong verbs: the case of past tense *sang* vs. *sung*." In Alexandra N. Lenz and Albrecht Plewnia, eds. *Grammar Between Norm and Variation*. Amsterdam & Philadelphia: John Benjamins.

Anderwald, Lieselotte, and Susanne Wagner. 2007. "FRED – The Freiburg English Dialect corpus." In Joan Beal, Karen Corrigan and Hermann Moisl, eds. *Creating and Digitizing Language Corpora*. Vol. 1: *Synchronic Corpora*. London: Macmillan, 35–53.

Anttila, Arto. 2002. "Variation and phonological theory." In J. K. Chambers, Peter Trudgill and Natalie Schilling-Estes, eds. *The Handbook of Language Variation and Change*. Oxford & New York: Blackwell, 206–43.

Aronoff, Mark. 1994. *Morphology by Itself: Stems and Inflectional Classes*. Cambridge, MA: MIT Press.

Aronoff, Mark, and Kirsten Fudeman. 2005. *What Is Morphology?* Oxford & Cambridge, MA: Blackwell.

Baayen, R. Harald. 2003. "Probabilistic approaches to morphology." In Rens Bod, Jennifer Hay and Stefanie Jannedy, eds. *Probabilistic Linguistics*. Cambridge, MA & London: MIT Press, 229–87.

Bartlett, John Russell. 1848. *Dictionary of Americanisms: A Glossary of Words and Phrases, Colloquially Used in the United States*. 1st edition. New York: Bartlett and Welford.

Bauer, Laurie. 1997. "A class of English irregular verbs." *English Studies* 78: 545–55.

Baugh, Albert C., and Thomas Cable. 1978. *A History of the English Language*. 3rd edition. London: Routledge.

Berko Gleason, Jean. 1958. "The child's learning of morphology." *Word* 14: 150–77.

Biber, Douglas, Edward Finegan, and David Atkinson. 1994. "ARCHER and its challenges: Compiling and exploring A Representative Corpus of Historical English Registers." In Udo Fries, Gunnel Tottie and Peter Schneider, eds. *Creating and Using English Language Corpora*. Amsterdam: Rodopi: 1–14.

Biber, Douglas, Stig Johansson, Geoffrey Leech, Susan Conrad, and Edward Finegan. 1999. *Longman Grammar of Spoken and Written English*. Harlow: Longman.

Blevins, Juliette. 2004. *Evolutionary Phonology: The Emergence of Sound Patterns*. Cambridge: Cambridge University Press.

Boersma, Paul, and Bruce P. Hayes. 2001. "Empirical tests of the gradual learning algorithm." *Linguistic Inquiry* 32: 45–86.

Burzio, Luigi. 2002. "Missing players: Phonology and the past-tense debate." *Lingua* 112: 157–99.

Bybee, Joan. 1985. *Morphology: A Study of the Relation between Meaning and Form*. Amsterdam & Philadelphia: John Benjamins.

    1995. "Regular morphology and the lexicon." *Language and Cognitive Processes* 10: 425–55.

    1996. "Productivity, regularity and fusion: How language use affects the lexicon." In Rajendra Singh, ed. *Trubetzkoy's Orphan*. Amsterdam & Philadelphia: John Benjamins, 247–69.

Bybee, Joan, and Carol Lynn Moder. 1983. "Morphological classes as natural categories." *Language* 59: 251–70.

Bybee, Joan L. 1988. "Morphology as lexical organization." In Michael Hammond and Michael Noonan, eds. *Theoretical Morphology: Approaches in Modern Linguistics*. San Diego: Academic Press, 119–41.

Bybee, Joan L., and Dan I. Slobin. 1982. "Why small children cannot change language on their own: Suggestions from the English past tense." In Anders Ahlqvist, ed. *Papers from the 5th International Conference on Historical Linguistics*. Amsterdam & Philadelphia: John Benjamins, 29–37.

Bye, Patrik. 2005. "Coaffixation and subcategorization in phonology: Unifying gaps, allomorphy and crazy rules through morpholexical control." Paper presented at *ICLaVE 3*, Amsterdam 23–5 June 2005.

Campbell, A. 1959. *Old English Grammar*. Oxford: Clarendon Press.

Campbell, Lyle. 1998. *Historical Linguistics: An Introduction*. London: Bloomsbury.

Carstairs-McCarthy, Andrew. 1992. *Current Morphology*. London & New York: Routledge.

    2002. *An Introduction to English Morphology*. Edinburgh: Edinburgh University Press.

Cassidy, Frederic G., and Richard N. Ringler. 1971. *Bright's Old English Grammar and Reader*. 3rd edition. New York: Holt, Rinehart and Winston. (First published 1891.)

Cassidy, Frederic G., and Joan Hall Houston. 1991. *Dictionary of American Regional English*. Vol. II. *D–H*. Cambridge, MA: Belknap Press of Harvard University Press.

Cedergren, Henrietta, and David Sankoff. 1974. "Variable rules: Performance as a statistical reflection of competence." *Language* 50: 333–55.

Chambers, J.K. 1995. *Sociolinguistic Theory: Linguistic Variation and its Social Significance*. Oxford: Blackwell.

2003. *Sociolinguistic Theory: Linguistic Variation and its Social Significance*. 2nd edition. Oxford: Blackwell.

2004. "Dialect typology and vernacular universals." In Bernd Kortmann, ed. *Dialectology Meets Typology*. Berlin & New York: Mouton de Gruyter, 127–45.

Chambers, J. K., and Peter Trudgill. 1998. *Dialectology*. 2nd edition. Cambridge: Cambridge University Press.

Cheshire, Jenny. 1982. *Variation in an English Dialect: A Sociolinguistic Study*. Cambridge: Cambridge University Press.

1994. "Standardization and the English irregular verbs." In Dieter Stein and Ingrid Tieken-Boon van Ostade, eds. *Towards a Standard English: 1600–1800*. Berlin & New York: Mouton de Gruyter, 115–33.

Chomsky, Noam, and Morris Halle. 1968. *The Sound Pattern of English*. New York: Harper & Row.

Croft, William. 1990. *Typology and Universals*. Cambridge: Cambridge University Press.

2000. *Explaining Language Change: An Evolutionary Approach*. Harlow: Longman.

Dahl, Östen. 2004. *The Growth and Maintenance of Linguistic Complexity*. Amsterdam & Philadelphia: John Benjamins.

Daugherty, Kim G., and Mark S. Seidenberg. 1994. "Beyond rules and exceptions: A connectionist approach to inflectional morphology." In Susan D. Lima, Roberta L. Corrigan and Gregory K. Iverson, eds. *The Reality of Linguistic Rules*. Amsterdam & Philadelphia: John Benjamins, 353–88.

Dossena, Marina. 2005. *Scotticisms in Grammar and Vocabulary*. Edinburgh: John Donald.

Dressler, Wolfgang U., Willi Mayerthaler, Oswald Panagl, and Wolfgang U. Wurzel. 1987. *Leitmotifs in Natural Morphology*. Amsterdam & Philadelphia: John Benjamins.

Durrell, Martin. 2001. "Strong verb Ablaut in the west Germanic languages." In Sheila Watts, Jonathan West and Hans-Joachim Solms, eds. *Zur Verbmorphologie germanischer Sprachen*. Tübingen: Niemeyer, 5–18.

Earle, John. 1892. *The Philology of the English Tongue*. 3rd edition. Oxford: Clarendon Press. (First published 1880.)

Ekwall, Eilert. 1980. *A History of Modern English Sounds and their Morphology*. (Translated and edited by Alan Ward.) Oxford: Blackwell. (First published 1914.)

Esser, Jürgen. 1988. "Die unregelmäßigen Verben im heutigen Englisch aus diachroner und synchroner Sicht." *Zeitschrift für Anglistik und Amerikanistik* 36: 26–46.

Foulkes, Paul, and Gerard Docherty, eds. 1999. *Urban Voices: Accent Studies in the British Isles*. London: Edward Arnold.

Francis, W. Nelson, and Henry Kučera. 1982. *A Frequency Analysis of English*. Boston, MA: Houghton Mifflin.

Giegerich, Heinz. 1999. *Lexical Strata in English: Morphological Causes, Phonological Effects.* Cambridge: Cambridge University Press.

Görlach, Manfred. 1996. "Morphological standardization: The strong verbs in Scots." In Derek Britton, ed. *English Historical Linguistics 1994.* Amsterdam & Philadelphia: John Benjamins, 161–81.

Green, Lisa. 1998. "Aspect and predicate phrases in African-American vernacular English." In Salikoko S. Mufwene, John R. Rickford, Guy Bailey and John Baugh, eds. *African-American English: Structure, History and Use.* London & New York: Routledge, 37–81.

2002. *African American English: A Linguistic Introduction.* Cambridge: Cambridge University Press.

Grimm, Jacob. 1819. *Deutsche Grammatik.* Vol. 1. Göttingen: Dieterich.

Guy, Gregory. 1991. "Explanation in variable phonology: An exponential model of morphological constraints." *Language Variation and Change* 3: 1–22.

Guy, Gregory R. 1996. "Form and function in linguistic variation." In Gregory R. Guy, Crawford Feagin, Deborah Schiffrin and John Baugh, eds. *Towards a Social Science of Language.* Vol. I: *Variation and Change in Language and Society.* Amsterdam & Philadelphia: John Benjamins, 221–52.

Halle, Morris, and Karuvannur P. Mohanan. 1985. "Segmental phonology of Modern English." *Linguistic Inquiry* 16: 57–116.

Halliday, M. A.K. 1992. "Language as system and language as instance: The corpus as a theoretical construction." In Jan Svartvik, ed. *Directions in Corpus Linguistics.* Berlin & New York: Mouton de Gruyter, 61–77.

Hansen, Erik, and Hans Frede Nielsen. 1986. *Irregularities in Modern English.* Odense: Odense University Press.

Harnisch, Rüdiger. 1988. "Natürliche Morphologie und morphologische Ökonomie." *Zeitschrift für Phonetik, Sprachwissenschaft und Kommunikationsforschung* 41: 426–37.

Harris, John. 1989. "Towards a lexical analysis of sound change in progress." *Journal of Linguistics* 25: 35–56.

Haspelmath, Martin. 2002. *Understanding Morphology.* London: Edward Arnold.

Hayes, Bruce P. 1996. "Phonetically-driven phonology: The role of Optimality Theory and inductive grounding." (Available on Rutger's Optimality Archive.)

Henry, Alison. 1995. *Belfast English and Standard English: Dialect Variation and Parameter Setting.* New York & Oxford: Oxford University Press.

Hockett, Charles F. 1987. *Refurbishing our Foundations: Elementary Linguistics from an Advanced Point of View.* Amsterdam & Philadelphia: John Benjamins.

Hogg, Richard M. 1998. "*Snuck*: The development of irregular preterite forms." In Graham Nixon and John Honey, eds. *An Historic Tongue: Studies in English Linguistics in Memory of Barbara Strang.* London & New York: Routledge, 31–40.

Huddleston, Rodney D., and Geoffrey K. Pullum. 2002. *The Cambridge Grammar of the English Language.* Cambridge: Cambridge University Press.

2005. *Student's Introduction to English Grammar.* Cambridge: Cambridge University Press.

Jespersen, Otto. 1924. *The Philosophy of Grammar.* London: Allan & Unwin.

1942. *A Modern English Grammar on Historical Principles.* Vol. VI. Copenhagen: Ejnar Munksgaard.

Katamba, Francis. 1993. *Morphology*. Houndmills and New York: Palgrave.

Kiparsky, Paul. 1982. "Lexical morphology and phonology." In I. S. Yang, ed. *Linguistics in the Morning Calm*. Seoul: Hanshin, 3–91.

Kortmann, Bernd, and Benedikt Szmrecsanyi. 2004. "Global synopsis: Morphological and syntactic variation in English." In Bernd Kortmann and Edgar W. Schneider, eds. *A Handbook of Varieties of English*. Vol. 2: *Morphology and Syntax*. Berlin & New York: Mouton de Gruyter, 1142–202.

Kretzschmar, William A., Jr. 2002. "Dialectology and the history of the English language." In Donka Minkova and Robert Stockwell, eds. *Studies in the History of the English Language: A Millennial Perspective*. Berlin & New York: Mouton de Gruyter, 79–108.

Kretzschmar, William A., Jr, and Susan Tamasi. 2003. "Distributional foundations for a theory of language change." *World Englishes* 22: 377–401.

Kroch, Anthony. 1978. "Toward a theory of social dialect variation." *Language in Society* 7: 17–36.

1989. "Reflexes of grammar in patterns of language change." *Language Variation and Change* 1: 199–244.

Krygier, Marcin. 1994. *The Disintegration of the English Strong Verb System*. Frankfurt a. M.: Lang.

Kytö, Merja. 1996. *Manual to the Diachronic Part of the Helsinki Corpus of English Texts: Coding Conventions and Lists of Source Texts*. 3rd edition. Helsinki: Department of English, University of Helsinki.

Labov, William. 1969. "Contraction, deletion, and inherent variability of the English copula." *Language* 45: 715–62.

1998. "Co-existent systems in African American vernacular English." In Salikoko S. Mufwene, John R. Rickford, Guy Bailey and John Baugh, eds. *African-American English: Structure, History and Use*. London & New York: Routledge, 110–53.

LALME. 1986a. *A Linguistic Atlas of Late Mediaeval English*. Vol. 1. *General Introduction, Index of Sources, Dot Maps*. Aberdeen: Aberdeen University Press.

1986b. *A Linguistic Atlas of Late Mediaeval English*. Vol. 4. *County Dictionary*. Aberdeen: Aberdeen University Press.

Lass, Roger. 1990. "How to do things with junk: Exaptation in language change." *Journal of Linguistics* 26: 79–102.

1994. "Proliferation and option-cutting: The strong verb in the fifteenth to eighteenth centuries." In Dieter Stein and Ingrid Tieken-Boon van Ostade, eds. *Towards a Standard English: 1600–1800*. Berlin & New York: Mouton de Gruyter, 81–113.

1999. "Phonology and morphology." In Roger Lass, ed. *The Cambridge History of the English Language*. Vol. III: 1476–1776. Cambridge: Cambridge University Press, 56–186.

Lightfoot, David. 1991. *How to Set Parameters: Arguments from Language Change*. Cambridge, MA & London: MIT Press.

2006. *How New Languages Emerge*. Cambridge: Cambridge University Press.

Lowth, Robert. 1762. *A Short Introduction to English Grammar*. London: Hughs. (Reprinted in 1967 Menston: Scolar Press (facsimile)).

Macaulay, Ronald. 2001. "You're like 'why not?': The quotative expressions of Glasgow adolescents." *Journal of Sociolinguistics* 5: 3–21.

Mayerthaler, Willi. 1981. *Morphologische Natürlichkeit*. Wiesbaden: Athenaion.
  1987. "System-independent morphological naturalness." In Wolfgang U. Dressler, Willi Mayerthaler, Oswald Panagl and Wolfgang U. Wurzel. *Leitmotifs in Natural Morphology*. Amsterdam & Philadelphia: John Benjamins, 25–58.
  1988. *Morphological Naturalness*. Ann Arbor: Karoma.
McCarthy, John J. 2002. *A Thematic Guide to Optimality Theory*. Cambridge: Cambridge University Press.
McMahon, April. 2000. *Lexical Phonology and the History of English*. Cambridge: Cambridge University Press.
  2003. "On not explaining language change: Optimality Theory and the Great Vowel Shift." In Raymond Hickey, ed. *Motives for Language Change*. Cambridge: Cambridge University Press, 82–96.
MED. 2002. *The Macmillan English Dictionary for Advanced Learners*. UK edition. Oxford: Macmillan.
Mencken, Henry L. 1921. *The American Language*. 2nd edition. New York: Knopf. (First published 1919.)
Miller, Jim. 2003. "Syntax and discourse in modern Scots." In John Corbett, J. Derrick McClure and Jane Stuart-Smith, eds. *The Edinburgh Companion to Scots*. Edinburgh: Edinburgh University Press, 72–109.
  2004. "Scottish English: Morphology and Syntax." In Bernd Kortmann and Edgar W. Schneider, eds. *The Handbook of the Varieties of English*. Vol. 2: *Morphology and Syntax*. Berlin & New York: Mouton de Gruyter, 47–72.
Milroy, James, Lesley Milroy, Sue Hartley, and David Walshaw. 1994. "Glottal stops and Tyneside glottalization: Competing patterns of variation and change in British English." *Language Variation and Change* 6: 327–57.
Mohanan, Karuvannur P. 1986. *The Theory of Lexical Phonology*. Dordrecht: Reidel.
Mugglestone, Lynda. 2003. *Talking Proper: The Rise of Accent as Social Symbol*. 2nd edition. Oxford: Oxford University Press. (First published 1995.)
Murray, Thomas E. 1998. "More on *drug/dragged* and *snuck/sneaked*: Evidence from the American Midwest." *Journal of English Linguistics* 26: 209–21.
Nevalainen, Terttu, and Helena Raumolin-Brunberg. 2003. *Historical Sociolinguistics*. London: Longman.
Nielsen, Hans F. 1985. "Tendencies in the evolution of the modern English irregular verbs." *Journal of English Linguistics* 181: 41–53.
ODEE. 1966. *Oxford Dictionary of English Etymology*. Oxford: Clarendon Press.
OED. 1994. *Oxford English Dictionary on CD-ROM*. 2nd edition. Oxford: Oxford University Press.
Oldireva, Larisa. 1999. "*Catched* or *caught*: Towards the standard usage of irregular verbs." In Irma Taavitsainen, Gunnel Melchers and Päivi Pahta, eds. *Writing in Nonstandard English*. Amsterdam & Philadelphia: John Benjamins, 263–84.
Orton, Harold, and Wilfrid J. Halliday, eds. 1962–64. *Survey of English Dialects*. Vol. 1. Leeds: Arnold.
Orton, Harold, and Martyn F. Wakelin, eds. 1967–68. *Survey of English Dialects*. Vol. 4. Leeds: Arnold.
Orton, Harold, and Michael V. Barry, eds. 1969–71. *Survey of English Dialects*. Vol. 2. Leeds: Arnold.

Orton, Harold, and Philip M. Tilling, eds. 1969–71. *Survey of English Dialects.* Vol. 3. Leeds: Arnold.

Orton, Harold, Steward Sanderson, and John Widdowson. 1978. *The Linguistic Atlas of England.* London: Croom Helm.

Penke, Martina. 2006. *Flexion im mentalen Lexikon.* Tübingen: Niemeyer.

Pinker, Steven. 1998. "Words and rules." *Lingua* 106: 219–42.

1999. *Words and Rules: The Ingredients of Language.* London: Weidenfeld & Nicolson.

Pinker, Steven, and Alan Prince. 1991. "Regular and irregular morphology and the psychological status of rules of grammar." In Laurel A. Sutton and Christopher Johnson, eds. *Proceedings of the Seventeenth Annual Meeting of the Berkeley Linguistics Society, February 15–18, 1991: General Session on the Grammar of Event Structure.* Berkeley, CA: Berkeley Linguistics Society, 230–51.

1994. "Regular and irregular morphology and the psychological status of rules of grammar." In Susan D. Lima, Roberta L. Corrigan and Gregory K. Iverson, eds. *The Reality of Linguistic Rules.* Amsterdam & Philadelphia: John Benjamins, 321–51.

Poplack, Shana, and Sali Tagliamonte, eds. 2000. *The English History of African American English.* Oxford: Blackwell.

Poplack, Shana, and Sali Tagliamonte. 2001. *African American English in the Diaspora.* Oxford: Blackwell.

Poplack, Shana, Gerard van Herk, and Dawn Harvie. 2002. "'Deformed in the dialects': An alternative history of non-standard English." In Richard Watts and Peter Trudgill, eds. *Alternative Histories of English.* London & New York: Routledge, 87–110.

Preston, Dennis. 2004. "Three kinds of sociolinguistics: A psycholinguistic perspective." In Carmen Fought, ed. *Sociolinguistic Variation.* Oxford: Oxford University Press, 140–58.

Prince, Alan S., and Paul Smolensky. 2004. *Optimality Theory: Constraint Interaction in Generative Grammar.* Oxford & Malden, MA: Blackwell. (First published 1993, online at Rutgers Optimality Archive http://roa.rutgers.edu/.)

Quirk, Randolph, Sidney Greenbaum, Geoffrey Leech, and Jan Svartvik. 1985. *A Comprehensive Grammar of the English Language.* Harlow: Longman.

Rissanen, Matti, Merja Kytö, and Minna Palander-Collin, eds. 1993. *Early English in the Computer Age: Explorations through the Helsinki Corpus.* Berlin & New York: Mouton de Gruyter.

Rumelhart, D. E., and J. L. McClelland. 1986. "On learning the past-tenses of English verbs." In D. E. Rumelhart and J. L. McClelland, eds. *Parallel Distributed Processing: Exploration in the Microstructure of Cognition.* Vol. 2: *Psychological and Biological Models.* Cambridge, MA: MIT Press, 216–71.

Russell, Kevin. 1997. "Optimality Theory and morphology." In Diana Archangeli and D. Terence Langendoen, eds. *Optimality Theory: An Overview.* Oxford: Blackwell, 102–133.

Sampson, Geoffrey. 2002. "Regional variation in the English verb qualifier system." *English Language and Linguistics* 6: 17–30.

Sankoff, David. 1988. "Sociolinguistics and syntactic variation." In Frederick J. Newmeyer, ed. *Linguistics: The Cambridge Survey.* Vol. IV: *Language: The Socio-cultural Context.* Cambridge: Cambridge University Press, 140–61.

Saussure, Ferdinand de. 1959. *Course in General Linguistics*. London: Peter Owen.

Seiler, Guido. 2006. "The role of functional factors in language change: An evolutionary approach." In Ole Nedergaard Thomsen, ed. *Competing Models of Linguistic Change: Evolution and Beyond*. Amsterdam & Philadelphia: John Benjamins, 163–82.

Singh, Rajendra. 2001. "Constraints, preferences, and context-sensitivity in morphology." In Katarzyna Dziubalska-Kolaczyk, ed. *Constraints and Preferences*. Berlin & New York: Mouton de Gruyter, 339–58.

Spencer, Andrew. 1998. "Morphophonological operations." In Andrew Spencer and Arnold M. Zwicky, eds. *The Handbook of Morphology*. Oxford: Blackwell, 123–43.

Spencer, Andrew, and Arnold M. Zwicky, eds. 1998. *Handbook of Morphology*. Oxford: Blackwell.

Stampe, David. 1979. *A Dissertation on Natural Phonology*. New York: Garland.

Stedman, Edmund Clarence, ed. 1895. *A Victorian Anthology, 1837–1895*. Cambridge: Riverside Press. (Reprinted in 2003: online edition by Bartleby.com, www.bartleby.com/246/.)

Stein, Dieter. 1998. "Syntax and varieties." In Jenny Cheshire and Dieter Stein, eds. *Taming the Vernacular: From Dialect to Written Standard Language*. London: Longman, 35–50.

Stemberger, Joseph Paul. 2001. "Overtensing within Optimality Theory." Online. Last updated 20 November 2001.

Stenström, Anna-Brita, Gisle Andersen, and Ingrid Kristine Hasund. 2002. *Trends in Teenage Talk: Corpus Compilation, Analysis and Findings*. Amsterdam & Philadelphia: John Benjamins.

Stockwell, Robert, and Donka Minkova. 2001. *English Words: History and Structure*. Cambridge: Cambridge University Press.

Strang, Barbara. 1970. *A History of the English Language*. London & New York: Routledge.

Swann, Joan, Ana Deumert, Theresa Lillis, and Rajend Mesthrie. 2004. *A Dictionary of Sociolinguistics*. Edinburgh: Edinburgh University Press.

Szmrecsanyi, Benedikt. 2006. *Morphosyntactic Persistence in Spoken English: A Corpus Study at the Intersection of Variationist Sociolinguistics, Psycholinguistics, and Discourse Analysis*. Berlin & New York: Mouton de Gruyter.

Tagliamonte, Sali. 2001. "*Come/came* variation in English dialects." *American Speech* 76: 42–61.

2006. *Analysing Sociolinguistic Variation*. Cambridge: Cambridge University Press.

Tiersma, Peter Meijes. 1982. "Local and general markedness." *Language* 58: 832–49.

Trudgill, Peter. 1999. *The Dialects of England*. 2nd edition. Oxford: Blackwell. (First published 1990.)

2001. *Sociolinguistic Variation and Change*. Edinburgh: Edinburgh University Press.

Upton, Clive, David Parry, and John D. A. Widdowson. 1994. *Survey of English Dialects: The Dictionary and Grammar*. London & New York: Routledge.

Wales, Katie. 2000. "North and south: An English linguistic divide?" *English Today* 61: 4–15.

2006. *Northern English: A Social and Cultural History.* Cambridge: Cambridge University Press.

Werner, Otmar. 1987. "Natürlichkeit und Nutzen morphologischer Irregularität." In Norbert Boretzky, Werner Enninger and Thomas Stolz, eds. *Spielarten der Natürlichkeit – Spielarten der Ökonomie: Beiträge zum 5. Essener Kolloquium über 'Grammatikalisierung: Natürlichkeit und Systemökonomie' vom 6.10. 8.10.1988 an der Universität Essen.* Bochum: Universitätsverlag Dr. N. Brockmeyer, 289–316.

1989. "Sprachökonomie und Natürlichkeit im Bereich der Morphologie." *Zeitschrift für Phonetik, Sprachwissenschaft und Kommunikationsforschung* 42: 34–47.

1990. "Wenn keine 'morphologische Natürlichkeit' – was dann?" In Norbert Boretzky, Werner Enninger and Thomas Stolz, eds. *Spielarten der Natürlichkeit – Spielarten der Ökonomie: Beiträge zum 5. Essener Kolloquium über 'Grammatikalisierung: Natürlichkeit und Systemökonomie' vom 6.10. – 8.10.1988 an der Universität Essen.* Vol. 2.2. Bochum: Universitätsverlag Dr. N. Brockmeyer, 157–83.

West, Jonathan. 2001. "The Newcastle Weak Verbs Project." In Sheila Watts, Jonathan West and Hans-Joachim Solms, eds. *Zur Verbmorphologie germanischer Sprachen.* Tübingen: Niemeyer, 51–61.

Wolfram, Walt, and Natalie Schilling-Estes. 1998. *American English: Dialects and Variation.* Oxford: Blackwell.

Wright, Joseph. 1898–1905. *The English Dialect Dictionary.* Oxford: Frowde.

1905. *The English Dialect Grammar.* Oxford: Frowde.

Wurzel, Wolfgang U. 1984. *Flexionsmorphologie und Natürlichkeit: Ein Beitrag zur morphologischen Theoriebildung.* Berlin: Akademie-Verlag.

1987. "System-dependent morphological naturalness in inflection." In Wolfgang U. Dressler, Willi Mayerthaler, Oswald Panagl and Wolfgang U. Wurzel. *Leitmotifs in Natural Morphology.* Amsterdam & Philadelphia: John Benjamins, 59–96.

1990. "The mechanism of inflection: Lexicon representations, rules, and irregularities." In Wolfgang U. Dressler, Hans C. Luschützky, Oskar E. Pfeiffer and John R. Rennison, eds. *Contemporary Morphology.* Berlin & New York: Mouton de Gruyter, 203–16.

Wyld, Henry C. 1927. *A Short History of English: With a Bibliography and Lists of Texts and Editions.* 3rd, revised and enlarged edition. London: John Murray.

Zwicky, Arnold M. 1975. "Settling on an underlying form: The English inflectional endings." In David Cohen and Jessica R. Wirth, eds. *Testing Linguistic Hypotheses.* New York: John Wiley, 129–85.

Index

AAE, 149, *see* African American English
AAVE, *see* African American Vernacular
    English
abide, 56
ablaut, *see* vowel change
ablaut classes, 5, 17, 25
ablaut rules, *see* vowel change
ablaut series, 5–6, *see also* ablaut classes,
    vowel change
A-curve, 71
adequacy
    of a model, 24, 47
affix /t/, *see* dental suffix
affix ordering, 23, *see also* level ordering
African American English, 149
African American Vernacular English, 134
American English, 39, 47, 62, 99, 117, 127,
    133–34
aorist, 2
apocope, 12, 57
ARCHER, 13, 103, 105, 106, 107, 108
arrive, 63
ask, 2
attractor
    stable word class as, 9, 11, 97

bake, 191
be, 10, 45, 188
bear, 5, 194
beat, 10, 58–59, 60, 61, 64, 136, 140
become, 10
begin, 5, 100, 103–5, 107, 110–11, 118
bend, 6, 25, 57
bereave, 56
Berkshire, 74, 77, 109, 127
Berwick, 81
beseech, 56, 92
beset, 12
bet, 8, 12
bid, 3, 12
bite, 6, 53, 194
blocking, 24
blow, 79–83, 91, 96, 194

BNC, 1
Bracket Erasure Convention, 22
break, 6, 25, 53, 67
bring, 20, 56, 194
Buckinghamshire, 129
build, 57
burn, 57, 169
burst, 12, 72
bust, 3, 93
buy, 6, 26
Bybee verbs, 10, 53, 63, 98–120, 136–37,
    146–47, 169, 181–82, 184, 187–90,
    194

can, 3, 10
cast, 6, 12
catch, 6, 56, 89–91
Cheshire, 81, 109, 137, 159–60, 162, 172, 176
choose, 6, 25, 53
class stability, 9, 43–44, 51–52, 54–55, 57–58,
    91, 96, 99, 101, 115–16, 147, 168, 180,
    182, 184
cleave, 56
climb, 191
cling, 10–11, 55, 101, 115, 169, 175, 184
COLT, 13, 95–96, 113–15, 124–25, 132,
    141, 144–46, 165–66, 179, 183,
    186–88
come, 10, 58, 60, 65, 67, 94, 149–68, 179, 182,
    184, 188–89, 194
comparative, 23
compounding, 21
connectionism, 31, 33, 35–38, 190
connections
    lexical, *see* network model
constraint ranking
    in OT, 27, 29, 31, *see also* constraints
    in stochastic OT, 32
constraints
    in OT, 27, 31, *see also* constraint
        ranking:in OT
    language-specific, 30
    violation of, 27, 29

conversion, 21, 24
cop, 90
Cornwall, 14, 77, 81, 127
cost, 6, 12
could, 10
Cumberland, 109, 160
cut, 12

Danish, 155
dental suffix, 5–7, 50–52, 57
Derby, 74, 127
derivation, 3, 21–22
devoicing, 6, 52, 57
Devon, 14, 77, 81, 128, 158, 160, 170
dig, 101
do, 10, 64, 98, 136, 147, 182, 184, 187–188, 189
dominance
   in natural morphology, 43–44, *see also*
      class stability, verb class: dominant
done, 105–6
Dorset, 129, 141, 160
drag, 47, 62, 99, 117
draw, 79–83, 91, 96
dream, 7
drink, 10, 11, 53, 55, 63–64, 98, 99–102,
      105–7, 111, 115, 118, 120, 136, 169,
      175, 184
drive, 53
dual route theory, 33–36, 188–90
Durham, 14, 160, 162
Dutch, 5, 9

Early Modern English, 2, 67, 80, 89, 102,
      108, 157, 172, 192
earn, 3
East Anglia, 74, 81, 109, 121, 129, 158, 160,
      164
eat, 10, 63, 98, 136–41, 146–47,
      187–88
economy
   hearer, 40, 65, 166
   of a model, 24–25
   speaker, 40, 65, 166
   system, 45
Elsewhere Condition, 23–24
emergence, 36, 38–40, 47, 189, 191
Essex, 128–29
EVAL
   in OT, 27, 30
exaptation, 2, 64, 184

faithfulness constraints, *see* constraints: in
    OT
fall, 10, 53, 60–61
family resemblance, 39, 54, 58–59, 61, 99,
      118, 190
Faroese, 154
feed, 30, 194

find, 8, 56, 67
fit, 3, 12
flee, 56
fling, 101
fly, 53, 80, 83
forbid, 12
freeze, 5, 53
future tense, 49

g-Deletion, 192
GEN
   in OT, 27
Generative Grammar, 21, *see also* SPE,
    LPM
German, 5
Germanic, 1
gird, 3
give, 51, 64, 73–74, 78–79, 91, 97,
    194
   past tense *give*, 78, 96, 98, 136, 146,
     147–48, 188
Gloucestershire, 74, 127, 129, 158,
    160
go, 10, 25, 45, 73–74, 91, 93–94, 168
Great Vowel Shift, 6, 19, 26, 151–52, 192
grow, 53, 67, 72, 79–83, 91, 96, 194

Hampshire, 127, 129
hang, 101, 182
have, 6, 10, 57–58, 194
heave, 56
help, 191
Helsinki corpus, 13, 103, 105–8, 157, 172,
    174
Herefordshire, 74, 121, 127
hit, 4, 6, 12, 25, 42, 59, 61, 194
hold, 55–56, 60, 65
hunt, 22, 25, 33, 41, 66
Huntingdonshire, 74, 158
hurt, 12

Icelandic, 154
iconicity, 41–42, 45, 59, 64–66, 77–78, 147,
    166–67, 180
Indo-European, 1–3, 5, 17, 66, 68
inflection, 21–22
   base form, 43
   stem, 43
irregular, *see* strong verbs
Isle of Man, 14
Isle of Wight, 160
isomorphism, 46, 188–89
I-umlaut, 56

keep, 41, 51, 66, 194
ken, 87
Kent, 14, 85, 103, 121, 128–29, 141, 176
kneel, 21

knit, 3, 12
know, 5, 30, 62, 67, 71, 79–83, 91, 94, 96–97, 194–95

LALME, 154, 169, 171–72, 174, 176, 179
Lancashire, 14, 74, 85, 137, 144, 159–60
language academy, 13
Leicestershire, 14, 74, 127, 129, 141
lend, 57, 61
let, 12
level ordering, 21, 27, 195, *see also* affix ordering
levelling, 9, 10, 59, 63, 64, 77, 96, 100–5, 113, 115, 126, 148, 150, 153, 165–66, 168, 172
lexical autonomy, 38
Lexical Phonology and Morphology, *see* LPM
lexical strength, 38
lie, 53
light, 56
Lincolnshire, 74, 77, 81, 141, 158–60, 162, 176
London, 95–96, 113–14, *see also* COLT, Middlesex
look, 2
LPM, 18, 21–27, 33, 35, 189, 191, 194–95
L-vocalization, 185

made, 58
make, 6, 10, 25, 57–58, 67–68, 94, 168, 194
markedness, 66, 166
markedness constraints, *see* constraints: in OT
markedness reversal, 41
may, 3
M-co, *see* Mossé-coefficient
M-coefficient, *see* Mossé-coefficient
mean, 6, 25
meet, 56
melt, 191
MEOSL, 6, 20
Middle English, 4, 53, 56, 66, 74, 76, 78, 80–81, 87, 89–90, 99, 101, 103–4, 108, 113, 137–38, 141, 150–54, 157–58, 167, 169, 171–76, 181, 192
Middle English open syllable lengthening, *see* MEOSL
Middlesex, 14
Midlands, 74, 77, 80–81, 83, 85, 91, 105, 109, 112, 113, 120–22, 124, 127–30, 138–40, 142, 152, 154, 158, 162, 165, 174, 178
minim-environments, 101, 150
modals, 1
Monmouthshire, 121, 129

morphological theories, 1, 17–48, *see* connectionism, dual route theory, LPM, natural morphology, network model, OT, Panini, SPE
Mossé-coefficient, 69, 95
motivation, 43, 51, 57
mow, 54, 80

natural morphology, 39–66, 193, 196–97
language-specific, 42–46
universal, 40–42, 66
natural phonology, 40–41
naturalness, 40–46, 51, 61–62, 66, 96, 148, 168, 180, 183, 186–88, 193
negation, 1
Neo-grammarians, 17
network model, 34, 38–40, 47, 99, 190–91, 196
networks
artificial neural, *see* connectionism
niman, 153–54, 157
Norfolk, 77, 129, 158, 172, 174
North, 69, 71, 73–77, 81, 83, 85, 87, 90–91, 99, 101, 109, 113, 121–24, 130, 138–40, 143, 152, 154, 161–62, 165, 178
Northamptonshire, 74, 158, 160
Northern preterite, 101–2, 113
Northumberland, 14, 81, 160, 162
Norwegian, 154–55
Nottinghamshire, 14, 74, 77, 105, 127, 158, 160

OE reduplicating verbs, 59
OE verb class I, 53, 101
OE verb class II, 53
OE verb class III, 53, 55–56, 99, 101–2, 106, 114, 169
OE verb class IV, 53, 137, 150, 154, 194
OE verb class V, 53, 137, 194
OE verb class VI, 53, 56, 82
OE verb class VII, 53–54, 56, 101
OE weak verb class III, 6
OE weak verbs, 6, 74
OGREVE, 138, 141, 176
Old English, 2, 4–6, 10, 12, 51, 53, 66, 68, 74, 75, 79, 85, 87, 89, 96, 102–3, 105–6, 111, 115, 120, 137–38, 141, 150–54, 167, 169, 192
strong verb classes, *see* OE verb classes I to VII
weak verbs, *see* OE weak verbs, OE weak verb classes
Old High German, 2
Old Norse, 76, 154
Optimality Theory, *see* OT
OT, 25–33, 196
stochastic, 32–33, 196

owe, 80
Oxfordshire, 14, 74, 121, 129, 160

Panini, 17, 21
parallel processing, 26, 27
partial suppletion, 5, 6
participle <-en>, 7, 52, 55, 60–61, 80, 91,
    103, 184
participle <-en>, 53
passive, 1, 50
past tense, 1
    formation of, 1, 17, 24
    regular allomorphs, 2, 19
    role in theory debate, 1
pattern associator, *see* connectionism
pattern PRES = PAST = PPL., 59, 166
pattern PRES = PAST ≠ PPL., 136, 140, 148, 188
pattern PRES = PPL ≠ PAST, 58–59, 166, 168
pattern PRES ≠ PAST = PPL., 50, 51, 55, 63–64,
    100, 115–16, 134, 136, 147–48, 187–88
pattern PRES ≠ PAST ≠ PPL., 52, 115
Pembrokeshire, 74
perfect, 1, 49
persistence, 196
person, 50
phonological rule, 22
plural, 23
prefix, 3
preterite I, 101, 111, 137, 141, 181
preterite II, 101–3, 111, 141, 181
Primärberührung, *see* spirant law
productivity, 23–24
progressive, 1, 49
pronoun exchange, 164
put, 6, 12, 67

Quirk et al., 2
quit, 12
quotatives, 185

redundancy, 10, 23, 118–19, 135, 166
    'dumb', 118
    smart, 45, 119, 136
re-functionalization, 64, *see also* exaptation
regular, *see* weak verbs
regular verbs, *see* weak verbs
regularization, 3, 12, *see also* strong verb shift
re-morphologization, 64, *see also* exaptation
rend, 57
retention
    of a historic form, 74
reverse vowel gradation, *see* rückumlaut
rid, 8, 12
ride, 49, 51
rin, 154
ring, 24, 100, 108–9, 111, 115, 118
rise, 5
r-metathesis, 78, 169

rückumlaut, 4, 6, 56
rule ordering, 23–24, 193
rules, 4, 192
    input-output, 191
run, 10, 26, 58, 92, 97
    past tense *run*, 65, 77–78, 184, 188–89,
        194
    past tense *runned*, 77–78
Rutland, 74

saw, 54
say, 8, 10, 168
schema, 39
    product-oriented, 47, 99, 182, 184, 190–91
    source-oriented, 39
Scotland, 15, 69, 73–77, 87, 89, 91, 112,
    124, 130, 137, 140, 143, 150, 165,
    179
SDSP, 43, 46, 115–16, 119
SED, 67–68, 76, 81, 85, 89, 138, 144, 151,
    162, 176
see, 53, 91
    past tense *see*, 98, 136, 146–47, 188
    past tense *seed*, 87, 144
    past tense *seen*, 85, 98, 125, 145, 188
seem, 2
sell, 56, 62, 67, 69, 73–77, 91, 96, 185
semantic irregularity, 24
send, 52, 57
serial processing, 26–27
set, 12
sew, 54
shake, 7, 82
shall, 3
shear, 54
shed, 6, 12
shibboleth, 69
shine, 56
shit, 3, 12
shoe, 56, 91–92
shrink, 5, 22, 100, 115
Shropshire, 14, 74, 81, 109, 137, 158,
    160
shut, 12
sing, 5, 10–11, 19, 22, 24–25, 33, 35,
    42, 55, 66, 100, 107–9, 111,
    115, 184
single route theory, 36
sink, 100, 106–7, 111
sit, 56
slay, 80, 83
slide, 56, 61
slink, 11, 101
slit, 12
sneak, 3, 35, 39, 47, 62, 99, 117
snow, 80
Somerset, 14, 77–78, 127, 129, 138, 158, 160,
    170

South, 74, 77–83, 99, 103, 105, 121, 128,
  144, 150, 152, 154, 157, 165, 169, 174,
  188
South East, 70, 71, 83, 85, 88, 95, 112–14,
  120–25, 129–30, 138–40, 143–46, 165,
  169, 178–79, 185
South West, 74, 83, 85, 112–13, 120–22, 124,
  129–30, 138–40, 142, 158, 164–65,
  169–70, 177–79
sow, 61
SPE, 18–21, 26, 189, 191
speed, 56
spend, 57
spill, 6
spin, 101
spirant law, 4, 6
spirantization, 56
spit, 12
split, 12
spread, 12
spring, 100, 115, 118
squeeze, 63
stability, 44, *see also* class stability
Staffordshire, 81
stand, 5, 25, 56
standard English, 12
standardization, 67, 96, 102, 118, 157, 181
stem in /t/ or /d/, 22–23, 30, 59
stems in /t/ or /d/, 12, *see also* dental affix
stick, 10, 101
sting, 51, 101
stink, 100
stratum model, 23, *see* LPM
Strict Cycle Condition, 22
strike, 39, 101, 182
string, 39, 99, 101–2, 118, 184, 189
strong verb shift, 2, 42, 54, 62, 65–67, 81, 83,
  92, 96, 183, 191
strong verbs, 2–5, 19, 21, 25, 30–31, 33, 37,
  39, 42, 46, 47, 51, 63, 66, 68, 91, 97,
  99, 115, 183, 189
  non-standard forms, 61–65, 69, 147,
  98–182
strong-weak verbs, 20, 41
Suffolk, 14, 103, 127, 129, 158
sunk, 113
suppletion, 38, 45
supralocalization, 97, 185, 188, 197
Surrey, 81, 127, 141, 159, 176
Sussex, 85, 121, 127, 160
swear, 53, 83
sweat, 3, 12
Swedish, 155
swell, 54
swim, 53, 100, 109
system congruency, 43, 55, 100, 140, 148

take, 6, 10, 25, 53, 55, 67, 154, 157, 168

teach, 4, 6
tear, 5
tell, 20, 56, 73–77, 91, 96, 185
T-glottalization, 185
thaw, 80
thrive, 3
throw, 79–83, 91, 96–97
thrust, 12
token frequency, 2, 10, 33, 35, 38, 40, 43, 45,
  47, 57, 67, 88, 92, 191
transparency, 41–42, 45, 66
tread, 53
Trisyllabic Shortening, 192
turn, 2
type frequency, 2, 10, 33, 35, 38, 40, 42–44,
  46, 47, 51, 191

umlaut, *see* vowel change
umlauting verbs, 56
uniformity, 41, 42, 66
Universal Grammar, 18, 25, 27
upset, 12

variable rules, 195
Velar Softening, 26, 192
verb class
  dominant, 44, 51, 58, 96, 100
verb classes, 5, 51–61
  competition of, 44
  criteria, 5–12, 52
vernacular primitive, 100
vernacular roots, 100
vernacular universals, 100, 149
vowel alternation, *see* vowel change
vowel change, 3–7, 10, 20, 46, 51–53, 56,
  61, 66, 91, 101, 114, 184
vowel gradation, *see* vowel change
Vowel Shift Rule, 19, 192

wait, 39
Wales, 70, 77, 112, 124, 130, 143, 179
want, 2, 49–50
Warwickshire, 14, 81, 85, 121, 127, 160
weak verb class, 2, 55–58, 91, 114
weak verbs, 2–5, 19, 21, 25, 30–31, 33, 35, 37,
  41–42, 51, 54–55, 57, 59, 63, 66, 97,
  100–1, 115, 117
  non-standard forms, 61–62, 67–97, 186,
  187
wed, 12
West Germanic, 5
Western preterite, 102, 113
Westmoreland, 14, 137, 160
wet, 12
Wexford, 127, 137
will, 3, 10
Wiltshire, 14, 109, 129
win, 10, 101

Worcestershire, 74, 81, 85, 121
word-and-rules theory, *see* dual route
theory
wring, 101, 118
write, 51, 53
wug test, 35, 37, 189

x-deletion, 6, 192
x-insertion, 192

yod-insertion, 192
Yorkshire, 14, 74, 81, 85, 109, 129, 137,
158–60, 162, 170, 176

Lightning Source UK Ltd.
Milton Keynes UK
UKOW030248300113

205579UK00004B/108/P